# BRENT D. PETERSON

*God's Invitation to*
*Become Fully Human*

# CREATED TO WORSHIP

BEACON HILL PRESS
OF KANSAS CITY

Copyright 2012 by Brent D. Peterson and Beacon Hill Press of Kansas City

ISBN 978-0-8341-2792-0

Printed in the
United States of America

Cover Design: J.R. Caines
Interior Design: Sharon Page

Library of Congress Cataloging-in-Publication Data

Peterson, Brent D., 1975-
   Created to worship : God's invitation to become fully human / Brent D. Peterson.
     p. cm.
   Includes bibliographical references (p. ).
   ISBN 978-0-8341-2792-0 (pbk.)
  1. Public worship.  2. Worship.  I. Title.
   BV15.P47 2012
   264—dc23

                                  2012000014

To my parents, Dave and Linda Peterson, and my grandparents,
Donna and Leonard Peterson and Ruth and Rudy Huber.
These people fostered and embodied a deep love for God,
the church, and communal worship.
"To whom much has been given,
much will be required" (Luke 12:48).

# CONTENTS

# ACKNOWLEDGMENTS

I would like to thank several friends and colleagues who read portions of early drafts, including Diane Leclerc, Dave Peterson, Eric Frey, Michael Scarlett, Todd Stepp, and Kevin Timpe. Their assistance has strengthened this entire conversation. I am grateful for their contribution. I would also like to thank my colleagues in the School of Theology and Christian Ministry at Northwest Nazarene University who provided encouragement all along the way.

Thanks also go to my editor at Nazarene Publishing House, Richard Buckner, who provided insightful comments and a keen eye for detail. I would also like to thank the churches I have had the privilege of attending and serving during my lifetime. Those experiences of worship continue to shape who I am and who I am becoming.

Lastly I would like to thank my family. My parents and grandparents taught me by example a love and passion for God, the church, and communal worship. This book is dedicated to them for the ways in which God has used them to show me how to become more fully human. I also want to thank my wonderfully supportive and encouraging wife, Anne, who continually carved out space for me to work on the book, and my wonderful children, Noah and Alexis, who were gracious on several Saturday mornings to let me steal away to write. Finally, I want to thank God for the inspiration and help God has bestowed on such feeble hands. *Soli Deo gloria.*

# INTRODUCTION

The battlefield testified as a silent witness to the carnage and atrocities of the conflict. Beginning in fits and starts, the dispute had escalated in a way few could have imagined. What began as minor disagreements and skirmishes among several people grew to include millions. Many never saw it coming. The intensity of this conflict turned friends and loved ones into combatants. As the violence increased, many people caught up in it were shocked it was happening. "Here?" "In this place?" "With these people?" "Clearly humans are capable of such cruelty, but not us. We should have been better." The longer the conflict continued, the more widespread were the casualties.

In the midst of the conflict the leaders and *prime* ministers tried a variety of tactics to reduce the animosity and hostility. Some concessions eased surface tensions, but in the end there was no reconciliation. Physical separation seemed to lessen the enmity between the parties, but relationally the discord between opposing sides surpassed all appearances to the contrary.

Eventually the seething anger and open hostility subsided; fights and clashes lessened. But this reduction in violence did not result from peace and restored relationships. It was accomplished through truces struck without reconciliation. It is one thing to seek the end of violence; it is another to seek friendship and communion with one's enemy. The combatants were tired. The cost of this war was beyond calculation. After a while, many were not sure what the point of the war had been. Fresh wounds caused by anger and rage became hardened scars of despair and pessimism. Anger turned to cynical apathy. Instead of seeking a resolution, people often gave up and simply left their homeland, family, friends, and places they had known their entire lives.

As the battles were subsiding, many were shell-shocked from what had taken place. The effects of posttraumatic stress were everywhere, producing an epidemic of pain and fear. The leaders and ambassadors sought peace at all costs. However, the peace they sought did not mean health, prosperity, and friendship; rather it was simply the absence of open conflict. Some leaders were so busy trying to ad*minister* triage to those who were left that little time was spent reflecting on the reasons this war began. This war exposed problems that had been germinating for a long time. The questions remained: Will the combatants learn from this war? Or will the hostility rise again, with later generations ready to inflict new wounds over the problems that had not been resolved? Unfortunately, the carnage of this conflict not only affected those in the war but also confirmed to those on the outside that they were correct in their assessment that the communities involved were hypocrites.

The so-called worship wars of the late twentieth and early twenty-first centuries were devastating for Christianity in many parts of North America and in places around the world. Throughout the history of the Christian church, Christians have often engaged in brutal fights and disputes among themselves. The reasons for such conflicts are many: doctrinal, political, economic, sociological, and so on. Likewise, these conflicts over worship were fueled by a variety of issues. Where did these wars come from? Were they simply a result of generational differences? Are they part of the transition from modernity to postmodernity that is occurring in the church? Or are they simply battles of hymns versus choruses, choirs versus worship teams, or organs versus drums?

We may still be too close to these matters to ascertain all that fueled such hostility within the church. What can be discerned is that these wars over worship exposed some areas of theological bankruptcy that must be addressed if the church hopes to move beyond these feuds. Three areas in particular stand out. First, at the very roots these wars exposed a poor ecclesiology (doctrine of the church); second, they revealed that there was lacking an orthodox (right) theology of worship; and third, these wars were caused by—and sadly have cemented for many—a dominant individualism in Christianity. It seems that a "Jesus and me" Christianity both fostered these conflicts as well as confirmed for some that the church is not good or necessary.

So how will the church move forward? The conversation in this book attempts to offer some suggestions by remembering several important realities:

- Conflicts over worship span the history of Christianity
- Church history and tradition offer a theology and practice of Christian worship that has not been fully captured by many Christians today
- Christian worship invites people to become more fully human for the glory of God

In this process of remembering, the present conversation is divided into three main sections:

Section I probes and proposes a Christian theology of worship that celebrates the transforming and healing power of God and the invitation offered to humanity.

Chapter 1, "Removing the Debris and Lamenting the Carnage," inspects poor theologies of worship that both led to and resulted from the wars over worship. Before exploring a Christian theology of worship, some deconstruction and "palate cleansing" is needed. This chapter also exposes how a poor theology of worship grows out of a poor theology of the church and how a poor theology of the church grows out of a poor view of Christian soteriology (doctrine of salvation) that idolized the individual.

After clearing the worship landscape, the remaining chapters of section I explore a dynamic theology of worship specifically in the Wesleyan tradition. This conversation will consider how communal worship is imagined as the *glorification of God and the sanctification of humanity*. This image of communal worship is further envisioned through the following theology of worship mosaic:

> Christian communal worship is the glorification of God and the sanctification of humanity as a divine-human event where God offers transformation and healing to help people become more fully what God created them to be and do. God breathes (inhales) and gathers in individual Christians to heal, transform, and renew them as the body of Christ to breathe (exhale) them out to continue the ministry of the incarnation that participates in the kingdom of God more fully coming. The consummation of the kingdom will come and God will be all in all.

Communal worship is a practice and calling of the church that does not exist in a theological vacuum. A theology of worship springs forth from ecclesiology (doctrine of the church), soteriology (doctrine of salvation), and theological anthropology (who God created humans to become). A Wesleyan understanding of salvation—that God is redeeming, transforming, and healing people to become a holy people set apart to love—offers a proper imagination for the engaging of a theology of worship. Interspersed within this guiding theology of worship, this section considers how communal worship participates in the further healing of people to become fully human as they are renewed into the *imago Dei* (image of God): to love God, love themselves, love others, be loved, and care for creation as an extension of the first three. In this way, people are *created to worship as God's invitation to become fully human*. Worship is a loving response to God's invitation to become fully human.

Chapter 2, "Worship: The Glorification of God and the Sanctification of Humanity," explores how the sanctifying of humans is a healing that also glorifies God, where creatures enter into the very love of the triune God.

Chapter 3, "Created for Worship," explains that communal worship is the primary reason God brought forth creation (1 Cor. 15:28 and John 17:21-23).

Chapter 4, "Healing Through Communal Worship," discusses how communal worship is a divine and human encounter where people are healed as an invitation to become more fully human as members of the church, the body of Christ (1 Cor. 12:27).

Chapter 5, "The Rhythmic Breathing of Communal Worship," explores how God, by the Spirit, breathes in the church for an event of communion, healing, and empowerment to exhale the church to be God's broken body and shed blood in the world.

Chapter 6, "Forming Christians in the Church," discusses how participation in a local church is imagined as God's gift and *ordinary* way in which people are being renewed and healed.

Chapter 7, "The Full Imagination of the Kingdom of God," examines the invitation to become fully human and how it envisions the kingdom of God coming in all its fullness where God may be all in all.

Section II draws upon the theology of worship explored in section I to suggest some practical ways in which local churches can imagine, create, and lead communal worship. Drawing upon the theological moorings of soteriology, ecclesiology, and theological anthropology, this section provides some practical suggestions and ideas for assisting local congregations in the work of creating worship services appropriate for each local congregation. This section attempts to assist local congregations in finding their own particular Christian liturgical voice. While this conversation argues for a robust theology of worship, this book will *not* prescribe one monolithic *ordo* (order), style, or instrumentality for worship. Even as Christian congregations share an important theology of worship, each local congregation must do the work (liturgy) to find its own most faithful worshipping voice. This book seeks to equip and assist congregations in finding this voice so it can be joyfully sung as part of the great Christian chorus.

Section II explores the following:

> Planning worship well begins with giving attention to the worship team, the process for planning worship, the people in a local community, the worship space, and the season of the Christian year; it also means planning worship services that are Christian. The service of Word and Table emphasizes God's gathering and calling while also empowering humanity's response. Planning worship well further includes paying attention to the final details and leading with excellence.

Planning worship services that are Christian and contextually appropriate is tough but rewarding work. This book makes the case that such work is of the utmost importance as the primary work of the church.

Chapter 8, "Who Plans Worship?" is about discerning *who* is planning worship. How these people are selected and cared for is a crucial first step.

Chapter 9, "How Is Communal Worship Planned?" will offer some ideas for seeing that worship is planned with excellence. The process for planning worship is just as important as the actual worship event itself.

Chapter 10, "The Local Context: Who Are We? Where Are We?" discusses how discerning the local body of Christ and worship space guides worship that is both Christian and contextually appropriate.

Chapter 11, "What Time Is It? The Christian Year," explores how the seasons and rhythms of the church year provide rich opportunities for faithfulness in Christian formation.

Chapter 12, "What Do We Do? Worship Services That Are Christian," explains that by drawing upon the model of the service of Word and Table, worship planners will be guided into crafting an order of worship that is locally appropriate and faithful to the Christian traditions and church year. The subtext of this chapter affirms the importance of the question, "How do we know our worship is Christian?"

Chapter 13, "Service of the Word: Scripture and Sermon," reflects on the call of God through the proclamation of Scripture and the sermon.

Chapter 14, "Service of the Word: Spoken Prayer as Humanity's Response," discusses the idea that as the church is called by God, the church responds through prayer.

Chapter 15, "Sung Prayers: Music in Communal Worship," notes that music's role in worship cannot be overstated, even though some theological and practical wisdom is needed. Guided by a robust theology of worship, this chapter scrutinizes and envisions the possibilities for music in communal worship.

Chapter 16, "Service of the Word: Response Through the Creeds and Tithes and Offerings," explores the important work of confessing creeds as well as the giving of tithes and offerings.

Chapter 17, "The Worship Event: Excellence and Perfection in Worship Leading," is about the communal worship event itself. After all the planning, the event of communal worship serves as an important climax to the entire process of worship planning. This chapter looks at the final details of preparation as well as considering practices of excellence in worship leading.

Section III ponders the beauty, mystery, and majesty of the sacraments in communal worship. This section provides a brief theology of the two sacraments of baptism and the Lord's Supper as well as liturgies and suggestions for their use in communal worship.

Chapter 18, "Baptism: The Waters Through Death to New Life," explains that the sacrament of baptism celebrates the new life of believers who are initiated into the church. Special attention is given to the theological and pastoral issues in regard to infant baptism, adult (believer's) baptism, and infant dedication.

Chapter 19, "The Celebration of Baptism in Worship," drawing upon the theology of baptism, offers both baptismal liturgies as well as practical suggestions for the celebration of baptism in local churches.

Chapter 20, "The Lord's Supper: The Renewal of the Church as the Body of Christ," considers the theological significance of the Lord's Supper as the primary place for Christians to encounter Christ and each other in a renewal of their covenant to God and one another. This covenant renewal is a further healing to love. As a sacrament, in the divine-human encounter the church offers itself to God as a living sacrifice. Furthermore, as the church is renewed as the body of Christ, it is sent out to be Christ's broken body and shed blood in the world.

Chapter 21, "Pastoral Issues at the Table," attends to some pressing pastoral issues in celebrating the Table, exemplified in questions such as, Who can partake? What is a proper bread sign? How often? Are the ordained necessary?

Chapter 22, "Service of the Table: The Celebration of the Lord's Supper in Worship," looks at the eucharistic liturgy of the Great Thanksgiving.

Chapter 23, "Benediction: Exhaled by and with the Spirit to Be Doxologically Broken and Poured Out," affirms that as God breathed in the church, the church is sent empowered by the Holy Spirit to be doxologically (in praise) broken and poured out before the world.

Despite this robust conversation, this book will not attend to all the questions a reader may have concerning Christian communal worship. This book does not pretend to be exhaustive. However, this book will assist in raising important questions and offer ideas that too often are neglected but are vital to the imagining, planning, and leading of Christian communal worship.

## A Word of Caution and Encouragement

*Created to Worship: God's Invitation to Become Fully Human* examines a theology of worship and provides practical helps that will enable each congregation to find a worshipping voice that is grounded historically and theologically. Within this conversation the concept of *imagination* plays an important role in this discovery of a theology of worship. While seeking clarity and precision in articulating a theology of worship, my goal is not to define or exhaust all that Christian worship can be. In offering a thesis on communal Christian worship, I hope it will not be received as restrictive or narrowing, demanding a literal obedience. However, within this imagination there are several postures and practices that I would argue are essential and must be attended to. My hope is that this conversation on worship offers new opportunities and possibilities that empower fresh creativity and inspiration. Rather than constructing a tight *definition* of worship that attempts to limit and restrict, I suggest an *imagination* of Christian worship that provides general boundaries while also creating space for Spirit-filled, contextually appropriate innovation.

At the beginning, I want to offer some important *lenses* as this conversation unfolds. In section I, there are areas when considering a theology of worship that are for me *nonnegotiable*. Furthermore, as section II draws upon the theoretical and moves to the practical, there are several issues, postures, and practices I am passionate about. However, many of the recommendations in section II need to be examined in light of each unique and particular congregation. In other words, section II is not meant simply to be "cut and pasted" into any local congregation. Some of what I suggest here will not work in your local context. I have attempted to offer enough practical suggestions that you can imagine and dream about what might work in your context.

Furthermore, in what follows, you may find yourself responding in several different ways. First, you may think, "This is impossible; no one can do this."

I would say that in what follows I have seen and encountered many churches doing much of what I propose. Second, your response may be, "I think this is a terrible idea; I have tried it and it does not work." In this case, I hope the word "suggested" is clearly felt. Not all of the ideas presented will work in every context. I am sure many of the suggestions are tied to my leadership personality and unique history. I am very content with some of my ideas not being helpful in all places. Some of you are doing many wonderful things in worship planning that I have not recommended or touched on. Nowhere do I pretend or claim that this conversation is comprehensive or conclusive. One of my primary desires for this project is that people will fall more in love with the gift of communal worship. In section II, I offer a model for worship planning with the hope that it will help spark new ideas. While this model may come across as a bit too structured, it has an underlying fluidity that allows for improvisation and adaptation.

Third (this is the one I am most concerned about), you may think, "I've been doing it all wrong. I just can't do a good job planning worship." Too many Christians, especially pastors and worship leaders, live in an atmosphere of insecurity and inadequacy. After considering what follows you may begin to feel poorly about your worship-planning process. That is precisely the opposite of my intention. This conversation is an invitation to look at where you are and see how God might bring about greater vibrancy—both in your communal worship settings and in your worship planning. Perhaps this conversation will spark a couple of new ideas or infuse new energy for doing what you are doing. Even though I have served often in helping to imagine, dream, plan, and lead communal worship services, those services and the process itself were far from perfect. Many times we struggled to make it from week to week.

I hope this book opens up new ideas and possibilities and confirms what is going well in your communal worship and planning processes. So I want you to repeat after me (verbally if possible).

1. I will not feel worse about myself as a worship leader after reading this book.
2. Our process for worship planning is not horrible.
3. I am open to God offering me new insights into how communal worship services may be imagined for my local context.
4. I will not feel worse about myself as a worship leader after reading this section but will celebrate the good things God is doing and the good things God will do.

Did you do it? Okay, maybe you should do it again, just to make sure. I know it is cheesy, but it is really important that you can hear my heart in what follows. I have attended many worship conferences where people come up on stage (typically people from big and "successful" churches) touting (really testifying) about how they plan worship. Instead of getting great ideas, all I hear is how poorly I am doing. Perhaps I am alone in this. If not, I hope what follows can just tweak and tickle your imagination a bit and provide new inspiration, joy, and excitement for imagining, planning, and leading worship.

Some pastors of small churches are not only the preaching pastor but also the music pastor, the secretary, the building administrator, and the janitor. In such contexts, some pastors perhaps long for any volunteers to help. My prayer is for many of you who are desperately wanting and needing assistance in planning worship but, as the landscape is surveyed, have few willing and capable helpers to call on. To those who feel all alone, may God bring people to you either from your community or from outside who can help you make your communal worship all you imagine it can be.

# SECTION I
# Toward a Theology of Worship

Mosaics are a medium of art where pictures and images emerge by assembling small pieces of colored pottery, glass, stone, or other materials. In mosaics separate and unique elements come together to form a powerful portrait. A mosaic is a helpful metaphor when considering a theology of worship that is layered, rich, and thick in texture and cannot be fully comprehended, exhausted, or extracted from the whole. The mosaic of a theology of worship draws deeply upon multiple conversations, all of which serve as important pieces that come together to form a dynamic imagination of Christian worship.

To begin, we acknowledge that care and consideration for God's full hope and desire for creation provides the lens that colors the entire landscape of the worship mosaic. God's creation of people to become one by the Spirit as the body of Christ has one goal, one end, one purpose—doxology, the praise and glory of God. It is in praising and glorifying God as the body of Christ that God's love flourishes and people enter the communion of the triune God. Within this design, the role and function of the church also needs attention.

Finally, these beginning conversations draw upon central Christian doctrines, each of which is a piece of the mosaic of communal worship as an *invitation to life*. A brief list includes the following:

- *Theological anthropology:* the conversation of who humans are called to be in light of who God has revealed God to be.
- *Soteriology:* the conversation of salvation that celebrates God's healing and transformation that enables humans to fully become what God imagined them to be.
- *Ecclesiology:* the conversation about God's people who are called to worship God as part of their continuing healing and who are empowered to continue the ministry of Jesus Christ in the world.
- *Hamartiology:* the conversation about the disease and destructiveness of sinning—choosing to resist or move away from God and desiring something or someone in the place of God.

- *Eschatology:* the conversation celebrating the healing and life available to people now by the Spirit and the future hope that the kingdom of God will be fully consummated.

All of these conversations (and others) come together into the mosaic of a Christian theology of worship.

As with all art, the best way to view a mosaic is to remove all obstructions, and so we begin our first chapter by doing just that.

# ONE
# REMOVING THE DEBRIS AND
# LAMENTING THE CARNAGE

At the beginning of this conversation, we need to clear away some debris remaining on the battlefield from the wars over worship. Some cleaning and deconstruction must take place to make room for a proper Christian theology of worship. This chapter will critique some poor theologies and practices of worship that caused and resulted from the wars over worship.

## Worship as Music: Hymns or Choruses?

The wars over worship were not about whether communal worship should happen but about what should be done during worship. During these wars, as a pastor in charge of worship, I found myself asking what now seem to be the wrong questions. Some were, "What songs will make folks happy?" and "What can I do to attract new people and have a bigger attendance?" Too often my local church's worship was centered on a vision of music. In fact, the language used by many of us underscored this way of thinking. When people used the word "worship," they often thought only about music. Those with the title worship pastors were often the ones in charge of music and choirs. Worship teams were those who led the congregation in singing. After a Scripture reading and just prior to leading the singing, a leader might retort, "Let's start worshipping again."

In light of this, much of the warfare and emotional angst revolved around musical issues: "Should we sing hymns or choruses?" "Can we play organ or drums?" "Should we use hymnals or PowerPoint?" On the surface these issues appear to be mostly about music, but they are theologically loaded. Music is crucial to Christian worship, but a full imagination of worship includes more than music; it encompasses all of a communal worship service and the way Christians live during the week. The musical side of the worship wars was especially bloody. Lifelong members of the church suddenly felt as if the hymnody they had grown up with was being taken away. What was familiar had become alien. Still others felt there was no space for the new and creative worship songs. The selection of songs chosen seemed to be guided more by musical transitions and flow rather than theological maturity.

## Worship as Marketing: "How Can We Get Bigger?"

Other battles, those that were not music centered, were equally toxic and seductive. Worship was imagined as a marketing strategy. Some members would ask, "What are the big and successful churches doing?" "Is our worship creative and edgy enough?" "Will it attract new people?" Attracting a bigger crowd was equated with fulfilling the Great Commission and with worshipping "in spirit and truth" (John 4:23). This exposes not only a poor theology of worship but also an anemic ecclesiology. Moreover, not only is worship poor when it is designed to "attract the masses," but it is also inferior when it is fashioned to avoid offending longtime constituents. Some of the guiding questions that arise when crafting this kind of communal worship include, "Will it make everyone happy?" "What did we do last week?" "Will it appease our tithers?" These questions often produce worship services that fail to encourage people to be present to God while also increasing their tendency to view worship as entertainment. There must be a better way.

In recent years churches have confused bigger crowds, stages, projector screens, and movie theater sound systems with faithfulness. Certainly numerical growth can be a sign of God's blessing and the authenticity of a faithful church. However, bigger is not always better. Conversely, there is nothing particularly holy about staying small or slowly declining to a "holy huddle." The lurking danger here is the confusion that equates faithfulness with increased membership or with sustaining the happiness of the "saints."

## Worship as Personal Preference: "Can We Do What I Want?"

One of the primary biological weapons of the wars over worship was personal preference. While much of the consternation focused on music, all facets of worship came under scrutiny. Let me offer an example.

The pastor just finished her morning coffee. She sat down at her desk for her Monday morning routine. It was a ritual she did not look forward to, but knew it could be put off no longer. On some Mondays it brought great hope and joy, but most days it offered pain and sadness; she opened her email. Too much of her email was junk, even though some of it came not from a company, but her parishioners. Some emails offered gracious words about the message. Some emails—couched with pleasantries and praise—leveled critiques. "Pastor, why did we sing this song?" "Pastor, the drums were too loud." "Pastor, the Bible reading was too long." "Pastor, why do we never sing any new choruses?" "Pastor, why do we never sing any of the old hymns? Would it hurt to sing a hymn every now and again?" "Pastor, do you know that someone on your worship team did (fill in the blank) this week?" "Pastor, when are you going to let me sing my special song?" "Pastor, I do not like any of the songs we are singing!" The pastor turned her computer off and wept.

Hopefully, such a narrative is foreign to your experience. Sadly, it occurs often. Too many people determine where they will worship on the basis of their personal preferences being met. While a worship service must be *familiar* to each local context, there is a profound idolatry at work when I can only worship when the church's worship is what I want, what I am comfortable with, or what I am used to.[1]

At this juncture, a word must be said about many local churches who, for the sake of the lost, alienated people who had decades of worship history in the church. There is something far beyond preference at work when people no longer know any songs and find the rhythms and practices of worship unfamiliar. Those with a lifetime in the church do not simply prefer hymns out of taste, but their own spiritual journey and growth in Christ through the years are intertwined with the use of hymns and specific worship practices. This larger conversation argues that those hymns, prayers, and practices shape the very core of what it means to be Christian, and thus human. This is not to deny that God can be at work in new songs and worship practices, but there was a pastoral transgression when those with a lifetime of worship memories felt as if someone "had stolen their worship."

## Worship as an Emotional Drug: "Can I Feel Something?"

Another poisonous way of imagining worship asserted that worship is only valid or spiritual if I *feel something*. Certainly, communal worship is an event that should impact the full person: intellectually, spiritually, physically, and emotionally. The poor theology of worship that must be avoided, however, claims that a worship service is only valid if a person has a deep emotional response. When worship leaders believe that a person "feeling something" is the final goal of a worship service, they tend to create worship experiences that feel more like emotional manipulation than genuine encounters with God. There is nothing particularly Christian about singing the same chorus first slowly then quickly then slowly again ten times.

A pastor friend of mine told me of an interchange that occurred as he was greeting his parishioners after a Sunday service. The exchange went something like this: "Pastor, I did not like any of the songs today. Because of this I did not feel God in worship today." The pastor looked lovingly at his friend and said with conviction and sincerity, "Then it is a good thing worship is not about you." While this exchange may be a bit curt, the pastor is correct. Worship's primary goal is not about me feeling something but about God receiving praise and glory.

Certain feelings often come from true worship, but those same feelings can be caused by other things besides worship. This is not suggesting that people's emotive and attitudinal posture when encountering God is irrelevant. God created people with emotions, and worship should affect people at the cognitive and emotional level. However, when communal worship is first about God, humanity can then more fully encounter God and become more fully human.

## Worship as Consumer's Choice: "What Options Do I Have for Worship?"

As the wars over worship waged on, many worship leaders tried to create peace by offering a smorgasbord of options. Instead of making people unhappy, churches offered a variety of worship styles. Early on, these services were often given one of two titles: traditional or contemporary. *Traditional* generally meant a service for the "old-timers" who wanted the same worship they had growing up. This service promised to keep things the way they had always been. The organ, robed choir, hymns (maybe even from a hymnal), special music, and sermon (with a pastor still wearing a suit) were all safeguarded so the saints would feel at home. *Contemporary* services were often created to appease people who wanted to have as little as possible of what they had growing up. Choirs were replaced with worship teams, hymns with choruses, organs and pianos with drums and guitars, and suits with jeans and sweater-vests (now designer T-shirts). Sermons were shortened to create space for more music and videos. The lights were turned down, and the volume was turned up. With multiple options, people could choose which service style they wanted. This menu approach seemed to ease some of the surface problems temporarily. However, this was not a true reconciliation but peace through segregation.

Another style emerged that attempted to bring folks together, allowing each person to have something in the service he or she liked. This style was often called *blended*. In these services you would often see choirs and worship teams, organs and drums, hymns and choruses, and the pastor in jeans and suit jacket. On the surface this seemed like a great compromise; unfortunately this felt more like worship schizophrenia than a thoughtful, contextually appropriate worship service. As a consequence of the menu approach, people developed loyalties to their preferred styles that often perpetuated or deepened divisions in local churches.

## Worship as Evangelism: "How Many Were Saved Today?"

While each of the previously described worship postures were easy to critique, some might be initially misidentified when challenging *worship as evangelism*. The Great Commission is a calling given to all Christians: "In your coming and going make disciples of all nations, baptizing them in the name of the Father, Son, and Holy Spirit" (Matt. 28:19, translation mine). If this task is so important, why would this not be the most prominent feature of communal worship? Christians from evangelical traditions often structured worship as a service of music, sermon, and altar call. While this is foreign to some, many may find this representative of much of the worship during the 1940s through the 1990s (and beyond for some).

As a child raised in such an evangelical tradition, I "learned" that people measured the success or failure of the pastor's sermon (and by extension the entire worship service) by how many came to the altar in response to the message.

I can remember being nine years old and seeing my pastor at the back of the sanctuary after a sermon when no one came forward to the altar. Attempting to be encouraging, I said, "Don't worry, pastor. I am sure your sermon will be better next week." It is noteworthy that several evangelical traditions that had weekly altar calls at the conclusion of their worship services have stopped offering them with any regularity.

Certainly, in the event of communal worship, it is God's hope and desire that people be transformed, but there is more to a full imagination of a worship service. A Christian communal worship service's end and goal is the glorification of God. While the healing and transformation of people in communal worship is extremely important, even this is not the ultimate hope and goal of communal worship.

As a pastor responsible for planning and executing worship during the height of the worship wars, I was influenced by all the above approaches. Offering this list here is not an indictment of the past. I am convinced most pastoral and lay leaders were trying to seek God's will in navigating those turbulent waters. Even as I was trying to manage all of those theologies of worship, something was not quite right in my spirit. I have few doubts about the sincerity of most worship leaders (preachers and music ministers), but as I look back on this era, including where we are today, it seems we *were* and perhaps still *are* asking all of the wrong questions. Rarely do we ask a very basic question, "Why do we worship?" or "How do we know our worship is Christian?"

Many more poor theologies of worship could be added. Yet the goal of this conversation is not to ridicule or condemn the past but to shed light on more faithful Christian theologies of worship. In my estimation most of the theologies of worship I critiqued contain an element of truth. My primary goal here is to help local churches articulate a theology of worship that will inform and guide their congregations into imagining, planning, and living worship that is Christian.

So now that some debris has been cleared, let's begin the mosaic of a Christian theology of worship—God's invitation to become fully human.

## Questions for Discussion and Reflection

1. What theologies of worship did you most resonate with in this chapter?

2. What scars, if any, do you have from the wars over worship?

3. How did your local congregation navigate these issues?

4. What new ideas and insights were raised that can be used as your local church moves forward?

# TWO
# WORSHIP: THE GLORIFICATION OF GOD AND THE SANCTIFICATION OF HUMANITY

*Christian communal worship is **the glorification of God and the
sanctification of humanity as a divine-human event where
God offers transformation and healing** . . .*
—Theology of Worship Mosaic[1]

The question for people is not *if* they will worship but *what* they will worship. What will capture their hearts? What will capture their imaginations? What will they desire to be and become? While all worship is religious, not all worship is Christian.

Roman Catholics have imagined Christian worship as the "the glorification of God and the sanctification of creation."[2] God creates in order that God's love may flourish. As God's love flourishes in creation, people glorify God. To glorify God literally imagines God's love shining between human faces and finally back to God. Humans glorify God as they are loved by God and respond to that love by loving fellow creatures, themselves, and God. Humans are set apart (sanctified) as God is glorified.[3] The Westminster Confession offers a similar sentiment when considering the primary purpose of humanity: "Q. What is the chief end of man? A. Man's chief end is to glorify God, and enjoy him forever."[4] This enjoyment of God is the love of God, love of oneself, love of others, and being loved. The glorification of God is the fulfillment of being created in the image of God. Within this rich imagination of Christian worship, some residual debris needs to be named and cleared to create a holy space.

## Worship Does Not Primarily Convey Ideas but Forms Habits of Kingdom Imagination

Too often Christian communal worship is only envisioned as a way to help people think correctly. When worship is deemed to be about conveying ideas and convincing people of them, it exposes a doctrine of salvation (soteriology) that assumes the human problem of sin is simply a matter of poor thinking that leads to poor behavior. Evangelism through communal worship attempts to solve the wrong thinking by offering the "right" ideas that are to be thought. Once people begin to think correctly, so it is thought, they will then choose to behave and love well. James K. A. Smith states that too often conversion in communal worship is reduced simply to giving mental assent to certain propositional beliefs, with the danger being the reduction of Christianity to a kind of intellectualism. This turns the Christian, not into a loving or doing being, but into a "thinking thing."[5] Smith suggests that this central and dominant anthropology (viewing people as thinking machines) shaped Protestant Christianity and subsequently Protestant Christian worship: "It is just this adoption of a rationalist, cognitivist anthropology that accounts for the shape of so much of Protestant worship as a heady affair fixated on 'messages' that disseminates Christian ideas and abstract values (easily summarized on PowerPoint slides)."[6] Smith goes on to suggest that sadly too often Christian formation centers around a fixation on doctrines imagined simply as propositions.

In naming the problem, Smith does not suggest that the remedy is to turn people into irrational "headless" bodies in which doctrines and creeds become irrelevant. Rather, the doctrines, creeds, and Scriptures are not simply to be mentally assented to but to be confessed and lived as the continual healing (sanctification) occurs. "What defines us is not what we think—not the set of ideas we assent to—but rather what we *believe*, the commitments and trusts that orient our being-in-the-world."[7] Smith understands belief as more bodily than mere mental assent; it is an imagination into which one's life is oriented. Smith notes that "before we are thinkers, we are believers; before we can offer our rational explanations of the world, we have already assumed a whole constellation of beliefs—a *worldview*—that governs and conditions our perception of the world."[8] A child learns to trust that his or her parents are loving and nurturing, not through an ability to rationally articulate a theory of nurture, but through experience and faith. The remedy for combating the reduction of people to thinking things is not that they should cease thinking and move into an immature or naive irrationality. There is a wonderful place of union where belief opens and orients people so that they begin to trust.

So instead of seeking to reconfirm or crystallize a person's set of ideas, worship must embody a set of practices that orients him or her to be renewed into the image of God. Worship invites people not simply to be intellectually convinced that what is happening is true. Christian worship breaks open an imagination of the kingdom of God and invites people into this grand story. "It is not primarily our minds that are captivated but rather our *imaginations* that are captured, and when our imagination is hooked, *we're* hooked."[9] This move to imagination is not antirational but recognizes that propositional statements fail to captivate and convert as effectively as stories.

Let me offer an illustration. My son has become a passionate basketball player. This is something he has caught largely from observing his father's own passion. While I have never forced my son to play sports, early on he saw the joy and fulfillment my wife and I experienced from playing sports. He also saw a movie on the life of Peter "Pistol Pete" Maravich. That movie offered a story about a young boy who wanted to be the best he could be. Pete practiced constantly; he lived and breathed basketball. Pete was gifted, but his gifts were not enough. Pete worked harder than anyone else. In the end the hard work paid off, and now Pete Maravich is often recognized as one of the best basketball players of his era. After watching that movie, without one word from me, my son started dribbling a basketball everywhere just as the young Pete had done. He began using all of his free time dribbling and shooting. My son's imagination had been captured, and so he began to imitate the practices of someone who was truly great. This is true for all of us. We often live into the imagination of some story. This emphasis of habit and imagination is also not antieducational. Rather, education is viewed, not as the data-dumping of information—although students still have skills to master and rules to learn—but as the formation of imagination through story and habitual practices.

Instead of allowing him to watch a movie and experience my love for basketball, I could have sat my eight-year-old son down with a handout filled with ten bullet points on why and how to be a great basketball player. My bullet points could have included statements such as, "If you work hard, you can become a great player," "Excellence requires a great deal of energy, desire, and devotion," and "Do not give up when you fail or other people will not believe in you." I am sure my passion and charisma would have been very convincing. In fact, I am sure if I were to ask my son at the end of this lecture whether he agreed with (mentally assented to) all these statements, he would no doubt say yes. I am also sure after my lecture was over, he would have asked if he could go and play video games. My son did not need a lecture. My son would not be impressed with my ten bullet points, even if he agreed they were true. His imagination would not have been captured as powerfully as it was by seeing the passion of his parents and entering into the story of Pistol Pete. Such an imagination would grow even more robust as he began to engage in the bodily practices designed to develop his playing skills.

In worship, the goal of the gathering is not to offer bullet points (propositional statements) for people to give mental assent to and then leave with lives unchanged. Worship must be about capturing people with the story and imagination of the kingdom of God. Such an imagination is not devoid of propositions but invites people into practices much deeper than mental assent. The power and hope is offered in and through Jesus Christ by the power of the Holy Spirit, by the will of the Father. Notice that worship is not antirational, nor should teaching be dismissed. Christian education must be about formation. It is very likely that my son would hear my lecture very differently after watching the movie on Pistol Pete. Why? Because his imagination had been captured.

Christian worship offers practices and habits that open new possibilities and insights into what God is doing in bringing the kingdom of God. Christian worship is a place for a renewed vision and further participation in this imagination of becoming more fully who God has created people to be. Christian worship is about a further practicing, embodying, and living into God's wonderful story of redemption. This helps to frame how we think of conversion. Conversion is not simply a rational attempt to logically prove that following Jesus is cognitively correct. Rather, as a person is captivated by the life of Jesus, who invites the church to enter into and continue this story, it reshapes the person's desire. As a person desires, so shall he or she do. Once a Christian imagination has been captured, a person desires to learn the habits and practices of Christians. "Thus we become certain kinds of people; we begin to emulate, mimic, and mirror the particular vision that we desire. Attracted by it and moved toward it, we begin to live into this vision of the good life and start to look like citizens who inhabit the world that we picture as the good life."[10] Too often Christianity has had the assertion that once a person believes rightly he or she will then live rightly. It seems humans are wired a bit in the reverse of such an idea. A person's habits can also help to reconfigure his or her desires.

A few students have come to me over the years confessing sadness over their loss of faith. Some recount that the beliefs they had when they were younger are shifting and that they are not sure they can still believe in God in the same way. I offer a remedy many before have suggested. Pray, read Scripture, and worship with a body of believers. This prescription is not legalistic, magical, or manipulative but formative. Aristotle noted that people can become virtuous by following a master's habits. A person's desires are shaped by his or her habitual practices. Similarly, John Wesley affirmed that through practices that become habits, one's attitudes, actions (tempers), and desires would be healed and matured to love more rightly.[11] When students tell me they are not sure they can believe, I encourage them to simply do what Christians do.

As another example, suppose I say, "I want to run a marathon, but I am not athletic and I do not believe I can do it." I could hire a motivational speaker to encourage me to think positively, to discipline my mind and envision myself running a marathon successfully. This motivational coach might even be passionate and persuasive. He or she might be effective enough to really make me believe I could run a marathon. Yet even if I "believe," I doubt I would ever lace up my shoes. I would do much better if I found someone who runs marathons and just go out and start training with him or her. I would not become a marathoner instantly but would develop the habits and practices of a marathoner over time, building up stamina and endurance by mimicking the habits of a master. If I keep following and doing what marathoners do, eventually I would be able to run a marathon and become a marathoner.

This process of being Christian must be learned in community. Being renewed and transformed into the image of Christ is not about an individual quest done in isolation, drawing only from the resources within. Handing a person a Bible and saying, "Go for it," is clearly disastrous. Paul, who was trained by the leaders of the church in Jerusalem, describes the importance of being mentored by others. Christian formation is learned in community by following and mimicking the habits of those who are mature Christians. However, too often discipleship or catechism is reduced to facts, figures, dates, and Bible trivia. Even theological truths are emphasized as something merely to be mentally believed. Rather, catechism and discipleship should be about following in step with the way of life of those who are more mature in their Christian formation. This is the wisdom of having a sponsor when going through the catechumenate (period of catechism—instruction and formation). This relationship between novices and sponsors involves formation, but this formation goes beyond merely downloading and intellectually assenting to facts, doctrines, Scripture, and creeds. Christians are formed not only cognitively but also bodily through doing—that is, mimicking or copying what other Christians do both in communal worship on the Lord's Day and in lived worship throughout the week.

As a person continues in the habits of Christian practice, he or she continues to be more fully captured by the Christian imagination and hope of the kingdom of God. Smith is clear that this is not erasing the importance for Christian thinking—that is, reflecting on the creeds, the doctrines, and Christian theology.[12] In some places discipleship is reduced to a person mentally assenting that he or she is a sinner and that Christ offers forgiveness for his or her sins. Encountering the power of the gospel and the love of Christ is more than just agreeing to ideas about Christ. Remember, "Even the demons believe [in God]—and shudder" (James 2:19).

What is being encouraged here is not that people should *decide* to be shaped more by fostering habits than by assenting to ideas. Rather, Smith's claim is that habits, leading us to either virtues or vices, are the primary means by which we are shaped and formed. In many ways *as we do, so we become.* Therefore, all habits are loaded; they all have an agenda, and some narrative and imagination is forming us. It is also true that we are habituated from many different stories. While I want to claim that the habits of Christianity and Christian worship are the most formative, I must also be aware that my habits of watching sports, consuming things, being entertained, and so on, all vie to be the most powerful and captivating story. Christian worship, like other habits, reflects and shapes "what matters to us."[13] In other words, habits not only speak about who we are becoming but also help to shape us to become what the habits open us to be.

## Questions for Discussion and Reflection

1.  What ideas were the most helpful in this chapter?

2.  What ideas are the most challenging?

3.  In light of this chapter, what should we consider to be the point and purpose of worship?

4.  How has Christianity become reduced to mentally assenting to propositional statements?

5.  How can communal worship form habits of the imagination of the kingdom of God?

# THREE

# CREATED FOR WORSHIP

*Christian communal worship is the glorification of God and the*
*sanctification of humanity as a divine-human event where God*
*offers transformation and healing **to help people become more fully***
***what God created them to be and do**. . . .*
—Theology of Worship Mosaic

I had the privilege of being a youth pastor for over fifteen years and now teach undergraduates at a liberal arts Christian university. While the faces and hairstyles change, many of the same questions remain: "Why am I here?" "What is my purpose in life?" "What does it mean to be human?" When my students ask these questions, some are not interested in answers—they simply like to see their professor squirm. I suggest to them that the story of Christian theology is audacious enough to offer some very simple responses to these big questions of human existence. Yet the very beginning of the Christian narrative switches the primary subject: "In the beginning God . . ." (Gen. 1:1, KJV).

## Genesis: Created in the Image of God

What follows both in Scripture and in life is the story of God, not the story of *me*. In this story all people really matter. They matter because God formed and breathed life into them (Gen. 2:7) and created them good (1:31).[1] Genesis 1–2 also affirms that the only thing worthy of worship is that which is not created. According to the Genesis narrative, that excludes everything except God. Worship is giving something your ultimate allegiance, devotion, or obedience. Idolatry is worshipping anything that is created. Genesis 1–2 thus describes the greatness and glory of God, the One who rightly ought to receive all worship.

Furthermore, as the Jews and Christians tell it, from the very beginning of God's story, all of creation is birthed from God's love (*creatio ex amore*—creation out of love). God's story also suggests in Gen. 1:26 that humankind is created in the *image of God*. Genesis 1 and 2 suggest that being created in God's image includes being in relationships with other humans as well as God. Genesis 2:18 asserts that God did not want Adam to be alone and thus made Eve as Adam's partner and helper. Created in the image of God also comes with a calling from God to have dominion and stewardship over the rest of creation. This stewardship of creation is an extension of humans' love for God and each other. Therefore, in the very beginning of God's story, the big questions of human existence are answered with a purpose and an appropriate order. Genesis 1–3 suggests the following:

1. The story of life is God's story.
2. God alone is worthy of worship.
3. Humans are created out of love to love.
4. Created in the image of God, humans are to love God, love themselves, love other humans, be loved, and care for creation as an extension of the first four.

While this story is about God, we learn about God in order to learn how to be human as created in God's image.

This is emphasized positively in Gen. 1 and 2 and tragically in the stories of the tree and slain brother in Gen. 3 and 4. God's appraisals of pleasure, "and God saw that it was good," in Gen. 1 and 2, are contrasted with penetrating questions of sadness in chapters 3 and 4. In these stories of failure, God's questions offer a haunting reminder of what it means to be human. After Adam and Eve ate the fruit from the Tree of Knowledge of Good and Evil, they hid from God. Instead of walking and talking with God in the garden, they hid and heard God say, "Where are you?" (3:9). This question is not asked because God needed a GPS to find the couple. God's question points to something of deeper significance; having been created in the image of God means that Adam and Eve were created for relationship with God. Because of Adam and Eve's disobedience, God was proclaiming through questions the brokenness in their relationship with God.

Unfortunately, this couple's offspring continued to fall short of being human. Abel's offering pleased God while Cain's did not. Out of jealousy and anger Cain killed his brother. Just as with his parents, God's first response is a question, "Where is your brother?" (4:9). Cain attempts to deny his responsibility for his brother and fellow human, "Am I my brother's keeper?" (v. 9). God's answer leaves no doubt: "Your brother's blood is crying out to me from the ground!" (v. 10). It is interesting that Cain's failure to love himself and insecurity over an inferior offering fostered violence against a fellow human, his brother. In this tragic narrative, the story of God suggests that being created in the image of God means to love oneself and other creatures well.

The punishments God inflicts on Adam, Eve, and Cain are noteworthy. Adam and Eve were removed from the garden, and now Adam must toil on the land to survive while Eve will experience tremendous pain during childbirth. Cain, who was a "tiller of the ground," would now find the ground barren: "It will no longer yield to you its strength" (vv. 2, 12). Instead of using the ground as a means of life, Cain must now wander the earth. Implicit in these punishments is the idea that when relationships with God and fellow humans are broken, a broken, barren, and difficult relationship is also created with the rest of creation humans are charged to steward. Within God's story, humans find their purpose and calling, which is to love, and broken relationships result from a failure to respond properly to this purpose and calling. So how does this calling or invitation to love connect to worshipping?

## New Testament: Communion in Love

When asked what the greatest commandment is, Jesus answered, "Love the Lord your God with all your heart, and with all your soul, and with all your mind, and with all your strength" (Mark 12:30). Too often Christians fail to consider the implications of this first commandment and move quickly on to the second commandment: "Love your neighbor as yourself" (v. 31). In no way do I want to separate these two important commandments, but I want to consider the idea that there is a hierarchy of loves. In focusing on the first and greatest commandment, I wonder what it looks like to have one's primary focus be on loving God. Jesus seems to imply that the most important thing humans do is to worship God, which then makes a proper love of self and others possible.

When I suggest to my students that God created us to worship God, several of them become agitated. Some respond, "So God really created us because God is either narcissistic or codependent." On the surface, it might seem that such a critique is fair. I have known a few couples whose marriages were on the verge of implosion. As a last ditch effort to "keep love alive" these couples decide to have a child. In the end, the child is not conceived in a communion of love but out of selfishness. "Child, we birthed you, not because we love you, but so we could use you to keep Mommy and Daddy's marriage together." Yikes! Is this why God created? Absolutely not! God created as an extension of who God is—Love. The doctrine of the Trinity celebrates that God is not needy in any way. God did not create to help offset an anemic divine ego. Rather, God created so that *love might flourish*. Therefore, God created humans so they might receive life in the very love of the triune God.

Within a robust theology of worship it becomes evident that God's *invitation to* and *purpose of* creation is so that all things may participate in the very love and intimacy of the triune God. Remember, this is the story of God and not the story of *me*. I can only become fully human as I am doing what God created me to do. As creation declares and embodies the glory and splendor of God, being fully human finds its ultimate end in glorifying God, which is precisely creation's sanctification. Jesus notes that the supreme end of creation is that creation may be united in God. As the gospel of John records in Jesus' Gethsemane prayer,

As you, Father, are in me and I am in you, may they also be in us, so that the world may believe that you have sent me. The glory that you have given me I have given them, so that they may be one, as we are one, I in them and you in me, that they may become completely one, so that the world may know that you have sent me and have loved them even as you have loved me. (John 17:21-23)

Christ came so that the world may be redeemed and become one in God. Too often people who follow the story of *me* narrate a "gospel" that focuses on *me* having both a "happier" life here while also securing *my* eternal destiny. The Christian gospel is perverted when the sole focus is on the idea that "I become a Christian so that I can get to heaven." Furthermore, heaven is often envisioned as "my personal utopia where I get to have all my desires fulfilled." Sadly, this describes not the Christian gospel but hedonism (the story of *me*). Hedonism is a doctrine or way of life where my pleasure and happiness is the primary or sole good in life. Conversely, in Paul's writings and in the book of Revelation, heaven is portrayed very much like an eternal worship service (e.g., the saints before the throne of God in Rev. 7). Communal worship provides both a proper vision and empowerment to keep our lives grounded in and lived for God. Moreover, communal worship offers a proper vision and empowerment for our ethics in the world. As the church is encountered, transformed, and then sent from the Word and Table, it is invited to join the *missio Dei* (mission of God) by continuing the ministry of the incarnation. What happens in communal worship shapes (for better or worse) how people live in the world.

## Sin: Failing to Be Human

So this leads to the question, how does worship open people to receiving the life and love of God? To answer this, attention must be given to the possibility of choosing death.

The Wesleyan tradition affirms that even though original sin is destructive, through the gift of forgiveness through Christ, humans have been given the freedom to choose God or not, which is the choice of life or death. As the stories of Adam, Eve, and Cain show, God desires us to love well, but God does not force or coerce our love. The freedom to choose for or against God provides the very context for how we discuss love and sin. If God determines or controls all human actions, if there is no human choice, there is no human action that is *loving* or *sinful*. So with this God-powered gift to choose life and love comes the possibility to *be* and *do* what humans were created and invited to *be* and *do*. Yet humans have not always chosen well; at some point all have chosen to move away from God. The irony is tragic. Many humans choose to move away from God, not because they are seeking death, but because they believe that distance from God is the space where life can be found. Somehow a narrative outside of God captivates, forms, and draws people away. In searching for life outside of God, people treat themselves as though they are of greatest worth. In the search for life, people try to be fully human by treating themselves as divine. When people worship themselves, they move away from the gift of personhood that God desires to give them.

While this is true for many, other people fail to be human by failing to love themselves well. Diane Leclerc suggests that for some people worshipping (being fixated on) another person causes them to love themselves less.[2] When individuals sin, they become less than human. Part of the invitation to worship God removes the lure of finding life through worshipping the self or another person (treating the self or another person as ultimate) and enables one to properly love oneself, love others, and be loved. Humans were created to love. Worshipping God assists in keeping those loves properly ordered and enables us to be more fully human.

As a person receives life and love from God, he or she responds first by loving God. This is why the first and greatest commandment is to "Love the Lord your God" (Mark 12:30). As God's story describes God's desire for Adam *not* to be alone, humans are also invited to appropriately love themselves, love others, be loved, and care for creation as a continuation and extension of their love for God. These loves are all connected. I cannot say I love God and hate another person (including myself). "Those who say, 'I love God,' and hate their brothers or sisters, are liars; for those who do not love a brother or sister whom they have seen, cannot love God whom they have not seen" (1 John 4:20).

Furthermore, people are not to love creatures above or instead of the Creator. "Therefore God gave them up in the lusts of their hearts to impurity, to the degrading of their bodies among themselves, because they exchanged the truth about God for a lie and worshiped and served the creature rather than the Creator, who is blessed forever! Amen" (Rom. 1:24-25).

In creating creatures for relationships in love, God created humans to worship. Worship is the ability God gives to every human so that he or she can respond in thanksgiving to God that "I am not all that is; I am not ultimate—and thus I have hope and joy in God." There is a better way to be human, to find life, than through the story of *me*. It is only when I do not seek to make myself or someone else the center that I can truly embrace love for God, myself, and others. It is only then that I can become fully human for the glory of God.

Humans often choose to follow the story of *me* and not God. This disease of sin is disastrous. As a disease, sin is an intruder and virus feeding off a healthy body, moving it away from life. As a disease, the body often fails to *remember* what health looks and feels like. However, God does not leave us alone in our sickness and disordered loves. Since we are created in God's image, God desires to heal us from the habits of life where we choose self or another over God. Hence, through worship, God continues to make us more fully human by offering healing and forgiveness. When our lives are fixated on God, and God's love flows through us, we can better reflect God's glory back to God and to our fellow creatures and ourselves. When reflecting God's glory in loving relationships, we then become what God created us to be, caught up in the very love of the triune God. Humans were created so that love might flourish all for the glory of God.

Thus we receive the gift of life by worshipping God, and in that worship we love ourselves, love our fellow creatures, and are loved rightly.

## Questions for Discussion and Reflection

1. What ideas were the most helpful in this chapter?

2. What ideas are you struggling with or challenged by?

3. In light of this chapter, what should we consider to be the point and purpose of worship?

4. What do you like or dislike about the claim that to worship God is a proper way to be more fully human?

5. How does this chapter inform what communal worship should be about?

## FOUR
# HEALING THROUGH COMMUNAL WORSHIP

*Christian communal worship is the glorification of God and the sanctification of humanity as a divine-human event where God **offers transformation and healing** to help people become more fully what God created them to be and do. . . .*

—Theology of Worship Mosaic

Through communal worship God continues to sanctify people, healing them from the disease of sin so that they can live a life of loving and being loved abundantly. As a divine-human healing and transforming event, communal worship is a means of grace.[1]

Thus far, I have suggested that God created humans to love God, love themselves, love other creatures, be loved, and care for creation as an extension of the first four. A properly ordered love exalts God as ultimate and the only One worthy of worship. To worship any created thing (including ourselves and others) is idolatry. When our loves are disordered, it prevents us from being fully human. The disease of sin cannot be healed through individual determination and human effort. Communal worship is not only *the* primary activity humans were created to do but also a primary healing event to help people reorder their loves and receive healing from the disease of sin.

## Narratives of Healing

She was scared to death. She did not have time to be humiliated. Fear for her life outweighed any sense of self-worth. Everything had happened so swiftly she was disoriented. The men had grabbed her and dragged her through the streets. She knew the penalty for adultery, and she knew women often received this penalty while the men were left alone. Her accusers had stones in their hands, and she knew they were taking her to the temple. Her accusers brought her to a man at the temple to ask him what should be done. She wondered if he was an expert in the Law who would offer a legal pronouncement of her death sentence. She was forced to stand before him, her shame, fear, and pain causing her to become feeble.

As she awaited her death, her accusers said to this man, "Teacher, this woman was caught in the very act of committing adultery. Now in the law Moses commanded us to stone such women" (John 8:4-5). The man did not speak but stooped down and began drawing something in the sand. She could not see what it was. Fear continued to grip her for what this man would do to her. Then he spoke. "Let anyone among you who is without sin be the first to throw a stone at her" (v. 7). Suddenly her accusers dropped their stones to the ground and left. Now what would happen? This man was the only one who remained. She was too ashamed to look at him and still fearful about what he would do. He then spoke to her with a gentle warmth and firmness. "Woman, where are the ones who condemn you?" (see v. 10). She looked around and saw no one but this man. She spoke in a choked whisper. "No one, sir" (v. 11). Then he looked not only at her but also right into her with a piercing look of tenderness and compassion and said, "Neither do I condemn you. Go your way, and from now on do not sin again" (v. 11). She was speechless. From humiliation, to anticipating her death, to a word of compassion—but a word of compassion that invited her into a different *way* of life, perhaps to follow this man who was *the way*. This encounter with Jesus was not simply an encounter that saved her from death but an encounter that invited her to begin living for the first time in a long time.[2]

He found his spot again on the busy road. Even though he could not see them, he knew many of the people who were passing by. When your sight is gone, other senses become almost superhuman. People were not very generous this day. He had received very little money on this day of begging. Only three pockets of his cloak had any coins. That would barely be enough for a loaf of bread later in the day. Then he began to hear something that was unusual. There was a crowd approaching. As people rushed by, he heard someone say that Jesus was coming. He had heard about this Jesus and his ability to heal people. He believed this was his chance. As the crowds grew louder he knew he had to try something. He took a deep breath and yelled with all of his might, "Jesus, Son of David, have mercy on me!" (Mark 10:47).

Those in the crowd were trying to hear what Jesus was saying and told the blind man to shut up. He would not be deterred; he yelled again, "Son of David, have mercy on me!" (v. 48). Suddenly everything grew quiet. Those who had just told him to shut up were encouraging him to rise and go see Jesus. He only had an instant to think about it. He threw off his cloak, which held his little pittance and was the only source of warmth, and went to where he heard Jesus. Jesus then asked him what he felt was a stupid question. "What do you want me to do for you?" (v. 51). He replied quickly, "I want to see" (see v. 51). Jesus replied, "Go; your faith has made you well" (v. 52). The man who had been blind could see immediately. But this story is not yet over. After the man could see, he followed Jesus on the *way*. This encounter with Jesus provided not only sight but also an imagination to *see* how to become human, following Christ.[3]

Similarly, recall the woman Jesus met during the middle of the day at a well in Samaria (see John 4:1-42). Her encounter with Jesus moved her from confessor to worshipper to evangelist. She traveled back to the town from which she was an outcast and shepherded the town to the Great Shepherd of the Sheep. The Samaritan woman's testimony was compelling enough that the town asked Jesus to stay for two extra days. The result, many believed because of the woman's testimony and the face-to-face encounter with Jesus. The healing and reconciliation of this narrative was not only between Jesus and this woman but also between herself and her community.

## The Dynamics of Healing

In these narratives healing occurs in many dimensions. Believers look upon the physical healings of Jesus in the Gospels with amazement. However, a broader imagination is needed for healing. The blind receiving sight, the lame walking, and the dead being raised are demonstrations of God's power in Jesus over sickness and even physical death. This healing also proclaimed to those who felt their disease was a sign of God's curse that God loved and believed in them and was not punishing them. However, physical healing is not the primary healing Christ offers. All those who were physically healed eventually physically died. The fullness of Christ's healing was the restoration of relationship to love God, love oneself, love others, and be loved. To demonstrate this point let's reflect on an important healing narrative found in all three Synoptic Gospels (Matthew, Mark, and Luke).

A paralyzed man is brought to Jesus. Jesus looks at the paralytic and says, "Son, your sins are forgiven" (Mark 2:5). Did you catch what just happened? The man cannot walk and Jesus offers him forgiveness of sins. I imagine many were confused and perhaps thought Jesus had missed the point of why this man was brought to him. Some scribes were not confused, but angry. "Why does this fellow speak in this way? It is blasphemy! Who can forgive sins but God alone?" (v. 7). While the scribes were theologically correct concerning forgiveness, Jesus sensed their disapproval. He responded, "'Which is easier, to say to the paralytic, "Your sins are forgiven," or to say, "Stand up and take your mat and walk"? But so that you may know that the Son of Man has authority on earth to forgive sins'—he said to the paralytic—'I say to you, stand up, take your mat and go to your home.' And he stood up, and immediately took the mat and went out before all of them" (vv. 9-12).

I often ask my students the question Jesus asked the scribes, and most of them get it. It is much easier to say, "Your sins are forgiven"; after all, verification of such a proclamation would be impossible to deny. However, to say, "Get up," would require instant verification. The point of this narrative is not to undermine the importance of the physical healing but to affirm that healing also includes the restoration of relationships to love. Furthermore, healing encounters with God do not guarantee the physical healing of bodies; however, God's faithfulness to offer spiritual healing is offered to all who have the courage to respond. The full healing is a renewal into the *imago Dei* to love God, love oneself, love other creatures, and be loved.

## The Response to Healing

Some may be asking, "What in the world do these stories of healing and transformation have to do with worship?" In my mind, everything. They are illustrations of the Christian narrative celebrating that encounters with God offer dynamic healing and transformation from the disease of sin to a life of love. While God can be encountered in all times, in all places, and among all peoples, God birthed the church by the Spirit for the primary task of encountering God in communal worship. Thus an encounter with God that empowers me to be present to God and others can be a moment of dynamic healing and transformation. God's Spirit that invites and gathers people to worship creates a space for humans to respond to God. Simply being encountered by God does not guarantee I will respond well to the healing and life God offers. Recall that the rich man in Mark 10:17-27 (also Luke 18:18-23) went away very sad because he could not handle the invitation to life; he was drowning in his possessions.

## The Response of Sacrificial Obedience

All of these narratives describe a divine-human healing and transforming encounter that demanded a response by those who were encountered. Jesus offers not only forgiveness but forgiveness wedded to repentance, a command to life, a command to "sin no more." The transforming encounters with Christ imagine much more than relief from guilt; they offer the invitation to a life full of hope and love. Moreover, the healing encounters with the Samaritan woman of John 4 and Bartimaeus, the blind man of Mark 10, offered more than an easier life; they were healed so that they might become followers. The healing and transforming encounters with God open new possibilities of further participation in God's work of redemption in the world. A person's healing opens up possibilities not simply for that person but for his or her community as well.

While God can offer healing outside of communal worship, communal worship is a primary place for God to heal, renew, and redeem people. Through communal worship God is calling people to be renewed into the image and likeness of God (Gen. 1:27-28). Communal worship is not simply an outward demonstration of piety; rather, "the practices of Christian worship are nothing less than training to be *human*."[4] In worship, people are offered healing and are being habituated into practices of love. This call to worship is an invitation for people to respond to God's invitation to become. "This call to worship is an echo of God's word that called humanity into being (Gen. 1:26-27); the call of God that brought creation into existence is echoed in God's call to worship that brings together a *new* creation (2 Cor. 5:17)."[5] God's call to creation empowers a response by those who were created in love, for love. Within God's providence, this call to love must be responded to in order that people might fully become what God intended. Communal worship is an invitation by God to receive the healing, vision, and empowerment to become more fully human. While each personal healing is worthy of celebration, all healings participate in God's further redemption of the world.

This response to healing and God's call invites people into ministry in the world that requires every bit of the "living sacrifice" Paul imagines in Rom. 12. The dynamic healing encounters between God and Moses, Gideon, David, and Paul were invitations to a life that participates in God's further redemption in the world. The healing in worship offered by God empowers a response of sacrificial obedience to go wherever the Spirit leads. God offers healing so that all who are healed may become evangelists, pastors, and priests to those whom God has placed in their paths. Bartimaeus's recovery of sight was not only about his eyes but about a new opportunity for life in seeing and following Jesus. The woman at that Samaritan well would have missed out on the fullness of the healing God desired to do in and through her had she not testified to a town that had previously relegated her to the long shadows of the high noonday sun.

## Questions for Discussion and Reflection

1. What ideas were the most helpful in this chapter?

2. What ideas are you struggling with or challenged by?

3. In light of this chapter, what should we consider to be the point and purpose of worship?

4. How does communal worship offer healing to become more fully human?

5. How does this chapter inform what communal worship should be about?

# FIVE

# THE RHYTHMIC BREATHING
# OF COMMUNAL WORSHIP

*Christian communal worship is the glorification of God and the*
*sanctification of humanity as a divine-human event where God offers*
*transformation and healing to help people become more fully what*
*God created them to be and do.* ***God breathes (inhales) and gathers in***
***individual Christians to heal, transform, and renew them as the***
***body of Christ to breathe (exhale) them out to continue the ministry***
***of the incarnation that participates in the kingdom of God***
***more fully coming. . . .***[1]
—Theology of Worship Mosaic

I have regular contact with people who do not currently attend church or profess to being Christian. Engaging them about their views of Christianity and the church fascinates and saddens me. Some have experienced condemnation, judgment, and hypocrisy. Some have been deeply wounded and scarred by people at the church, including leaders. Some feel that Christians are only interested in coming together to form a mutual admiration society to affirm how righteous "we" are and how sinful "everyone" else is. Some feel that Christians only care about those "inside the walls" and not about those outside, in their local neighborhoods. Such pain and concern comes not only from those "outsiders" but also from God: "You that are accursed, depart from me into the eternal fire prepared for the devil and his angels; for I was hungry and you gave me no food, I was thirsty and you gave me nothing to drink, I was a stranger and you did not welcome me, naked and you did not give me clothing, sick and in prison and you did not visit me" (Matt. 25:41-43).

Jesus said plainly anyone can love those who love him or her. If you love me, you will love those unlike you. You will love your enemies and especially those who persecute you (see also 5:43-48). Certainly that includes people living in our neighborhoods and subdivisions, apartment complexes and under the bridges, rescue shelters and detention centers. Neglecting those outside the walls is a critique not only from those on the outside but also from those on the inside who recognize something is amiss.

Some of the people who are tired of the church's hypocrisy, judgment, and inward gaze attempt to follow Jesus' command of compassion but do so cut off from a worshipping community. Some who are honestly frustrated with local churches assert, "We are going to stop wasting our time in worship and instead go and feed the poor." While the motivation to care for those hurting is just, the remedy cannot include removing oneself from the empowerment and vision to love. What should be the relationship between communal worship and loving those who currently are on the margins, shadows, and gutters of our cities?

## The Rhythm of Breathing

A few years ago some friends of mine asked if my wife and I would join their Sawtooth Relay team. We enjoyed these friends, so we trusted them and signed up without fully grasping what we were committing to. As it turns out, this was a sixty-three-mile relay from Stanley to Ketchum, Idaho, in which each member runs two legs averaging over six miles. For avid distance runners this is nothing. For a middle-aged adult nonrunner, such as myself, training was mandatory. So I began to train.

As I set out around my university's track, the first lap was not too bad, but laps two and beyond became increasingly more difficult. I soon learned that running longer distances demands both mental and physical discipline. In my early training I quickly learned how important it was to breathe well. For nonrunners like me, this may sound comical. How hard can it be to breathe? Isn't this just part of our involuntary system? Yet when you run, if you do not develop a good breathing rhythm, you will collapse or pass out. If you breathe too quickly, with shallow breaths, you are literally starving the body of oxygen and you will pass out. Breathing too deeply and too slowly also yields disaster. Training taught me that breathing should be in tune with the rhythm of my pace. Developing a disciplined rhythm of breathing in and breathing out is essential to becoming a successful distance runner.

As observed earlier, in Gen. 1–2, God breathed into the dust and Adam came to life. God's Breath is the very thing that sustains all living creatures. While the rhythm of breathing in oxygen and expelling carbon dioxide gives life to our body, so, too, does God's Spirit desire to gather (breathe in) the body of Christ in order to send it out (exhale it) to participate in God's present and coming kingdom.

## Breathed In: Being Gathered for Christian Communal Worship

Glancing at the history of Christian worship offers intriguing insights. One of the most illuminating is the claim that Christians do not *go* to church; rather, God gathers the believers together by the Spirit. At first glance, this concept struck me as obtuse and a bit of theological mumbo jumbo. I get up and get ready on Sunday. My wife and I get the kids ready, drive to church, park, enter the sanctuary, and sit down. Nowhere in that scenario did I feel or sense God getting me there; it felt like a great deal of my effort. Furthermore, my students who attend "Bedside Baptist" do not report having to resist the Spirit from physically dragging them to communal worship.

Being gathered is a response to God's call. The Greek word for church is *ekklēsia (ek-kaleō), "the called-out ones."* The church is not a "voluntary society of those whose chief concern is to share, to build community, to enjoy fellowship, to have moral instruction for their children. Rather it is a society of those who have been chosen, redeemed, called, justified, and are being sanctified until one day they will be glorified."[2] The long tradition of liturgical theology has continually emphasized that God has first called, God has first beckoned. Furthermore, God, through the power of the Holy Spirit, makes possible our response to be gathered. The emphasis that humans are gathered by the power of the Holy Spirit is not made to minimize human response and activity as it is to recognize that God is the One who fashions, creates, and renews the church in and through local gathered bodies into one body, the body of Christ. God, as Creator, is always the primary Actor. This gathering of Christians is the means through which the Spirit opens us to the imagination of being God's called people. Stanley Hauerwas suggests the gift of being gathered (breathed in) for communal worship:

> Gathering indicates that Christians are called from the world, from their homes, from their families to be constituted into a community capable of praising God. . . . The church is constituted to be a new people who have been gathered from the nations to remind the world that we are in fact one people. Gathering, therefore, is an eschatological act as it is the foretaste of the unity of the communion of the saints.[3]

Yet upon greater consideration of the role of God's Spirit in the life of believers, the idea that God gathers and breathes in the believers offers a powerful image. Genesis 1 and 2 declare in praise that God breathes into people and this Breath sustains and empowers them so that without God's Breath they are unable to do anything (see the conversation on Pentecost later). At a basic level, I am only able to make breakfast, wash my face, and walk to the sanctuary as God's Spirit has empowered me physically and emotionally to do so. Moreover, the Spirit's gathering occurs not simply in getting us to the sanctuary or worship space but also in enabling us to be present to Jesus Christ, the Incarnate Word, and to fellow believers. Susan White notes, "It is the Word of God, read and preached and received, that calls the Christian community together to worship."[4]

So God's Spirit gathers and breathes in the church to encounter Jesus Christ, and this encounter between believers and Christ is at the center of the entire Christian worship service of the Word and Table. The gathering of the people of God around Scripture serves as a conduit to encounter Jesus Christ as the key and unique component of Christian worship. The centrality of Scripture as a means by which the body of Christ is made present to Christ is the basis for Christian worship. The image of the people of God gathered around God's Word is at the heart of the study of Christian worship. Being gathered by the Spirit to encounter Christ, oneself, and one another provides a healing context that sends us from communal worship to carry on the mission of Jesus Christ. As the church encounters Christ and offers itself with Christ in the offering and at the Eucharist Table, the church is renewed as the body of Christ. In this renewal as the body of Christ, the church is sent, blown out, by and with the Spirit to continue the ministry of the incarnation.

## Breathed Out: Sent Out for Doxological Mission

We are gathered and breathed in on the Lord's Day to then be sent out to worship all week long in the places where the Spirit leads us. It is not the case that Christians only worship God on Sundays. The church as the body of Christ is sent from that service in hope and joy to participate in God's mission in the world. The church continues its Sunday worship by living lives of thanks and praise from Monday to Saturday. Communal worship is shaped by a blessed rhythm of God gathering the believers (breathing them in) for a time of healing, praise, and transformation so that they can worship personally all week long as they participate in the further coming of God's kingdom.

Within this rhythm of being breathed in to be breathed out, a further word needs to be said to those who would rather remain blown out and never breathed/gathered in. As stated above, many who have critiqued local churches for neglecting those "outside" have attempted to solve this hypocrisy by neglecting to be in a gathered body, refusing the inhaling of the Spirit. While caring for the lost, broken, and marginalized is the church's vocation of doxology during the week, if individuals are cut off from the service of Word and Table, they run the risk of drawing on their own strength and not the Holy Spirit's. Furthermore, while God's Spirit can work love and hospitality through all people of the world, God intends Christians to be empowered and further healed in communal worship. When Christians resist the Spirit's inhaling, they run the great risk of failing to know how to properly love and care for those placed in their paths. Furthermore, when serving the lost, poor, and broken, it is tempting for us to think about how "holy, good, and righteous" we are for showing this benevolence. The service of Word and Table reminds the church that such ministry to others is done for God's glory; it is not a work that earns credit but an occasion through which people can give honor and glory to God.

This rhythm of breathing, healing, and ministry is a celebration *now* of the healing and redemption God has done and is doing in the world. Yet the encounter with God in communal worship also offers an imagination of what God will do as the kingdom continues to come. Hence, the church living into the hope of the future consummation of the kingdom is called to participate in God's further healing in all the places the Spirit blows the church.

## Questions for Discussion and Reflection

1. What ideas were the most helpful in this chapter?

2. What ideas are you struggling with or challenged by?

3. In light of this chapter, what should we consider to be the point and purpose of worship?

4. How does this rhythm of being breathed in to be breathed out illumine the role of communal worship and missional worship throughout the week?

## SIX
# FORMING CHRISTIANS IN THE CHURCH

*Christian communal worship is the glorification of God and the*
*sanctification of humanity as a divine-human event where God offers*
*transformation and healing to help people become more fully what*
*God created them to be and do.* ***God breathes (inhales) and gathers in***
***individual Christians to heal, transform, and renew them as the body***
***of Christ*** *to breathe (exhale) them out to continue the ministry of the*
*incarnation that participates in the kingdom of God more fully coming. . . .*
—Theology of Worship Mosaic

Participation in a local gathered community of faith is the central practice of Christians; however, some basic guidelines must be drawn for what is confessed to be genuine Christian communal worship. Christian communal worship should be public, contain certain practices, and be under the ministry of the ordained.

I have suggested that God created humans to worship. Worship is a participation in the ongoing healing from the disease of sin that offers reconciliation between God, ourselves, and others. However, some people who appreciate and value worship hesitate committing to Christian communal worship and participation in a local community of faith. Keeping this hesitancy in mind, this chapter will first argue—from the perspective of church history (tradition) and experience—for the importance of a person's participation in a local body. Second, this chapter will explore specific markers for what is the full embodiment of Christian communal worship. The underlying current of this entire conversation is an attempt to maintain a tension between the church's traditions and present context. Local worship teams must be careful to avoid being held captive to the tyranny of the present. The tyranny of the present often asserts that only what is new is good, with things traditional often being disregarded simply for their longevity. Of course some congregations lean too far in the other direction by privileging the old and critiquing anything new.

Some questions to explore include, "Can you be Christian and not attend a church, a local community of Christ?" "Can you and three friends have a Bible study over coffee and call that church?" "What do you need for Christian worship?"

I have grown up and lived my entire life in the Christian faith and in a local body of Christ. In many ways I never *converted to Christ.* Through the prevenient mercy of God and the power of the Holy Spirit, I have chosen to remain in the body of Christ. The Holy Spirit, through my parents and other family members, brought me into the local community of faith. As an infant this was not my choice but something that was imposed on me. Some may be dismayed at such a practice, asserting that my parents infringed on my freedom. This certainly was the case. As a young child, adolescent, and teenager I never had a choice about whether or not I would worship in a local church body and live in a home saturated by God and the Scriptures. While some may recoil at my parents' actions, I consider what they did a blessed gift from God. I have never known life apart from the love of God and participation in a local body of faith. Through the local communities of faith into which I have been privileged to be grafted, I have found God's grace, healing, and empowerment. I also realize this is not the experience of everyone. Some people have had horrific acts of evil done to them by people in a local community of faith and even by such a community's ordained leaders. Yet with all these challenges, the importance of participating in a local community of faith is a paramount practice for Christians.

## The Necessary Gift of the Church

Every semester I teach an undergraduate course titled Introduction to Christian Theology. Exploring God's story provides illumination into who God is and, in light of this, who humans are created to be. Within these conversations it is always intriguing which topics within God's story elicit the greatest passion from my students. Issues on the authority and inspiration of Scripture, the problem of evil, whether God knows the future (and does it matter), and a host of other topics generate lively conversations. However, there is one topic that always creates much emotional angst. It is the discussion about the importance of the church. When this topic is raised, many of my students are not pleased with my assertions (although that is changing). At the outset of my lecture, I offer three propositions:

1. You *cannot* be a Christian if you do not regularly worship communally with the body of believers.
2. You can go to church and not be a Christian.
3. Going to church does not make you a Christian.

The first proposition is so foreign and unsettling that many of my students immediately raise their hands. While most of my students anonymously self-report weekly church attendance, many do not. Several students are concerned that my first proposition automatically fosters a type of legalism. Propositions two and three clarify that attending church, a local community of faith, is not some work or deed that earns a person his or her Christianity or proves he or she is a Christian. The main point I make in this conversation is that the majority of Christians throughout Christianity's two thousand years of existence have participated in communal worship. Along with this historical observation, I also make a normative claim: *People do not get to decide what it means to be Christian*.

I often ask my students who are on our collegiate sports teams to answer this question: "What if you told your coach you had decided that practice was boring and not much fun, so you would only be joining the team at game times and not at practice? What do you think would be the response of your coach?" "We would get kicked off," they reply. "Why?" I ask. "Because we cannot set our own rules." I respond, "So why do you think you can set your own rules when it comes to being a Christian?" This question usually does not generate any confident rebuttals. These students are not unique. Many Christians feel they get to define for themselves what it means to be a Christian. I do not find many who claim to be Christian opposed to worshipping God. Many struggle with the importance of doing this as part of a local body. In this struggle the story of God and the story of *me* are often in opposition. Just as God's story notes that it was not good for Adam to be alone, and just as God's story implies that Cain is Abel's keeper, God's story likewise observes that people can only be fully human in a community of believers.

One can see the confusion that would occur if a person gets to decide for himself or herself what it means to be Christian. Too often in North America the word "Christian" evokes a multitude of images and emotions. The main point here is to suggest that Christians have always found it necessary to come together for singing, instruction, fellowshipping, breaking bread, and prayer (see Acts 2:42). If Christians stop doing those things, they are simply no longer doing what Christians have (largely) always done. This argument is not solely from tradition, "We have always done this." It is also a matter of observation that people who attempt to continue a dynamic Christian life apart from a community of believers will fail. As the author of Hebrews notes, "Let us consider how to provoke one another to love and good deeds, not neglecting to meet together, as is the habit of some, but encouraging one another, and all the more as you see the Day approaching" (Heb. 10:24-25). This passage does not conceive of meeting together as some law or rule but understands it as an invitation to life. In being gathered together, the hope is that by the Spirit and in the fellowship of the faithful, Christians will become more loving and spurred on to having compassion for people in their world. This emphasis on communal worship is not a new form of legalism but recognition that every Christian is part of the church universal, both present, past, and future.

## What Is Needed for Christian Communal Worship?

My bright, yet cynical students reply, "Okay, if you want us to be in community, and if Jesus affirmed that 'where two or three are gathered there I am,' then why can't three of us head to a dorm room on Thursday night and call that communal worship?" I agree that church is not a building but God's gathered and redeemed people. While I want to affirm that authentic Christian worship can happen in dorm rooms, Starbucks, parks, beaches, ski slopes, and trains, with a group of people or all alone, the Christian communal worship gathering imagines something greater.

The history of Christian worship offers rubrics and boundaries in the discernment process for things that *are* and *are not* Christian worship. The Christian communal worship gathering involves several things. First, the gathering must be public—open to all. As public, I cannot simply invite my closest friends and be a group closed off to others who are "not like us" and call that Christian communal worship. Second, Christian worship should incorporate several practices, including prayers, Scripture, a sermon, an offering, and the sacraments (I will explore the practices, disciplines, and order of a Christian communal worship service more fully below).

At this point my students are not deterred. "So, we will Facebook and tweet our entire campus and community and invite whoever wants to come to be there. See, we can have Christian communal worship." Yet another important element is needed for the fullest expression of Christian communal worship. The third thing God established for the church is ordained pastors and priests. Like their response to my first proposition declaring that people who do not attend communal worship services cannot be Christian, the students' angst and ire rise again.

## The Gift of Clergy for Christian Communal Worship

The apostle Paul articulates God's calling and specific ministry of the ordained: "The gifts [God] gave were that some would be apostles, some prophets, some evangelists, some pastors and teachers, to equip the saints for the work of ministry, for building up the body of Christ, until all of us come to the unity of the faith and of the knowledge of the Son of God, to maturity, to the measure of the full stature of Christ" (Eph. 4:11-13).

This passage highlights several important things about clergy. First, God has gifted individuals with specific and unique gifts. In the New Testament Paul has several lists showing that God has gifted each person with unique charisms (giftings) for the body. This diversity of the Holy Spirit's gifting is for the benefit of the entire body (see 1 Cor. 12). Some of those charisms are for the leadership and edification of the church. Just as God raised the Levites for the people of Israel, so, too, God raises, calls, and equips women and men for prophetic and priestly ministry in the church.

Second, those called to leadership in the church are gifted to "equip the saints for the work of ministry, for building up the body of Christ" (Eph. 4:12). Those given leadership in the church are called and empowered to minister in the body of Christ to help every Christian become a minister of the gospel in the world. What is fascinating is that Paul equates this empowering of the laity for ministry with the building up of the body of Christ.

Third, Paul notes that this ministry by the pastors, teachers, and evangelists will continue "until all of us come to the unity of the faith and of the knowledge of the Son of God" (v. 13). It seems to be the case that this "all of us" is not just people in my local congregation but all Christians in the one body, one church (v. 4). The full imagination of this unity also includes those who are not yet part of the one body. Moreover, this "knowledge" is not simply a matter of cognitive assent, like affirming that 2 + 2 = 4. The New Testament affirms that to *know* the Christ is to proclaim him as Savior and Lord over all creation. This is not simply the goal for clergy but the calling of the church.

While some Christians do not have the luxury of ordained clergy, when there are clergy within reasonable proximity, believers should participate under their ministry. The ordained are not the superelites of the faith. They do not have all the answers or power that can never be questioned. God raises and gifts each person for a unique function in the body. The priests and pastors are called and gifted by God to lead and shepherd the local flock. Those who are called are also trained, examined, and confirmed by the church to verify their gifting and to place them in positions of authority in the church. The dynamic event of ordination is when the church confirms and sets apart individuals for ministry and the Holy Spirit offers further anointing, authority, and power to lead a local body of believers. Acts 6 offers an important narrative about the church raising several people and confirming their gifts for work in the body.

However, my students are still not fully persuaded. They ask, "What about the persecuted church in China that has so few ordained ministers? What about places in Africa where educational opportunities are limited and thus ordained pastors are in short supply?" These are important questions. The response is simple. God is at work in all corners of the world, even in places where the ordained clergy are not present. However, that is not what God desires or intends. This is not to speak against the authenticity of a community's faith that does not have the ordained. Such depletion reminds the church that its task is still undone. The church continues to find and affirm those individuals gifted by God and called from such local contexts who can be trained and empowered for leadership in the church.

To celebrate the importance of the clergy I offer my students another illustration. My class generally includes about forty undergraduates. I say, "Imagine we are all stranded on a desert island and one of us needs an appendectomy. Who in here is ready to perform that surgery?" I often look at my nursing and premed majors and ask, "Are any of you ready and capable to perform this surgery?" Most quickly answer, "No." So I ask, "Would you nursing and premed students feel more comfortable if we could fly in a doctor to perform the surgery?" They all answer emphatically, "Yes!" Some do not yet see the parallel. While most people, including nurses in the operating room, desire a trained, examined, and licensed surgeon, some think they would prefer to be led by people not educated and trained in the traditions of the church.

*does ordination have to come from those already ordained?*

The ordained make mistakes; the ordained are not infallible. People can encounter God and find healing without the ordained. However, God and the body of Christ gifts, graces, and trains women and men to preach the Word, administer the sacraments, and order the church. God has given the church the ordained to help equip the saints for ministry until all the world proclaims Christ as Savior.

So people do not get to decide individually for themselves what it means to be Christian in their confessions or communal practices. The significance of communal worship for Christians is clear from the viewpoints of history and practice. God invites and gathers all believers to communal worship under the leadership of the ordained for the further coming of the kingdom.

## Questions for Discussion and Reflection

1. What ideas were the most helpful in this chapter?

2. What ideas are the most difficult or causing the greatest amount of tension?

3. What do you think about the importance/necessity of regular participation in a local church?

4. What do you think about the three aspects of Christian communal worship: Open to the public, incorporates certain practices (which will be explored more fully below), led by ordained clergy?

5. In light of this chapter, what should we consider to be the point and purpose of worship?

SEVEN

# THE FULL IMAGINATION
# OF THE KINGDOM OF GOD

*Christian communal worship is the glorification of God and the
sanctification of humanity as a divine-human event where God offers
transformation and healing to help people become more fully what God
created them to be and do. God breathes (inhales) and gathers in individual
Christians to heal, transform, and renew them as the body of Christ to
breathe (exhale) them out to continue the ministry of the incarnation **that
participates in the kingdom of God more fully coming. The consummation
of the kingdom will come and God will be all in all.***
—Theology of Worship Mosaic

So what is the point of it all? This chapter explores the full and final hope of
communal worship. However, the end to which communal worship draws us
is the full and final purpose of the church, sacraments, Scripture, evangelism,
missions, salvation, Christ's incarnation, and even the point and purpose of creation—*that God will be all in all.* This conversation moves way beyond the myopic
question of "Why am I here?" to "Why is anything here?" This chapter explores
how communal worship embodies and participates in the gift of the kingdom of
God, which is here but also not fully here. The trust and hope in the kingdom's
consummation invites Christians to the fullness of what God created creatures
to *be, do,* and *become.* Before this exploration, there is still some debris of popular
Christian thinking that must be cleared to make room for the fullness of hope
to which God is calling creation and in which communal worship places its hope
and confidence.

## It Is All About Me

As discussed earlier, most sin is about idolatry—an elevation, an exaltation,
and a fixation on any aspect of creation as ultimate. While there are some people
for whom their sin is a failure to properly love the self because they idolize a crea-

ture over the Creator, many people have an overindulgent love for the self that has become twisted, toxic, and tragic. Augustine and Luther both emphasized that sin is often the *incurvatus in se* (the self curved in upon itself). While the options for affection and desire are many, there are two primary alternatives where a person may focus his or her ultimate affection and desire—God and creation (oneself, other people, material goods or possessions).

Salvation is God's work of redeeming and restoring people who have become enslaved to a love for self that often causes hurt, pain, and violence to other humans and to the larger creation itself. As discussed earlier, because they were created in the *imago Dei*, humans were designed to love themselves, love fellow creatures, be loved, and care for creation. Sinning is a failure to love and thus a failure to be fully human. Here is the sad irony. People often attempt to find happiness, meaning, and security through the idolization of other creatures and creation, and in doing so they also fail to love themselves or God. As humans treat themselves or another as ultimate (divine), their actions push them away from humanity (*imago Dei*). God's invitation to redemption and reconciliation is an invitation to enter into the abundant life God created for us.

Many Christians probably agree with much of this. Yet a subtle virus has worked its way through the evangelical church in North America (and perhaps beyond). As an adolescent who had only known life in the church (and it had been a wonderful life), I had concluded that the goal of being a Christian was to get to heaven. Unfortunately, my youthful mind conceived of heaven as a personal utopia. I imagined it to include physical prowess on the basketball court, fast cars, big homes, and daily access to an amazing beach. The gospel was all about escaping hell and getting to the heaven of my dreams.

Later, as a young youth pastor, I would preach, teach, and evangelize to my young students that securing happiness by objectifying others and pursuing instant self-gratification was not what God desired. Embodying such postures would mean missing out on God's invitation to life. Unfortunately, in the next breath I would proclaim the hope of heaven, often depicting it as a place where "you will always be happy," a utopia where your dreams and pleasures are fulfilled.

Then in case the promise and hope of heaven was not enough, I could always resort to using scare tactics and show them movies about hell that envisioned it as a place of eternal torment, torture, and pain. I would next seal the deal by asking such diagnostic questions as, "So if you died tonight, would you go to heaven or hell?" Manipulation had never been so effective. I could line altars with frightened and emotional, twelve- to sixteen-year-olds who wanted to escape hell's unquenchable fires. To evade this terrible end all they had to do was follow the formula I was offering: "Just admit you are a sinner and ask Jesus into your heart." Not only did I think I was fulfilling the Great Commission, but I could also count on my pastor's report how many people I could get to "convert."

Such a form of Christianity offered mixed results. One of the by-products in evangelical circles was that people were not quite sure their conversion to Christianity "stuck," so they kept responding to the altar call to salvation time and time again just to make sure their latest sin had not disqualified them from the prize of heaven or unleashed on them the punishment and pain of hell.

As I continued to journey with these young people whom I loved, I realized that instead of forming them by the Spirit to love God, themselves, and others more deeply, I was preaching a gospel that actually reinforced selfishness, a grasping at securing happiness on individual terms. As I matured in my theological education, I became more reflective on both my imagination of heaven and the purpose of Christianity. I came to realize the gospel I was proclaiming and my pastoral methods needed conversion. It became clear that some people were interested in heaven but had no need or interest in God or other people. Repenting, confessing sins, and accepting Christ as Savior were simply a means to secure "my eternal destiny, my hedonistic utopia." Too often I felt I was selling a selfish "eternal-destiny insurance policy." So what is a better option?

While all the approaches to heaven and hell are too numerous to deal with here, the use of fear to manipulate must cease. One of my college jobs was in retail sales, and selling often involves manipulation. Manipulation must not be confused with bold proclamation. However, manipulation is employed when people either want immediate results no matter the cost or do not believe their product can stand on its own.

## God Will Be All in All

The main emphasis of this chapter is rather simple. The final purpose and goal of communal worship, the sacraments, Scripture, evangelism, missions, the church, Christ's incarnation, and creation itself is that God will be all in all.[1]

Paul writes in 1 Corinthians,

But in fact Christ has been raised from the dead, the first fruits of those who have died. For since death came through a human being, the resurrection of the dead has also come through a human being; for as all die in Adam, so all will be made alive in Christ. But each in his own order: Christ the first fruits, then at his coming those who belong to Christ. Then comes the end, when he hands over the kingdom to God the Father, after he has destroyed every ruler and every authority and power. For he must reign until he has put all his enemies under his feet. The last enemy to be destroyed is death. For "God has put all things in subjection under his feet." But when it says, "All things are put in subjection," it is plain that this does not include the one who put all things in subjection under him. When all things are subjected to him, then the Son himself will also be subjected to the one who put all things in subjection under him, *so that God may be all in all.* (15:20-28, italics mine)

Paul states boldly that Christ's resurrection from the dead defeats the final enemy of death and is an action whereby the Father has put everything in subjection under Christ's feet. This is the consummation of the kingdom. Recall again Jesus' prayer in Gethsemane as recorded in John 17 (highlighted earlier in chap. 3). Furthermore, "the glorification of God is the final end of God's mission that the church may be one in God. With that end (*telos*) in mind, the church is called to participate in God's mission in the world."[2] With John 17, as God is all in all, people may know God, may become one in God, may be sanctied in the truth, and may be in the triune God so that the world may believe the church. People become one in God by the mutual giving and receiving of love, which is their sanctification and God's glorification.

Moreover, communal worship offers a hope that invades an uncertain present. As Paul affirmed in 1 Corinthians, Christ's resurrection is an anticipation of and a hope for what Christ prayed for in Gethsemane as recorded in the gospel of John.

> Can Christians know with certainty that Christ will return to consummate the inaugurated kingdom of God? Will there be a general resurrection of the dead and the judgment thereafter? Will the whole creation finally recognize that "Jesus is Lord, to the glory of God the Father" (Phil. 2:11)? Yes! Both are confidently affirmed by the New Testament and the Nicene Creed. We don't know the details as to how all this will unfold. We do know Christ will return and that his kingdom shall have no end (Rev. 11:15).[3]

Christians live into the hope that the kingdom of God will come in its fullness. The kingdom of God is present and yet still to come. However, the church's hope and confidence in the kingdom's coming grounds all human activities, especially communal worship. The hope of what we will be invades an uncertain present. Therefore, the hope into which God gathers Christians for communal worship is not naive to present pain, death, torture, and evil. The church's proclamation by the Spirit is that this present challenge is not eternal. Furthermore, this hope of what will be empowers the church not to seek escape from this life but to participate by and with the Spirit to embody more fully the kingdom of God on earth as it is in heaven. I would affirm that communal worship is the church's primary activity whereby God inspires, empowers, and sends the gathered for such an end. The final goal and purpose of creation is that God may be all in all.

This first section has explored a mosaic of a theology of worship:

> Christian communal worship is the glorification of God and the sanctification of humanity as a divine-human event where God offers transformation and healing to help people become more fully what God created them to be and do. God breathes (inhales) and gathers in individual Christians to heal, transform, and renew them as the body of Christ to breathe (exhale) them out to continue the ministry of the incarnation that participates in the kingdom of God more fully coming. The consummation of the kingdom will come and God will be all in all.

From this theology of worship, section II will explore some practical ideas of how to imagine, plan, and lead communal worship.

## Questions for Discussion and Reflection

1. What ideas were the most helpful in this chapter?

2. What ideas are the most difficult or causing the greatest amount of tension?

3. What do you think of the idea of aiming the purpose of worship, life, and Christ's incarnation toward God being all in all?

4. What did you recognize in the discussion about the motivation for becoming Christian as it relates to heaven and hell? What did you appreciate about that discourse? What made you uncomfortable?

5. In light of this chapter, what should we consider to be the point and purpose of worship?

# SECTION II
## Worship That Is Christian:
## A Practical Guide to Imagining, Creating, and Leading Christian Communal Worship

Drawing upon the theology of worship mosaic from section I, this section offers practical suggestions to guide local congregations in imagining, dreaming, planning, and leading communal worship that is Christian. While a theology of Christian communal worship is essential, the process for creating Christian communal worship is equally significant. A question that has not been asked with enough intensity or regularity in the church is this: "How do we know our worship is Christian?" Simply because people gather in a sanctuary, read, sing, pray, and preach does not mean what they do is Christian. While a theology of Christian communal worship offers a prophetic lens and basic guideline, how congregations plan and what they do in communal worship enhances or obstructs the gift God offers in communal worship.

While this section offers many suggestions, each local pastor and congregation must do the hard work of conceiving, planning, and executing communal worship. This section provides tools and handles to help guide each local congregation in this process of finding its own faithful liturgical voice. Every context is unique, and just as each service must be faithful to the Christian tradition and be contextually appropriate, so each local church must work to plan in ways that are faithful to the tradition in each context. Some suggestions will pertain more to those in smaller churches while other suggestions will be more appropriate for larger congregations.

As John Wesley affirms in his sermon "Catholic Spirit," faithful Christian communal worship is not uniform.[1] While there are some aspects of Christian worship that are to be universal, there is also room for contextual beauty and flavor.

Please also remember the caution and encouragement offered at the beginning of section I. When employing the proposed practices of worship planning, some may feel overwhelmed and discouraged about their current worship planning process. My hope is that instead of being a burden this section can provide new ideas and stimulate fresh creative energy. This section celebrates the importance of the worship-planning process and the care given to all those planning and leading communal worship. It is my heartfelt desire that through these ideas and suggestions a fresh passion and fire for worship planning and leading will be ignited.

# EIGHT

# WHO PLANS WORSHIP?

*Planning worship well begins with **giving attention
to the worship team** . . .*[1]

———————

The worship-planning process is much bigger than the worship pastor holed up in his office charged with the task of creating, planning, and leading worship. The worship team is a vital component to this process, and care should be given to those entrusted with such a blessed task. Who this team is and how they work together is of vital importance.

Before considering the worship team approach, many pastors may find themselves in small-church settings where the idea of a worship team seems impossible. It is difficult enough finding someone to help clean bathrooms, let alone help in the imagining of communal worship. With that said, this section hopes to offer a vision of how worship teams can function even for small churches. Those who currently are planning worship alone because of a lack of resources can still plan faithful Christian worship. The hope is that God will bring people along to share with the clergy this joyful responsibility and important work.

## Caring for the Worship Team

Every Sunday afternoon it was the same scenario: raised voices, drama, hurt feelings, and often tears. Yet by 6:00 p.m. the teen worship service would always begin and "get done." The drama and craziness was not the fault of my wonderful, gifted, and emotional teens but mine. My teens were very talented and wanted to do it "on their own." The teen worship leader was highly gifted but did not always affirm the other members of the worship team. Whether it was not paying attention, missing a note, or messing up a lyric, for the sake of "excellence" harsh, reprimanding words would be spoken. There were times I had to step in and help my teens see the bigger picture.

I wish that such drama only occurred with teenagers. However, in many areas of the church, people are mistreated along the way for the sake of "getting things done." The reality is powerful. Sunday is always coming. The clergy recognize this pressure and are thus tempted to treat people like *little minions* doing the bidding of the pastor. Yet with all the pressure, worshipping well on Sunday certainly includes how each service is planned, including how people are loved and cared for during the planning process.

This point may be obvious, yet it is a persistent issue in the planning of worship. Intentionally focusing on the worship team is vital before considering the details of the worship service itself. However, too often the demands made by the awareness that "Sunday is always coming" causes problems by not attending to the people and process involved in the planning of worship. All churches draw upon volunteers to assist in either the planning of worship or the leading of worship through singing, reading Scripture, or playing instruments. In many ways these volunteers are doing much more than professional clergy who are paid to do these tasks. Clergy would be wise to never forget the sacrifice of volunteers who often have other full-time responsibilities in the workforce and at home. While the expectation for excellence should be in the atmosphere of worship planning and leading, this excellence begins with loving and nurturing the people involved in these tasks.

## Who Plans Worship?

### *How Many?*

It is Tuesday. The pastor gives the music minister a scripture, some bullet points, and a possible closing hymn and says, "Go for it." The music minister begins picking songs, putting the service together, figuring out who is in town this week, what instrumentalists are on, and what announcements must be made—and along with all of this and more, he or she must plan a service that will *transform people for eternity.* No pressure.

Many may find something familiar about this picture, for others it is foreign. Before considering how worship is planned, deciding *who plans* will dramatically affect the planning process. I have served at many churches of all shapes and sizes, observed and interviewed dozens more, and found that not any two churches are the same, nor should they be. So how many should help plan worship?

### Three Is Better Than One and Seven

In my experience, it is not optimal for people, including pastors, to plan worship in isolation from other people. It is intriguing that many lead/head/senior pastors do not spend much time planning communal worship. Many pastors feel their worship-planning time is consumed by sermon preparation. In congregations where there is a full- or even part-time music leader, the lead pastor may feel his or her obligations lie in the many other important tasks and duties of the church. This is misguided in my opinion. Recall from chapter 6 that elders are ordained to preach the word, administer the sacraments, and order the church.

Clearly two-thirds of this charge is directed toward communal worship, and the final third could easily be enfolded into communal worship as well.

Pastors and congregants need to recognize the limited and focused calling and gifting of the clergy. The recommendation here is not that a pastor should spend forty hours on sermon and worship planning. All extremes need to be avoided. Pastors must find within their calling and context the right balance for worship preparation with other important pastoral duties. What tends to happen is that pastors spend time doing things they most enjoy. There is some logic to this. Often those activities that are enjoyable are also things the pastor is good at. My hope for pastors and congregations is that they not dismiss the time spent in worship planning, even though such planning may not be the activity that brings the greatest personal joy.

Therefore, I suggest a team approach. In my opinion there is no magical number of members for a team, but what is best is a group that is creatively gifted and called. Group members must also work hard to develop among themselves mature relationships saturated with honesty, trust, and care. People gifted musically are important, but it is not advisable to have the entire music team at the planning meetings. Just because someone is an amazing singer does not mean he or she has the gifts to plan, dream, and imagine worship. There are some wonderfully talented people who are both gifted in their creative imagination and excellent in their performance on Sunday. But often there are people who are gifted in dreaming and imagining but unskilled in performing musically on Sunday, and vice versa.

This group can also be too big. My wife is amazing at many things, including being a fabulous chef. She is a very kind and considerate person, but when you step into the kitchen with her, you better have a plan and a purpose. Moreover, offering her any ideas or tips while cooking, unless she has asked for them or you are on the cooking team, is not usually prudent. I can attest to the truth of the old saying that having too many chefs in the kitchen is not a good thing. Likewise, there are a number of challenges with a worship-planning team that is too big. First, although the world is full of great ideas, not everything can be done. Often when a group is too big, it will end up affirming what the "main leaders" want to do. Second, there is often great inconsistency among the team members from week to week, making it harder to maintain a feeling of honesty and trust among the team. So what is the right number? Each local congregation must discern this on their own. I have seen groups work well that are as small as two or three and as large as eight, but to be honest I think the smaller groups get more done, even though the larger groups can offer a wider range of creative reflections.

## Expectations for Worship Team Members

Whatever the size of the group, there are some expectations for worship-planning members.

1. Consistent and Dependable: People can have many gifts and abilities, but if their schedules are so busy that they cannot be present regularly, they should probably not be included.

2. Creatively Gifted and Skilled: Most people are more creative than they believe, but some people are especially gifted for creativity in communal worship.

3. Humble and a Team Player: For a team to work well, an atmosphere of trust and humility is necessary, and it is mandatory that ideas not get personal. A person filled with insecurity will be a hindrance to having a successful group. People need to be relaxed enough so that personal feelings do not hamper the creative and decision-making process. As groups function in healthy ways, this spirit of trust and cooperation will facilitate creativity without anxiety.

### Who? Combine Clergy and Laity

Pastoral leadership is essential. It is crucial that both the person preaching the sermon and the person leading the music be present (realizing that in some contexts this may be the same person) on the planning team. It is also important to draw upon skilled, creative, and available laity. Creativity can arise imaginatively from all the bodily senses (vision, hearing, smell, touch, and even taste). Laity can also help guide pastors in planning a service by offering a unique perspective. Such insight is vital. A planning team should also reflect the diversity of the congregation. This diversity should include differences related not only to gender but also to socioeconomic levels, ethnicity, and length of church attendance—that is, long-term members as well as those newer to the church or faith. The intention here is not tokenism but genuine diversity.

Within this diversity of clergy and laity, a team must have a clear leader and decision maker. All functioning groups need a clear structure for decision making. Well-functioning teams will often make decisions by consensus, but there are occasions when someone must be decisive to keep the team from getting bogged down. This is another reason why a group made up of a smaller number of people attending to fewer opinions encourages efficiency—though, again, smaller groups will not generate as many creative ideas. On healthy teams, with shared trust and wisdom, the one(s) making the final decision may be fluid depending on the situation or issue at hand.

## Questions for Discussion and Reflection

1. What ideas were the most helpful in this chapter?

2. What ideas are the most difficult or causing the greatest amount of tension?

3. Who creates worship? What about this process is working well for you? What parts need attention?

4. What ideas in this chapter may be worth exploring and trying?

5. How is your church treating those who are assisting in the planning, organizing, and leading of communal worship?

## NINE
# HOW IS COMMUNAL WORSHIP PLANNED?

*Planning worship well begins with giving attention*
*to the worship team, **the process for planning worship** . . .*

───────────

After considering the team members involved in worship planning, care must be given to the planning process of Christian communal worship. This chapter offers a planning process for communal worship that celebrates the role of the Holy Spirit through planning ahead and consistency. There is a value pervading this chapter that is often believed but rarely embodied in practice: The process for creating and planning worship is just as important as the actual event of worship and should be an act of worship itself. Local churches must refuse the pragmatic attitude that *the end* (Sunday service) always justifies the means (whatever it takes) for Christian worship. The process of planning worship enhances or detracts from the communal worship event on the Lord's Day.[1]

## Prayer by the Spirit

As a pastor and worship leader, one of the most important things often appreciated in theory but not in practice is prayer. If you ask any pastor or worship team leader, he or she will affirm the importance of prayer. Yet too often prayer is used like a cordial beginning to a meeting. All that the church is and does for the kingdom only occurs by the empowerment of the Holy Spirit. Communal worship is no exception. The emphasis here is not a feigned piety but an intentional posture that recognizes the Spirit's wisdom and empowerment in all that occurs. Many worship teams and pastors regularly practice and rely on God's Spirit, and this should become a discipline for all in worship leadership.

Along with this emphasis I also believe prayer can be used to bog down or overspiritualize the worship-planning process. The Spirit can be at work in discourse and dialogue, not only when eyes are closed and heads are bowed. An attitude and posture of prayer offers both illumination and humility as people recognize the sacred calling and task that is upon them.

## Planning Ahead by the Spirit

As a professor I have often heard it said, "I did not plan ahead for this presentation; I just waited on the Spirit's inspiration in the moment." While most recognize the immaturity of such students, I have also heard this rationale used for worship planning. While all worship plans must remain open to the Spirit, laziness is often passed off as spirituality. In all areas of the church we must  exorcise such demonic thinking. I doubt many people would be interested in a surgeon deciding just to wing it during surgery as he or she feels led at the table. Yet how often has it been said in the church, "If we plan too far ahead, we will be stifling how the Spirit wants to work in the moment."

Similarly, I have also heard it expressed that for the sake of creativity, the event should not be too planned. Some people in the church believe the Spirit only works in the present moment and does not offer guidance in doing advanced planning. Such an idea should be rejected resolutely. I also believe that those who do not plan in advance actually make the Spirit's job more difficult. The Spirit is not a worker of chaos and disorder. Recall at Pentecost, when "the tongues, as of fire, appeared," that the Spirit brought unity through shared understanding (Acts 2). Furthermore, humans are creatures of habit, and when chaos and disorganization in worship is the norm, the congregation often misses the Spirit's powerful presence.

Furthermore, I am also persuaded that with advanced planning done in prayer by the Spirit, any plan or order of service can be preempted by a dynamic and authentic move of the Spirit (not something contrived through the manipulation of emotions). It cannot be emphasized enough how advanced planning creates new opportunities for the Spirit to be dynamically at work in a congregation. Clearly the Spirit can work in, around, and even outside of the plans; yet too often a lack of planning and attention to detail creates obstacles for the Spirit's movement. Plans must never become idols that demand strict obedience, but with Spirit-filled advanced planning, services can more fully be what God intended: dynamic and transforming encounters between God and brothers and sisters in the church.

Another important benefit that planning ahead provides is a calming effect for those planning and leading. Many creative people proclaim the blessings of inspiration during crunch time. However, the inspiration of last-minute planning usually comes at the cost of excellence and/or broken relationships.

## Pastoral Vision

Advanced planning begins with finding and naming a distinct theme and main idea for each service. To facilitate this practice the preaching pastor(s) may find planning retreats helpful. Some preaching pastors find inspiration in solitude; others through small groups. In one congregation I served, we had a preaching team that regularly offered preaching in our church's three services.

Once a quarter the preaching team would get together and go over the upcoming lectionary texts.[2] These times were enriching for the preaching team and provided a Spirit-filled pool of collective wisdom. For pastors who are the sole preachers in their congregations but enjoy this communal approach, members of the worship team or other people specifically gifted in scriptural discernment can be included in the sermon-planning process. For those churches that follow the lectionary, there are often local groups of pastors from a variety of denominations who meet for sermonic and scriptural insight and inspiration, since they are all preaching from the same group of texts. This is another occasion where there is not a right or wrong way. Each church, pastor, and worship team needs to find their own rhythm.

## Worship Vision Calendars

It is Wednesday night and the worship team gathers for the planning meeting. The pastor is so excited to share what the Holy Spirit has been speaking to her about concerning the upcoming service. The worship team is brainstorming wonderful ideas. Unfortunately, some of the best ideas cannot be implemented because there is just not enough time. So the team can only use ideas that can be easily realized in a day or two. When this scenario occurs over and over, the pastor and the worship team learn to limit the creative imagination to what the immediate present can afford. While some wonderful ideas can be generated on a Wednesday for a Sunday service, advanced planning provides space for a larger imagination than what two or three days can afford.

To provide more opportunities for advanced planning, a worship vision calendar can be created. No matter what the process, it is helpful when worship teams have available to them the next four to eight weeks of sermon themes and ideas. Some pastors like to plan one year in advance while other pastors feel on top of the game when they are two weeks ahead. Although flexibility is needed for each congregation, supplying worship teams with a four- to eight-week plan provides a healthy gestation period for creativity and the creation of intentional worship elements.

### What Does Such a Calendar Look Like?

Each local pastor and worship team needs to find out what would be the most helpful for advanced planning. While each worship team needs to find their own rhythm, it would be wise to interview or observe other worship-planning teams to see what is working for them. In my worship class at the undergraduate level, I expose my students to several worship teams so they are introduced to a variety of planning methodologies. There is always the danger of copying what other churches are doing. Some ideas and steps are transferable from local church to local church, but it is best for each local worship team to find what works best for it. However, looking at what others are doing can be a good start for those who are wanting to improve their process or feel a bit "stuck." Even though I will offer some suggestions, a question the worship team should ask is, "What information do we need in advance for planning?"

Here is one example of a process for planning. This may not work in each context, but it may provide some ideas and illumine some goals to strive for in the weekly planning.

### Week Zero (Last Sunday)

Week zero is an evaluation of the previous week's service(s). Here are some guiding questions to ask:

1. What stories of transformation did we hear or experience?
2. What worked well? How do we know? Why did it work?
3. What did not work well? Why? What specifically about that element do we think caused its failure? Consider the songs, Scripture readings, spoken prayers, sermon, transitions, worship space and furniture, sound, media, worship leaders, Lord's Supper, and other elements unique to that service.

Evaluating the previous service is one of the most important parts of worship planning that is often neglected. Worship teams that do not have a great deal of trust and security among their members often speak about the positive aspects of a worship event but on a very general level. As in life, failure often provides the greatest learning opportunity. To be honest about ideas that did not work is not a condemnation of any person or idea but a learning tool to assist in offering worship that better glorifies God. Giving and receiving critiques is a challenge for the worship team but especially for the preaching pastor or music leader. For this reason, it is crucial that all team members share their perspectives in grace and love. This is also why having valued and trusted laity on the worship team is essential.

It is also important to keep in mind that since Christian worship is a divine-human event of transformation, there are forces and powers at work that cannot always fully be discerned. There are times when something "working" or "failing" will not come with clearly detailed reasons. Care should be taken when assuming the worship team can fully exhaust and discern all the positive or negative things that occurred during worship.

Finally, there will not always be agreement about what went well or poorly. The goal in the end is not to decide whether something is good or poor but to discover ideas and issues that can assist in planning future worship services. This does not need to be a long and drawn-out process; it can take as little as five minutes. Taking notes during this time is helpful. Patterns of "success" or "failure" will then be illumined over a long period and should be helpful for the continual shaping of communal worship. A failure to evaluate is dangerous and careless. The evaluation process is another key element that necessitates strong, vibrant, and healthy relationships among the worship team members.

### Week One (The Upcoming Sunday)

1. The preacher offers any further developments in the sermon outline or illustrations, emphasizing how the sermon illumines the main emphases of the Scripture text(s). This should also include a final draft of how the congregation will be invited to respond to the sermon and service in general.

2. The order, main theme, and big idea of the service are reviewed:

    *a.* Assurance is given that the primary Scripture texts were distributed to the Scripture-reading team and that the team members have been practicing these texts for two weeks.

    *b.* The song leader shares when and what songs (perhaps with lyrics) will be sung.

    *c.* The prayer of invocation, offertory prayer, prayers of the people, and benediction are read.

    *d.* The worship space coordinator shares about any visual changes or arrangement of seating, banners, lighting, and so on, that will be used for this day.

    *e.* Transitions are discussed, clarifying when, how, and where people will be moving in the service.

    *f.* Final logistics and particulars to this week are discussed.

In many ways this conversation serves as a dress rehearsal and review. Comments and final revisions can be adopted from the insights and suggestions of team members. It is possible and advisable that a well-functioning team will spend most of its time on weeks two, three, and four in the weekly meeting.

### Week Two (Two Sundays Ahead)

Week two should receive the bulk of the time and attention during a planning meeting. The goal of this week's conversation is to come away with a solid rough draft of the order of worship. Any creative elements needing development should be presented for the team to view, discuss, and consider. Here is an agenda for discussion on week two.

1. The preacher offers a more developed outline of the sermon, emphasizing how the sermon illumines the main emphases of the Scripture text(s). The preacher may also suggest ways the congregation will be invited to respond. The team should also be ready to offer ideas and suggestions from any insights they have had while thinking about the congregation's response.

2. The order, main theme, and big idea of the service are reviewed:

    *a.* Assurance is given that the primary Scripture texts have been distributed to the Scripture-reading team to begin practicing.

    *b.* The song leader shares song ideas (perhaps with lyrics) that fit the main theme of the day.

  *c.* The prayer of invocation, offertory prayer, prayers of the people, laments, benediction, and so on, should be presented as a first draft for the team's comments.

  *d.* The worship space coordinator shares about any creative ideas for the visual space, including the arrangement of seating, banners, lighting, and so on, that may be used for this day.

  *e.* Any unique logistics for this Sunday are addressed and considered.

The primary goal of this conversation for week two is to walk away with a fairly refined order of worship. As noted above, when dealing with week one (the next Sunday) there are always moments of last-minute tweaking and adjustments. In fact, tweaking and fine-tuning create new opportunities if the bulk of the work has already been done two weeks in advance.

## Week Three (Three Sundays Ahead)

The conversation about week three seeks to ignite and gather creative ideas. This is a free brainstorming session about what could be.

1. The preacher offers a more developed theme and main idea based on the previous week's conversation. The team should be prepared to offer additional reflections and feedback on the theme, possible worship elements that could be employed, and other ideas that had come up during the week.

2. The song leader may share a few preliminary song ideas that may fit. The worship team should also offer some creative ideas for response through song.

3. Assignments can be handed out for things to be created: Those in charge of the prayers should make some suggestions about what kinds of prayers might be appropriate for the theme of the service. The worship team should also respond with some ideas, thoughts, and possible prayers for consideration. Someone should then be responsible for composing or gathering prayers. The Scriptures should be handed off to the Scripture-reading team. Media (not just digital) assignments should also be given for the team to review during the week-two conversation.

4. The worship space coordinator shares any creative ideas for the visual space, including the arrangement of seating, banners, lighting, and so on, that may be used for this day. Team members also offer suggestions and ideas.

5. Any unique logistics for this Sunday are addressed and considered.

The goal of week three is providing feedback based on week four's first proposal given by the preacher. The hope is that by the end of the week three's conversation a rough order of service can be built and people can be working to develop the necessary elements for week two's conversation. The week-three conversation will conclude with the handing out of assignments in preparation for that upcoming conversation.

### Week Four (Four Sundays Ahead)

This conversation is offered by the preacher as a rough draft about the scriptures and themes he or she is exploring. The pastor may also share any of the items that have been gathered by the worship team in the preceding five- to eight-week conversations. This conversation may offer some initial responses and ideas, but mostly the goal is to inspire the team to come back to the week-three conversation ready to offer some initial feedback and worship possibilities.

### Weeks Five Through Eight (One to Two Months Ahead)

As a pastor's vision calendar broadens, these weeks can be simply on the radar perhaps with a bullet point or two with Scripture texts. Being aware of weeks five through eight is helpful to get the creative juices flowing. Some pastors and worship teams simply create a folder (both digital and physical) with the date, Scripture passages, and an initial theme. As the team finds inspiration for these weeks, ideas can be collected into a file and then presented for the week-four conversation.[3] Brainstormed ideas can be anything from news stories to intriguing illustrations, movie clips, ideas from art or novels, songs, or anything from contemporary culture that might help connect and shape the main theme.

Let me offer a picture of what such a meeting may look like. I will assume the meeting is on Wednesday.

Worship-Planning Meeting for September 5
Agenda
1. Week 0, September 2 (5-10 min.): Evaluate what worked and what did not.
2. Week 1, September 9 (10-15 min.): Go over final order of service and discuss any fine-tuning that is needed.
3. Week 2, September 16 (45-60 min.): Work to create a fairly solid order of worship with most of the worship components already having been created. Offer final assignments for worship elements that need to be refined and adjusted.
4. Week 3, September 23 (10-15 min.): Brainstorming session and handing out of assignments for worship elements needing to be gathered or created. What prayers need to be composed? What Scriptures are going to be read? What media (not just digital) needs to be created?
5. Week 4, September 30 (5 min.): Preacher offers a preliminary main theme along with Scripture texts. Some preliminary feedback is warranted. This presentation by the preacher is mostly for the team to put in the "hopper."
6. Weeks 5-8, October 7, 14, 21, 28 (5 min.): The worship team receives the Scripture texts and some possible main ideas and themes. The preacher may ask if any ideas or contemporary illustrations for these weeks have come to the surface.

Worship Planning Meeting for September 12
Agenda

1. Week 0, September 9 (5-10 min.)
2. Week 1, September 16 (10-15 min.)
3. Week 2, September 23 (45-60 min.)
4. Week 3, September 30 (10-15 min.)
5. Week 4, October 7 (5 min.)
6. Weeks 5-8, October 14, 21, 28, November 4 (5 min.)

Let me stress again the fluidity of these recommendations. Adaptation and improvisation are strongly encouraged. What I have offered is a template for consideration.

*Strengths of the Worship-Planning Calendar*

### Planning Ahead

The creative worship process will not only alleviate some of the stress of the "Sunday is coming" urgency but also provide more opportunities for creative ideas and their implementation. Moreover, in accord with what was discussed in chapter 8, planning ahead also helps to keep in the forefront a significant but often neglected matter when the tyranny of the present overwhelms the worship leaders and team—the importance of caring for people.

### Planning Worship Takes Time

The time estimates provided above, while suggestions, emphasize the importance and value that planning worship deserves. It seems that at a minimum, two hours a week is needed. Some churches take four to five hours weekly to plan communal worship. For professional and lay ministers, time is precious. I would argue vigorously that the (lead, senior, preaching) pastor's primary task is the shaping and formation of worship. As mentioned above, there are always extremes, but the responsibility of the ordained leader to attend and care for communal worship must not be neglected. While this is not to be the only way a pastor cares for, nurtures, and disciples his or her flock, I believe it is the primary pastoral calling in shepherding the local body of Christ. Some pastors (lead, senior, preaching) may respond, "I do not have the time." I would encourage them to find the time and make planning worship a priority. This responsibility should not be put solely on the music leader. The preaching pastor is certainly a worship pastor, just as much as the pastor who organizes and leads worship in song.

### Worship Meetings Should Be Ordered and Organized

This is perhaps a personal passion connected again to my leadership style. It's true that some wonderful things can happen when agendas are built on the flow and are not explicit. However, more often than not such meetings get off task. Order and organization are usually far better at producing the best results.

### Excellence in Details

This topic will be more fully discussed below, but it warrants a brief remark here. The Scriptures are clear: any worship done to honor God must be done by offering our very best. Nothing less will suffice. Recall that animals and grains reserved for sacrifice were to meet a standard of purity (see Lev. 1:3; 2:7; 14:10). Leviticus is a book about precision in worship. Clearly, such precision can become an idol when the form of worship takes a higher place than God, which is one of the main critiques Jesus offered to the Pharisees. Nonetheless, God requires our very best. Not only did God strike down Uzzah for careless preparations in moving the ark to Jerusalem, but God also struck down Ananias and Sapphira for their dishonest worship (2 Sam. 6:6-7 and Acts 5:1-11). The goal here is not legalism but the glory of God, and so excellence must be pursued without carelessness. Planning ahead makes excellence in all the details more likely.

Let me offer a major caution about this process. Not all pastors are as skilled, gifted, or inclined to plan ahead as others. While I do not think that is a worthwhile excuse, a worship team must honor the pastor who *does* make the effort to plan ahead. There is nothing more discouraging to the preaching pastor, especially one for whom planning ahead takes tremendous initiative and effort, to have a worship team do nothing with those plans. Furthermore, I want to emphasize again that the process of listening, imagining, and planning worship is just as significant as the communal worship event itself. Local churches must resist the tendency to treat planning as a simple means to an end.

## Questions for Discussion and Reflection

1. What ideas were the most helpful in this chapter?

2. What ideas are the most difficult or causing the greatest amount of tension?

3. How does your local church plan worship? What is working well? What is not?

4. What ideas in this chapter may be worth exploring and trying?

5. Why is the process of worship planning just as important as the worship event?

## TEN

# THE LOCAL CONTEXT: WHO ARE WE? WHERE ARE WE?

*Planning worship well begins with giving attention to the worship team, the process for planning worship, **the people in a local community**, the worship space . . .*

---

In light of section 1 it may be tempting to assume that the only thing one needs for planning worship is a solid theology of worship. There are several preliminary things needed to plan well. In this chapter we will explore how planning worship well begins with the recognition and awareness of who comprises a local congregation and what type of worship space will be used. In striving for excellence in worship planning, the Spirit must guide the leaders to know their people and the worship space well so that it can become sacred.

Since transitioning from pastoral ministry to a teaching ministry, one of the areas of my life I have truly missed is the opportunity to journey with and pastor people. Not only do I miss hospital visits, marriages, and potlucks, but I often have preaching and worship-planning withdrawals. To help with my cravings I am often privileged to do interim preaching for churches going through pastoral transition or for pastors who are on vacation. While this opportunity is a blessing, it is difficult to preach or lead worship in a congregation if I do not know who the people are. I try to find out as much as I can about the congregants. At some level an awareness of who the people are must impact the planning of a worship service.

I can imagine that many who are planning worship for the same local context might find such a step silly or unnecessary. "I know my people," declares the pastor. Such an emphasis on knowing one's people is not an accusation that pastors are ignorant of their people, but it is an acknowledgment that *who* a local congregation is must inform and shape how worship is planned.

## Pastoral Eisegesis and Exegesis

In biblical scholarship two primary methodologies are set up as foils for how a person is to engage and encounter Scripture: *eisegesis* and *exegesis*. "Eisegesis" is the practice of bringing one's ideas to the text and finding verses that appear to "prove" your point. This is often known as proof-texting. I am very nervous when a preacher uses individual, scattered verses (or partial verses) from all over Scripture to "proclaim" the good news. In contrast, "exegesis" is about critically studying a text with as much objectivity as possible to draw out its true meaning. Good exegesis allows the text to speak for itself without imposing one's own ideas on it. Along with Scripture, eisegesis and exegesis can also be applied to people in the church.

How can pastors perform eisegesis on their own congregations? There are always extremes to be avoided. One pastoral danger is for pastors to be so focused on the members of the current congregation that the entire congregation can become inward focused and closed off to those in surrounding communities and neighborhoods. At a dangerous level, little to no objectivity is possible "because everyone is known so well." The other extreme is pastors who are not really interested in the people currently being gathered in their local community but in those who are not there.

Considering these extremes, pastoral eisegesis could be done in several ways. One way is for pastors to create worship services that will keep the saints happy. Another way would be to create services for the type of people the pastor wants to be there but are not. Some pastors want their congregations to be somewhere on either side of the spectrum: more *or* less educated, more *or* less affluent (really!), more *or* less ethnically diverse (despite what is said publicly), more *or* less urban, more *or* less rural, more *or* less concerned with communal worship, more *or* less churched, more *or* less professionally dressed, and so on.

Another form of eisegesis can occur through ignorance. The pastor simply does not know the people. I have heard some pastors say, "I just want to preach. I do not want to pastor." At some level, preaching is just an expensive speech for someone who does not want to shepherd the people. While the negative options are endless, a proper *exegesis* of a congregation involves several lenses.

## Pastoral Exegesis of a Congregation: Ethnography

Pastoral exegesis and ministry begins with those who are currently present in the church. Remember exegesis means learning about the "text," or congregation, without imposing personal ideas on it. So what type of information will help a pastor become more acquainted with his or her congregation? A myriad of options present themselves. Information worth gathering may include age, occupation, marital status, educational level, number of people living in the home, religious background, history with this present church, perceptions, hopes, and desires for the church and specifically for communal worship. Certainly more data could be gathered as appropriate for each local context.

So how can this data be gathered? Ethnography is a scientific research methodology that fosters the gathering of empirical data of human cultures and societies. Some of this data can be acquired through observation; other data can be collected through individual and group interviews.[1] The goal in such a project is not simply to accumulate data on parishioners but also to get personally acquainted with them. This is challenging for pastors of all sizes of congregations.

Here are some suggestions and tips for data gathering: Depending on the context and one's familiarity with the congregation, a pastor may use an outside consultant to help gather data, or if a pastor and staff are new, data gathering could become a relationship-building opportunity. If a pastor has served a congregation for a considerable time and has become blind to the local context, an outside consultant can help that pastor see a situation with fresh eyes. While the pastor, staff, or worship team can gather the data, it is highly recommended that a consultant or "secret shopper" at least be used to observe a congregation at worship. Even for a new pastor, a secret shopper offers a level of objectivity that can yield invaluable insights. Every context is unique, so the exact process for gathering data will be specific for each local congregation.

## Reminders

Depending on the methodology employed for gathering data from congregants and the size of the congregation, such a process of data gathering will take a substantial amount of time and is a considerable amount of work.

## Caution

When you gather such data—especially seeking the input of congregants on things they find helpful and unhelpful in the church and specifically in communal worship—the congregants need to be aware of how this data will be processed. Although it is doubtful that congregants will expect pastors to start shaping the church and communal worship based on their suggestions, if pastors ignore this data, some congregational harm may result. In other words, certain questions should not be asked if there is no plan to engage the data or comments of those questions.

## Benefits

Pastors new at a congregation may quickly see the benefits of this formal and informal ethnography (exegesis) of a congregation, but pastors who have a longer tenure may also find this process illuminating. Although a pastor has remained at the same church, the local body ebbs and flows with people coming and going. This shifting of people is often slow and subtle. Furthermore, it may be appropriate to share some of this data with the congregation. For congregants who are new, it will provide a fuller picture of their community of faith. For the saints who have been present awhile and who think they know their church, surprises will no doubt emerge. Even if a congregation enters this process of listening and gathering data to see more clearly "who we are" and few surprises come to light, that information still bears weight in planning and can give assurance to the pastor and worship team as they move forward.

*Frequency*

Depending on the intensity and comprehensiveness of an initial listening journey, it is not necessary to ask "who we are" every week as if things change that quickly. However, the pastor and worship team may find that a rhythm of formal and informal listening sessions can keep a certain awareness of the congregation active and dynamic.

## Know the Space

Another important contextual influence is the communal worship space used for each congregation. Similar to the need to know who we are, some people may also feel that an awareness of the worship space is obvious. However, for a congregant or pastor who has experienced any longevity with the same sanctuary or worship space, it is possible to become blind to the theological statements of a worship space.

Some questions that could be asked the worship team and even the congregants during the listening tour include the following:

- What theological statements does your worship space articulate?
- What theological symbols are present or absent? Where are these symbols?
- What liturgical furniture is used (lectern, pulpit, Communion Table, altar rail, baptismal font, mourners' bench, etc.) and where?
- What does the space encourage and discourage?
- How do people sit? Do they face each other or do they face the back of people's heads?
- Where do people lead in worship—through singing, reading Scripture, preaching a homily or sermon?
- Where do baptisms take place?
- How is the space used for the Lord's Supper?
- What is the lighting?
- What media technology is employed?
- What are the sound acoustics?
- How does the space facilitate people connecting and responding to God in worship?
- How does the space facilitate people encountering each other in communal worship?
- What physical opportunities and limitations does the space offer?

There are no right or wrong answers in this exegesis of a worship space, but such information can help make the church aware of the theological statements a space is making. While it is true that God does not need any specific physical accoutrements, some spaces are more sacred than others simply because of the care and attention to detail given by those who help adorn and create those spaces. Let me offer an example.

I have worshipped in all types of buildings and spaces, cathedrals, sanctanasiums, front yards, pitched tents, sanctuaries, and open dirt fields. God was faithfully and dynamically present in all of those times and spaces. However, I must admit that some spaces make encountering the awesome and holy God easier than others. Although my breath was taken away when I entered the cathedrals of Notre Dame and Sacré-Coeur in Paris, I have also experienced the holy God in a small chapel on an Indian reservation in South Dakota and in a batey in the Dominican Republic. The question remains: "What is your space saying theologically?" Does your space declare that God is holy, awesome, and sovereign or that God is your buddy? Does your space declare that God is close, present, and immanent or that God is distant, far removed, and absent? The question is not *if* your space is making theological statements but *what* theological statements your space makes.

A question that perhaps seems unnecessary is very important: "Is your communal space Christian?" What makes it so? Too often churches fail to take advantage of Christian symbols that can draw people and facilitate encounters with God. What makes your space sacred/holy, set apart specifically for communal worship? How is this space different from a community theater or civic office building? This is especially important for churches whose space has many uses. Similar to the listening journey and exegesis of a congregation, having an outside consultant, or "secret shopper," come to your worship space can be beneficial. A consultant can help you see what your space is saying about God and about humans encountering God.

There was a time in recent history when churches attempted to reach out to their communities by stripping away all of the Christian symbols and furniture (pulpits, Communion Tables, baptismal fonts, and even crosses). These symbols were thought to be obstacles to those who either did not know their meaning or were perhaps offended by them. However, people new to the Christian faith, along with those who have grown up in it, need education about Christian symbols and icons. It is dangerous and dishonest to hide Christian symbols because they might cause offense. The apostle Paul clearly said that the cross of Jesus Christ is "a stumbling block" for some (see 1 Cor. 1:23). Local churches do a disservice to all their congregants when fear or ignorance prompts them to hide Christian symbols.

Before communal Christian worship can be planned, it's important to be aware of who currently composes a local community. Also attention must be given to the worship space. Paying attention to who we are and what our space says theologically will reap important benefits in the crafting, planning, and dreaming of communal worship.

## Questions for Discussion and Reflection

1. What ideas were the most helpful in this chapter?

2. What ideas are the most difficult or causing the greatest amount of tension?

3. How well does your church know which people God has entrusted to you?

4. Would having a listening journey and exegesis of your congregation help guide your church and specifically communal worship?

5. What theological statements is your worship space making?

# ELEVEN

# WHAT TIME IS IT? THE CHRISTIAN YEAR

*Planning worship well begins with giving attention to the worship team,
the process for planning worship, the people in a local community,
the worship space, and **the season of the Christian year**. . . .*

---

My daughter and I play a fun game together. As she was learning to tell time, she would ask me, "Daddy, what time is it?" Early on she did not care or really understand what time was. She heard her brother and other adults ask this question, and she just wanted to join the game with them. As she grew up, she started to decipher the numbers and began to say, "It is three twenty-three." At first she did not associate these numbers with anything significant, but as she grew older and could understand more, she would repeatedly ask, "Daddy, what time is it?" So as any good father would do, I started giving her the nonanswer, "Game time," supposing she was able to figure out the time on her own. She would then respond, "No, seriously, Dad. What time is it?" And again, I would answer, "Game time."

Eventually knowing what time it was became very important. In getting ready for school, she has to stick to a schedule and be ready by 7:55 each morning. So even though we continue to play our game, when the pressure is on, as on such mornings, she really needs to know the time. Knowing the time becomes a helpful guide for her ethical and liturgical practices (getting dressed, eating breakfast, washing her face, brushing teeth, combing hair, and getting her backpack ready). My wonderful son, who often gets sidetracked and loses focus in the morning, is constantly being reminded by my daughter, "Don't you know what time it is! You better not be late."

Too often local churches do not know what time it is. I do not mean those who neglect to "spring forward" or "fall back" around the beginning or end of daylight savings. Too often local churches have neglected the church year. In fact, many are not even aware there is such a thing. Many evangelicals know that Christmas and Easter are important times in the church year; unfortunately, these days are exciting for churches often because they bring in the highest attendance numbers. In some evangelical circles there is even a category of church attendees called C and E Christians.

Some of this ignorance of the church year in the past may have been intentional. In many evangelical churches (and perhaps mainline Protestants more broadly) there has been a long-standing rubric: "We will not do anything the Roman Catholics do." In my lifetime I have been pleasantly surprised to see the gradual evaporation of this way of thinking in many places. It seems narrow-minded for denominations to refuse to participate and engage in conversations and practices simply on the basis of a Protestant bias. The Reformation was important, but there were many traditional practices neglected by Protestants that should be and are being recovered. Paying attention to the church year is one of these gifts of Christian tradition.

The Christian church year in many ways is birthed from the rhythm of feasts and festivals of ancient Israel. The Israelite worship calendar was marked by special times when the Jews remembered and were made present again to Yahweh's acts of redemption. The special times recalling the events of redemption include the Feast of the Passover (Pesach) and Unleavened Bread (Mazzot) celebrating the exodus (Exod. 12:14-20; 13:3-10); the Feast of Weeks (Pentecost or *Shavuot*) commemorating the giving of the Torah fifty days after Passover (Deut. 16:9-12); the Feast of Booths (Tabernacles or *Sukkoth*) remembering the forty years that the Hebrews wandered in temporary shelters or booths. In the Second Temple period it was an eight-day festival involving the imagery of water and light (Deut. 16:13-15). The weekly Sabbath (*Shabbat*) day of rest recalls the seventh-day of rest celebrated by God during creation and the Israelite's freedom from Pharaoh's brick quota (Exod. 20:8-11). New Year (*Rosh Hashanah*) celebrates the reestablishment of burnt offerings by the priest Ezra after the Babylonian exile (Lev. 23:23-25; Ezra 3:1-6; Neh. 7:73–8:18). The Day of Atonement (*Yom Kippur*) is an annual ritual of purification in which a sacrifice was offered for the purification of the temple, the land, and the people (Lev. 16:1-34).

These celebrations of past events are also fresh encounters with God. Past events are made present by the repetition of liturgical actions. This is the foundation from which Christians understand the word "remembrance" as translated from the Greek word *anamnēsis*. These actions are not magical incantations, but postures of faith in trust. They affirm that because God has been faithful in the past, God will continue to be faithful.

From this rhythm of thanksgiving and remembrance for past and present acts of deliverance, Christian worship arises. As the Christian calendar developed, the birth, life, death, and resurrection of Christ became the focal point of connection and remembrance. Moreover, the church year developed over time alongside the organization of Scripture being patterned in the lectionary. As each year narrates the Christ story, the church *re-presents* and embodies this story in its communal worship and in its practices in the world. The Christ event is narrated through the seasons of Advent, Christmas, Epiphany, Lent, Holy Week, Easter, and Pentecost. While Passover and Shavuot (Pentecost) formed the high points of the Jewish calendar, the Christian calendar affirms that a new time has been ushered in.

Robert Webber suggests that this new Christian time can be discerned through three emphases. First, time is fulfilled. Christ's coming is the fulfillment of the promised Messiah. This new time (*kairos*) has arrived in Christ. "Repent, for the kingdom of heaven has come near" (Matt. 3:2; 4:17). Second, the coming of Christ is the time of salvation. The Messiah's presence, birth, life, teachings, death, resurrection, and ascension offer healing to all of creation. Third, Christ's first coming and the inauguration of the kingdom of God celebrate the presence of God but also celebrate a time of the consummation of the kingdom as the *age to come*. Webber goes on to suggest that "in worship we sanctify the present time by enacting the past event of Jesus in time which transforms the present."[1]

Drawing upon the Jewish framework of remembrance is not about a sentimental nostalgia but about a Spirit-filled divine-human encounter with Christ offering the church healing and transformation. Worship is not simply about "telling stories about the good ol' days." Worship lives in thankful remembrance that the God who has been faithful is present and desires to heal and transform today (the affirmation of *anamnēsis*). Because God has been faithful, the church acts out in faith and hope that God will be faithful. The Christian church lives into this Christian narrative as a celebration of what God has done and is calling the church to embody now.

## The Seasons of the Church Year

The primary seasons of the Christian year include Advent, Epiphany, Lent, Easter, Pentecost, and Ordinary Time.[2] Although the church's high and holy days of Christmas and Easter provide important celebration markers, when they are abstracted from the entire Christian year and most especially from Advent and Lent, their full meaning is lost.

### Advent (Liturgical Color: Purple or Blue)[3]

Advent is the beginning of the church year. Advent means "coming" and is a season of expectation and imagination of Christ's first and final coming. Three main emphases shape the climate of expectation of Advent. First, the church must remember the Jews' deep longing and waiting for their Messiah. Second, just as the Jews longed for the Messiah, the church also considers its sinfulness and need for a Savior. In this desperate need of a Savior the church reflects upon death, judgment, heaven, and hell.[4] Third, while the church lives in the light that Christ came, the church also lives in the hope and expectation that Christ will come again in the consummation of the kingdom.[5] Advent is a season of discipline; a time of preparation for Christ's coming. This is a season of waiting, longing, and hoping.

## Challenges

The cultural marketing power of Christmas is overwhelming in North America (and beyond). Christmas decorations pop up in stores right on the heels of Labor Day. The primary reason is that Christmas sells. As hard as Christians try to keep Jesus "the reason for the season," it is difficult. Advent was an appointed time of preparation of Christ's coming; however, too often Advent becomes little more than "Christmas lite." Advent is to be a season of waiting, longing, and hoping. In a culture of instant gratification and self-indulgence, the church must resist the temptation to indulge in the gluttony of impatience. If there is little fasting, hoping, and longing, Christmas's arrival becomes the next day of indulgence rather than a true day of encountering the long-expected One.

## Opportunities

Advent provides the church an opportunity to discipline its life, to recognize the desperate need for Christ. While Christmas has become a cultural season of materialism and indulgence, the church is to mark this time by preparing, longing, and waiting for what really offers life, Jesus Christ. While the church, even in Advent, lives out the hope of Christ's first coming, the church also longs, waits, and yearns for Christ's coming again.

## Tips and Suggestions

The communal worship team has many challenges during this season. The cultural context of joy and happiness in December is difficult to hold in check at the door. The atmosphere of Advent must be one of disciplined expectation. While it is hard and difficult, most Christmas carols are not theologically appropriate in Advent. "Joy to the World" is a wonderful song for Christmas, but singing it in Advent leads to great confusion for the local congregation. Part of the challenge is that Christian hymnody does not provide many songs of expectation and longing; however, there are some carols and hymns that do fit within the season of Advent. Some carols and hymns can also be sung, omitting some verses that are more fitting for Christmas. A strong musical anchor for Advent can be the hymn "O Come, O Come, Emmanuel." Laments are also appropriate in Advent, recognizing the church's desperate plight of waiting for Christ's presence and return.

In this atmosphere of delayed gratification, it is helpful to live in the Minor Prophets of the Old Testament that bring Christians into the desperate world before the Messiah came. Recognizing the desperate longing and waiting for the Messiah guides the church's expectation and longing for Christ's return. The Old Testament texts, especially in Isaiah, help to demonstrate that while Christ's first coming fulfilled many of the promises of God, the consummation of the kingdom of God is yet to come and thus should be sought after.

The season of Advent is four weeks long and the primary colors are blue or violet to symbolize the atmosphere of confession and penitence of the season as well as the royalty of Christ.

Worship teams can also lead a Hanging of the Greens service. Manger scenes can be designed in fitting ways that can show the holy couple moving toward Bethlehem. If manger scenes are used in the decorations, it is also wise to not put the baby Jesus in the manger until Christmas.

### Christmas (Liturgical Color: White and Gold)

Christmas comes from the celebration of "Christ's mass." In Christmas the longing and expectation in Advent finds a hopeful celebration that Christ did come. God has not left creation mired in its sin, despair, and hopelessness. The darkness of despair in a season of anticipation, waiting, and longing is pierced by the light of God. As Mal. 4:2 notes, "For [those] who revere my name the sun of righteousness shall rise, with healing in its wings." John 1 also offers a doxology of the light of God that has invaded that darkness: "In him was life, and the life was the light of all people. The light shines in the darkness, and the darkness did not overcome it. . . . The true light, which enlightens everyone, was coming into the world" (vv. 4-5, 9). The good news affirms with joy and hope that God is with us. God's presence brings light, hope, and healing. God's promises have been fulfilled. As the church is made present to that nativity, its longing and expectation for Christ's second coming are further encouraged as the church celebrates that just as God was faithful to send the Son, God will be faithful to send Jesus Christ to consummate the kingdom.

By 450 the church in the West universally celebrated December 25 as the appropriate day to celebrate the sending of the Son to become incarnate in Jesus Christ.[6] This date may have been selected to work against a pagan festival, the Birthday of the Invincible Sun (*sol invictus*).[7] The Eastern Orthodox have long recognized the season of Christmas, including the twelve days of Christmas, moving from Christmas to Epiphany.

## Challenges

Notwithstanding all the consumerist forces at work, the church must also *not* find Christmas's primary hope in Calvary. Too many Christmas Sundays are filled with images of the "real" importance of Christ's coming reduced to his death at Calvary. While Christ's death at Calvary is crucial, the emphasis here is misplaced. The Eastern Orthodox remind the church universal that Christ's coming—God becoming flesh—is the good news of healing. That God in Christ became fully human offers all humans healing from the disease, enslavement, and destruction of sin. Work with diligence to find the hope and joy in Christ's coming, Emmanuel—God with Us, without reducing the benefits and celebration to Christ's death. Moreover, Christmas is not a day but a season.

## Opportunities

Christmas is a reason for many people who do not normally attend church to make their annual or biannual (Easter) pilgrimage. As such this is an occasion to offer great hospitality in worship. In other words, the song selections should be well known by all. This is not the Sunday to try out the "cool" new song found on the Internet. Furthermore, singing Christmas carols is appropriate. However, one would be wise to look closely at the lyrics of such carols. Without careful attention sentimentality may replace orthodoxy (right worship).

## Tips and Suggestions

The world of consumerism has largely stolen Christmas from the church. The church should work with diligence to reclaim the hope of Christmas that is found, not in buying or consuming, but in giving. As Christmas is not a day but a season, the church can and should sing carols into the ordinary time after Epiphany. This is a season for feasting and joy, celebrating again the good news that into the darkness God has brought forth a great light. This good news and revelry should also celebrate giving to those who are lacking physically and spiritually. Rather than consuming, may the church live into the imagination of Christmas by finding creative ways to give joyfully and thankfully to a world in need, perhaps of things it is not aware of. Christians have also offered worship services on Christmas Eve and Christmas Day to anticipate and celebrate the Savior's birth.

### *Epiphany (Liturgical Color: White) and the Season After Epiphany (Green)*

Epiphany is the feast day concluding the twelve days of Christmas. Epiphany means "manifestation" or "divine revelation," celebrating specifically how Christ is revealed to be the Son of God. The church in the East likely saw Epiphany as solely connected to the baptism of our Lord.[8] A later development envisioned Epiphany as the celebration of Christ's birth, baptism, and first miracle—all testifying to God's glory being at work in Jesus Christ. It is noteworthy that Epiphany is older than the celebration of Christmas, and James White suggests that it has a deeper meaning than Christmas: "Instead of simply being an anniversary of the birth of Christ, it testifies to the whole purpose of the incarnation: the manifestation of God in Jesus Christ, beginning both with his birth and with the beginning of his ministry (the baptism when he is proclaimed 'My Son, my beloved')."[9]

Robert Webber notes that Epiphany may have gained prominence beginning in Egypt as a way to countermand the pagan winter festival on January 6. During that time January 6 came to be associated with the revealing of Jesus to the wise men as a manifestation to the Gentiles (the rest of the non-Jewish world) that Jesus was God.

The season after Epiphany is similar to the season after Pentecost called Ordinary Time. The season after Epiphany continues to celebrate the continual revelation that Jesus Christ is the Son of God and Savior for the world. This is powerfully celebrated with the Baptism of the Lord (liturgical color: white). This remembrance declares Jesus' divine sonship and is the inauguration of his ministry. In some churches this season after Epiphany ends with Transfiguration Sunday (liturgical color: white) celebrating the full revelation of Christ's divinity.[10] However, Transfiguration Sunday is not simply a day to remember what happened to Christ. With the Eastern Orthodox Church and especially those in the Wesleyan tradition, this is a Sunday to affirm that with Christ we will abide into the very glory of the triune God.

## Challenges

In many cultural contexts, Epiphany and the season after Epiphany come after all the parties are over. People recognize they have overindulged with their stomachs and credit during the holiday season. People return to regular patterns of work and school often in despair over the failed expectations of what they hoped the holidays would offer. Another challenge is a great lack of awareness about the significance of Epiphany. Many Christians have a hard time harnessing the joy of God's revelation in and through Christ, since "we already did that at Christmas."

## Opportunities

Epiphany and the season following are an opportunity to encounter again who God in Christ is. Too many Christians may be under the false premise that "I know who Jesus is." The worship team through its teaching, preaching, and singing may want to emphasize both historical and theological lessons focusing on Christology. One of the challenges for the entire Christian year, including Epiphany, Lent, and Easter, is that too many Christians cannot conceive of what it means that Christ is fully human. While Epiphany is a feast day celebrating God's manifestation in Christ, this manifestation should not be at the expense of the radical humanity of our blessed Savior.

## Tips and Suggestions

Epiphany and the season after Epiphany come at the beginning of the calendar year even in places that physically look and feel very dead. With the newness of the year, people in many local churches offer services of covenant renewal. In an atmosphere of New Year's resolutions, offering a renewal of covenants to God, oneself, other brothers and sisters, and creation is appropriate. Since Epiphany and the season after are largely unknown to a great deal of Christianity, worship teams would do well to emphasize the texts and songs celebrating why this encounter with Christ reveals who God is and the love of the triune God. The movement from Epiphany through the season following to Lent is critical. As Lent invites Christians to journey with Jesus into the shadow of the cross, people need to encounter the Christ again who does not simply do something *for* us. In this season we see that Christ invites us into the Way, where life begins and through which God is redeeming the world.

*Wesley Covenant Service*

On the first Sunday of each year Wesleyans have long participated in a Wesley Covenant Service. This service is a time for a local congregation to renew their commitment and covenant with God and each other. During a time when many are making New Year's resolutions, local churches can intentionally renew their covenants to serve God, one another, and their world.

*Lent (Liturgical Color: Purple)*

Just as Christmas without Advent offers the church a circumstantial and emotional high that does not last, without Lent, Easter's victory is a bit shallow, forced, and without staying power. Lent is a season of discipline, devotion, and preparation. The beginnings of Lent are not entirely clear or uniform in the early church.[11] As the season developed, the importance of forty days became increasingly more significant. The period of forty days of preparation is found throughout Scripture. Moses was with God on Sinai and Horeb for a period of forty days before going back to minister to the people (Exod. 24:18; 34:28-29). Our Lord, after his baptism, began to prepare himself for public life by a fast of forty days in the desert (Matt. 4:1-2).

Similarly, the church is invited to prepare itself for a journey with Christ all the way into the shadow of the cross. As Epiphany offered revelations and manifestations of who God is in Christ, the Lenten season continues to live in the life, teachings, and miracles of Christ. However, the teachings and scriptural encounters are not simply a history about what Christ has already done but an emphasis describing what God is currently doing and what God is inviting the church (Christ's body) to presently do.

Lent offers five emphases and postures as a way to prepare the church to journey with Jesus through Holy Week into the shadow of the cross.

1. Consider your mortality.
2. Consider your sin and your great need for God.
3. Consider what you might fast from this season—especially as a statement that your treasure is not in the things of this world but in God and a greater awareness and compassion for those who go without daily provisions through no fault of their own.
4. Consider increasing your time in God's Word, prayer, and service to others.
5. Consider the hope and healing offered in Christ and how such life invites us to participate in God's further redemption of the world.

*Ash Wednesday (Liturgical Color: Purple)*

Ash Wednesday is celebrated as the beginning of Lent. The ashes are a sign of mourning and mortality. Ashes had great meaning to God's people in the Old Testament. Job sat in ashes (Job 2:8), and ashes were used in the book of Esther as a sign of mourning (4:1-2). Even in our modern world ashes are a universal symbol of death, destruction, and nothingness. Ashes remind us of our helplessness and our dependence on God, who alone is our help and salvation. The church traces the use of ashes from these ancient traditions to outwardly remind us of the need to mourn our sin and turn to God in whom alone there is forgiveness.

Similar to Advent, this season is about confession and repentance. Repentance is not simply about getting relief from guilt but about the transformation of lives. Throughout much of Christian history, Christians have had ashes placed on their foreheads in the sign of the cross to show a spirit of humility and sacrifice. These ashes are often made from the previous year's Palm Sunday fronds mixed with oil.

Here is an example of the invitation to receive the imposition of ashes: "Tonight those who desire may come forward and receive the imposition of ashes. Along with our utter need for God, the ashes also remind us of our mortality on earth and that the only redemption is with our Lord. Remember, we are dust, and to dust we shall return. As we are called to be reconciled to God, we are also called to be open to the world. Imposing ashes in the shape of the cross on our foreheads is a sign of humility and penance."

This Lenten pilgrimage does not leave us on the ash heap. It begins with Ash Wednesday but leads us to Easter.

## Challenges

The celebration of Ash Wednesday services and participation in Lenten fasts and disciplines are becoming increasingly regular practices in many Protestant and evangelical circles. Within the opportunities of the Lenten disciplines and fasts, maturity is needed. What is chosen should be a matter of prayer. Fasts and disciplines are not "works" to show off personal piety but bodily reminders of and daily engagements with Christ's sufferings and my need to prepare for the journey with Jesus during Holy Week. One year God challenged me to fast during lunch. It was a difficult discipline, but it offered me a daily reminder of both my need for God and Christ's willingness to suffer in love for the world (including me). Moreover, it served as a bodily reminder of those who are forced to fast daily for lack of food.

## Opportunities

Lent offers the opportunity to observe certain biblical disciplines. While the Christian lifestyle of self-denial should characterize the walk of the believer throughout the year and not just during one season, the disciplines practiced during Lent have particular value in leading the church to a deeper experience of Christ's passion and the depth of God's love in preparation for the more joyous experience of Easter. The goal, as is noted in the Ash Wednesday 2 Cor. 5:20–6:10 passage, is that we are to be reconciled both to God and our neighbor. We enter a discipline, not to be seen by others, but through it to be reminded of God's love.[12] Spiritual disciplines should never leave us feeling prideful. Thus when we pray, fast, or give charity to others, we should do these things in secret.

The disciplines can be either giving some things up or taking on new spiritual disciplines.[13]

So what should people give up? The cynic might say, "How about broccoli?" As a matter of prayer consider what is the thing you think you cannot live without. Maybe it is the Internet, music, television, shopping, coffee, or sports. Things that are given up, offered to God, are not necessarily things that are bad in themselves, but things people think they need, things they "can't live without." Lent reminds us that if there are things we cannot go without, those things are most specifically our "gods." So we offer things up as a testimony that true treasures and happiness are not locked into this world.

Furthermore, God may call some people not to subtract but to add. God may call some people to devote more time in Scripture or praying or maybe spending time volunteering in a local school, food bank, or hospital. Maybe God's call will involve painting for those who cannot or writing notes of encouragement. A question offered to the congregation before Lent may be, "What practice is God asking of you that will help make you more aware of your sin, God's love, and the preparation you need to walk with Jesus during Holy Week?" The point is not that we become masochists, but when we remove things from our lives and then long for them, we are to immediately reflect on our sin and need of God's forgiveness and love. When we add things that are new habits, we recognize our daily desperation for God that often becomes muted.

## Tips and Suggestions

Lent is a season, like Advent, that is confessional, penitential, and, thus, somber and subdued. It is not dour, but worship is restrained in Lent. Liturgies that are often filled with "alleluias" are left out in Lent to mark the restrained worship. If you pay attention to numbers, you will note that not all the Sundays are included. Any Lenten fasting is broken on the Sundays in Lent, because even in Lent the church celebrates the Lord's Day, the day of Christ Jesus. However, just as Advent should not celebrate Christ's birth, so, too, the church's worship in Lent should provide deliberate spaces for confession and penance. Furthermore, Lent provides an intentional space for laments. Too often in the church's worship there is little opportunity given to those who are angry and in despair. Laments are a crucial part of worship and compose one of the largest categories of the Psalms. Within this restrained worship, each Sunday is a celebration of the Lord's resurrection, so living in this tension needs to be addressed. A church that engages Lent with intensity will provide a more dynamic encounter with and appreciation of the joy of Easter season.

### Holy Week

Holy Week is not a season of its own but a week of preparation for the high point of the Christian calendar. As Lent prepared the church for Holy Week, Holy Week invites the church to journey with Jesus right into the death, despair, and darkness of the cross. In the fourth century, Holy Week was known as the "Great Week" in Jerusalem. The drama of this week is more than a dramatic re-telling of past events; it provides the church an opportunity to liturgically retrace the week as a present journey with Christ.

## Passion/Palm Sunday (Liturgical Color: Purple)

Palm Sunday is the final Sunday of Lent and a day of great ambiguity in the Christian year. On the one hand, the church remembers the triumphal entry when many rightly praised Jesus as the Messiah. Shouts then and now should be heard, "'Hosanna to the Son of David!' 'Blessed is he who comes in the name of the Lord!' 'Hosanna in the highest!'" (Matt. 21:9, NIV). The church's praise of Christ is right and true and worthy. However, within this exaltation of Christ, the church also observes that many who were offering praises to Christ on that first day of the week were enraged at his refusal to destroy the Romans and that from those same mouths shouts of "Crucify him!" spewed forth. Within this narrative the church must reflect on its own inconsistency in worship. Just as those Jews had hopes and desires for Jesus, we also shift our loyalty away from Christ when he does not answer our prayers how and when we want. This tension must not be overlooked.

## The Great Triduum

The three days of Thursday night to Sunday morning make up what has been labeled the Great Triduum. "Triduum," or "three days," was the Latin term used by Augustine to emphasize the unity of the single three-day service.[14] Although the church celebrates these days as Maundy Thursday, Good Friday, and Holy Saturday, these three days point to the one great and terrible event of Christ's passion. It was not lost on the Christian church that the weekend of Christ's death and resurrection was during Passover. Christians thus consider how the events from Thursday to Sunday morning enable the church to encounter and be present to Christ's paschal (Passover or passion) mystery. Even though each day celebrates and encounters one aspect of the story, all three days should be seen in light of the entire narrative.

The emphasis of this three-day service is not sentimental nostalgia of past events. Rather, these services make the church present to a dynamic encounter with Christ, who invites Christians into this past, present, and future journey. When beginning to celebrate these Holy Week services, pastors and worship leaders must intentionally explain that these services are not opportunities for the super pious or devout to demonstrate their spiritual maturity. Rather, the worship leaders should articulate to the local congregation that a failure to attend the full Triduum will likely cause people to miss the full significance of encountering Christ on Easter.

### Holy Thursday/Maundy Thursday (Liturgical Color: Purple)

This service encounters, remembers, and re-presents two events depending on the lectionary year: the washing of the disciples' feet and the institution of the Lord's Supper.[15] John 13:1-15 narrates Jesus washing the disciples' feet on the night of his betrayal. This action embodies Jesus' new commandment (in Latin, *novum mandatum*—from which comes the word "maundy") given in John 13:34, "Love one another. Just as I have loved you, you also should love one another." While foot washing can be included in present-day services, the differences between the first-century context and the present context are so vast that some alternatives to foot washing can be explored. Worship leaders and pastors should be cautious of sentimental or "cute" options; however, creativity with theological and liturgical care opens up powerful ways to embody this command to love one another.

An emphasis on the institution of the Lord's Supper is also fitting for a service of Holy Thursday. The traditional Passover meal was transformed when Christ took the bread, gave thanks, broke it, and proclaimed, "This is my body, which is given for you" (Luke 22:19). Later he took the cup and offered it to them saying, "This cup that is poured out for you is the new covenant in my blood" (v. 20). While the Last Supper is familiar to most Christians, the tensions of this passage provide a helpful drama in which a present-day congregation can become immersed. Similar to the foot-washing narrative, this event happened on the night Christ was betrayed. Most eucharistic liturgies begin with this declaration.

Such familiarity must be made new again, recalling afresh that Jesus offered himself to his disciples in such an intimate fashion, even while sensing betrayal in the air. The betrayals were not limited to what Judas did; they included what Peter was soon to do—a betrayal Jesus predicted in response to Peter's ignorant and audacious declaration of faithfulness (vv. 33-34). Moreover, in light of the intimacy of this meal, Peter, James, and John were unable to stay awake and pray for Jesus in his intense time of need in the garden. When Judas and the guards approached, and after Jesus rebuked the use of the sword, all the disciples abandoned Jesus to the religious and civic powers. Craig Hovey suggests that even though Jesus offered the disciples his body and blood, "the disciples failed to drink deeply."[16]

To fully receive Christ's self-offering at the Lord's Supper requires Christians to offer themselves to Christ, to follow where he has led, come what may. Rather than ingesting Christ through the emblems, the disciples were invited to *drink deeply* by offering themselves with Christ for the glory of God. Moreover, past, present, and future disciples are invited not simply to consume Christ but also, in the reception of Christ, to offer themselves to Christ as their means of fully receiving him. Holy Thursday, in this sense, is an invitation to the church in all of its Lenten disciplines to allow the Spirit to give them courage to walk with Jesus all the way into the shadow of the cross.

## Good Friday: Tenebrae (Service of Shadows— Liturgical Color: Black or Red)

*Tenebrae* is Latin for "darkness and shadows." From the festivity and joy of Holy Thursday, the congregation is rushed into the darkness, stripped of all joyous trappings. The mood of Holy Thursday transitions from joy to somber discipleship. The power of Christ's love is again on display as the Light of the World lays down his life and allows the darkness of sin and death to vanquish him. Naming this day as *Good* Friday needs explanation. This day is not good because the Romans and Jews succeeded in killing Jesus; rather it is good only because Jesus was obedient to the will of the Father, even "to the point of death" (Phil. 2:8). Christ's example offers the church hope that Christians, too, when facing suffering, persecutions, and even death are not alone and thus should not be afraid. The magnitude of the love of the Father who gave up the Son and of the Son who gave himself up by the power of the Spirit to the world for the Father is the foundation of Christian hope and faith.

This is not the setting to recount a host of atonement theories celebrating how "good" it was that Jesus was killed. This is a day to be thankful for the sacrifice of Christ. But within this thankfulness arise two powerful assertions: first, Christ has died and we have killed him. Second, Christ invites us to journey with him all the way to his last breath when "it is finished" (John 19:30). This is precisely what the Lenten disciplines have prepared the church to do.

The service often contains three distinct movements.

1. *The Service of the Word*, where the passion account from John is read (18:1– 19:42).
2. *The Solemn Intercession*, where the church offers prayers of bidding for Christ and the world.
3. *The Adoration (Meditation) of the Cross*, where following the intercessions the church is offered to gaze deeply upon the cross. Careful lighting of a cross in the sacred space or carrying a cross into the service provides a stark new event moving toward a finality in this passion journey.

Worship leaders should creatively use light and the persistent and steady growth of darkness to move the worshippers into the atmosphere of total loss and despair that surrounds the killing of the Light of the World. At the conclusion of the service, the Christ candle is carried out and the congregation leaves in silence and darkness. The conclusion of the service offers blackness, not blessings; no benediction, but silence.

## Holy Saturday

Holy Saturday is a day when the heavens are shut. The heavens are silent and move the church to reflect deeply on the powerful offering of Christ's death for our sin.

*Easter (Liturgical Color: White)*

The Triduum concludes on the *Paschal Vigil*, the first service of Easter beginning late on Holy Saturday. This service often begins before dawn on Easter morning and is often a service of baptism for those who have been training and preparing for this covenant.

Easter is a high point of the church year, when light breaks through the darkness of despair and disappointment and shines again to conquer fear, sin, and death. With jubilation by the Spirit the church shouts its declaration of praise and hope, "He is risen!" To which the congregants respond in joy, hope, and faith, "He is risen indeed!" This celebration pierces all circumstances of death and despair. Easter, with its hope of resurrection, proclaims not only the eventual end of our present challenges but also victory over all sin and death. No longer do people need to be enslaved to sin (see Rom. 6). No longer do people need to fear enemies, hardship, or death. Easter is the proclamation in hope and joy that death (physical and spiritual) has been overwhelmed in the resurrection. The resurrection of Christ is also not simply about what happened to Christ but is also a firstfruits, a beginning of what will occur for all who accept the invitation to become fully human.

The hope of resurrection is also not relegated to the future. As celebrated in the hope of baptism, Christians are invited to let themselves be drowned to evil and sin and raised to new life in Christ, born of water and Spirit. Moreover, the resurrection of Christ is a testimony that Jesus lived "a life worthy of the calling to which [he was] called" (Eph. 4:1). The resurrection is confirmation that Jesus himself, along with the life he invited people to live, is the true Way to become fully human.

## Challenges

Like Christmas, most Christians "know" the story. In some sense familiarity produces apathy. Churches often try to counterbalance this by the implicit manipulation of emotions. Just as with Christmas, the joy of Easter is not about fabricating a superficial emotionalism. Like Christmas, Easter is not one day but a season of celebrations ending with Pentecost. Every Sunday through the year, even during Lent, is a day to celebrate the resurrection of Christ; the season of Easter invites people into a hope, a confidence, and a peace that provide courage to remain steadfast even in the midst of the daunting and painful storms of life. This posture of hope is not one of naive ignorance or blindness to our own pain or that of our neighbors but a statement of faith and trust and an invitation to hope when all the present circumstances invite despair.

A major theological challenge surrounding Easter is the atonement. The caution is similar to the earlier warning about not reducing the Christmas message to Christ's death at Calvary. If care is not taken, the hope of Easter can be reduced to "Christ died for us." Christians must not neglect Paul's assertion that if Jesus is not raised, there is nothing saving about Christ's death (see 1 Cor. 15:1-

19). With vigilance, worship leaders must proclaim that it is only through the life, death, and resurrection that salvation is possible. This is the full imagination of Christ and the life God is inviting people to enter.

## Opportunities

The season of Easter is a fifty-day feast ending with Pentecost and the birth of the church. These fifty days were also known as a "week of Sundays." Church tradition provides many songs and prayers for all seven Sundays. The powerful sense of hope and joy that belongs to the Easter season necessitates the Lenten season of denial that precedes it.

Along with the songs, prayers, and celebrations, Easter Sunday often gathers people who are not regular participants at church. This is a wonderful opportunity for the local congregation to welcome those who are rarely seen.

Finally, the realization that the focus of the resurrection is not only on something that has already happened but also on what is happening now is of paramount importance. Because Easter often celebrates the baptism of catechumens, and since each baptism and Lord's Supper is a present renewal of the covenant with God, resurrections continue to happen. Recall the force and imagination of *anamnēsis*. The church at Easter does not simply celebrate that Christ was raised but also that Christ is alive and present to us, here and now! Moreover, it is the presence and power of the Holy Spirit who raised Christ from the dead that the church encounters and anticipates as Easter is moving the church forward to Pentecost.

## Tips and Suggestions

Those churches that have celebrated a Good Friday Tenebrae service can begin the Easter service in darkness with the carrying of the Christ candle into the sanctuary. As the candle processes in, the church can then be filled with joy and light. Although the darkness was powerful, the light of God has once and for all overcome it. Joyful music and the acclamations of alleluias should saturate the atmosphere.

Certainly this is a season that welcomes celebrating the Lord's Supper weekly as a regular and present encounter with Christ, while also anticipating the future heavenly banquet (to which each celebration of the Lord's Supper points).

For many congregations whose current imagination of Easter is one day, it is wise to begin and regularly proclaim the Easter good news throughout the entire season: *He is risen! He is risen indeed! Alleluia!* Such intentional praise helps the congregation realize that the hope of the resurrection endures much longer than the joy-filled celebration of the first Sunday of Easter. Church tradition also offers many call-and-response litanies (prayers) that can help the congregation celebrate the resurrection during the entire Easter season.

Churches that have *sunrise services* should draw upon the great history of the Paschal Vigil service. This is a service of light in which the church has often celebrated the baptism of the catechumens.

## Ascension Sunday (Liturgical Color: White)

Ascension Sunday occurs on the fortieth day after Easter. For many Christians the ascension has not been presented in a way that has captivated the church's imagination. This has resulted in most Christians either ignoring it or announcing it on that Sunday as just another announcement among several others. Part of the challenge is that Christians often do not celebrate what they believe does not really matter to their salvation. This is problematic on many levels in more ways than it is possible to explore at this time, but briefly, some Christians find Jesus helpful only in his death and marginalize his birth, life, teachings, temptations, resurrection, and ascension. Ascension Day is a celebration that Christ is the ruler over all creation. The church is thus invited not only to participate in Christ's death and resurrection but also to affirm that he is both Savior and Lord of all creation. Ascension Sunday can also be an occasion to affirm the hope of the resurrection that one day Christ will return in the consummation of the kingdom of God.

## Pentecost: God's Spirit Poured Out in the Birth of the Church (Liturgical Color: Red)

Easter is a seven-week season concluding with Pentecost. Within the celebration of the life, death, resurrection, and ascension of Christ, at Pentecost God pours forth God's Spirit and the church is birthed. While Pentecost is the culmination of the season of Easter, it is also the beginning of the church's empowerment to be Christ's body and blood in the world. Historically, Pentecost was the conclusion of the Easter season.

## Challenges

Similar to many Christian holy days outside of Good Friday, most Christians have not been properly trained in the Christian narrative on the importance of Pentecost. This problem is not only liturgical (with regard to worship) but also theological. Some parts of Christendom need to properly remember and be present to the power and importance of the Holy Spirit. Without the outpouring of the Spirit there is no church, there is no salvation and redemption of the world. Pentecost is God's gift of life through God's Spirit, God's breath (*pneuma* in Greek).

## Opportunities

As Pentecost is largely undercelebrated in many parts of Christianity, a robust and dynamic teaching and communal worship can invite Christians into the full power and promise of God's presence in the world today. Church tradition contains many rich resources to draw upon as the church attempts to more fully celebrate the past, present, and future outpouring of the Holy Spirit.

## Tips and Suggestions

This Sunday provides new opportunities not only to offer theological instruction on the power and role of the Spirit but also for the local church to encounter the dynamic healing power of the Spirit. While appropriate in any season, services of healing and reconciliation find an especially wonderful space on this day. This day should also be used to offer special prayers for the healing and redemption of the world, as well as for the need to continually encounter the sustaining and powerful presence of the Holy Spirit.

### *Trinity Sunday (Liturgical Color: White)*

Trinity Sunday is celebrated on the first Sunday after Pentecost. This is an important feast day for the church that for many Christians has also not been included in the Christian liturgical imagination. While most feast days emphasize God's healing through events of redemption, this is a day of praise and honor to the triune God. It is a day to celebrate the glorious mystery of the triune God, whose nature and name is love.

### *Ordinary Time (Liturgical Color: Green)*

The season between Pentecost and Advent is a time without feasts called Ordinary Time. During this season many Christians emphasize the role of the Spirit in the church and its mission in the world. Since green is the liturgical color (as is the season after Pentecost), this is a season to grow. This season is an invitation to the church living in the power of the Spirit to faithfully live into the hope and grace of God in the Ordinary Time.

## Challenges

The church does not provide a specific theme and imagination into which to guide the local congregation during this season. Moreover, this season occurs during the months when many are on vacation and out of school. People floating in and out without a central guiding theme demand the full attention and intention of the worship team.

## Opportunities

What is viewed as a challenge is also a wonderful opportunity. For those following the lectionary, the summer months of Ordinary Time provide a wonderful chance to immerse the church in the books of the Bible. This season can also devote attention to saints or books from the Old Testament that are largely neglected throughout the year.

## Tips and Suggestions

This is a wonderful season for series as well as attending to the narrative of the Old Testament. A person misses out on the full imagination of the Christian narrative if he or she has not encountered the narrative and saints of the Old Testament in all their triumphs and failures. A study in the Old Testament opens the church to the wonderful mercies of God amid the continual unfaithfulness of God's people.

*Christ the King (Liturgical Color: White or Gold)*

Christ the King is the final Sunday of Ordinary Time after Pentecost. During the time of growth in Ordinary Time, Christ the King Sunday anticipates the hope of the kingdom of God coming in its fullness as Christ comes in glory as the King of kings and Lord of lords. In Christ's coming human suffering and weakness will be no more. This is a day to hope amid life's struggles and challenges that such present trials are not eternal and are incomparable to the glory that is coming. Similar to other days of celebration, this day offers hope from the past and future to an uncertain present.

## Questions for Discussion and Reflection

1. What ideas were the most helpful in this chapter?

2. What ideas are the most difficult or causing the greatest amount of tension?

3. What parts of the church year are being emphasized in worship? What is going really well?

4. What aspects of the church year are being neglected? What are some ways to allow a fuller imagination of the church year that guides the planning of communal worship?

5. What are some of the biggest challenges when the Christian year is the dominant guide to communal worship?

# TWELVE

# WHAT DO WE DO? WORSHIP SERVICES THAT ARE CHRISTIAN

*Planning worship well begins with giving attention to the worship team,*
*the process for planning worship, the people in a local community, the*
*worship space, and the season of the Christian year; it also means*
***planning worship services that are Christian.* . . .**

---

At the beginning of this conversation, it was suggested that an important question that is rarely asked in local churches is essential, "How do we know our worship is Christian?" Such a question may seem absurd or pejorative. However, a failure to attend to this question results in worship services that are not as faithfully Christian as they could be. Recall that the point of communal worship is the glorification of God and the sanctification of humanity (and creation). Some worship services do this more faithfully than others. I am sure there are many who would agree with all of these points. However, the tension comes with the *power* question. *Who* decides what faithful worship that glorifies God and sanctifies humanity looks like?

At this juncture let me offer two caveats to frame this question about what *is* and *is not* Christian worship. One of John Wesley's most important sermons is titled "Catholic Spirit." In this sermon Wesley calls for the church to find a unity in love even as people will not always share the same opinions. Most specifically he discusses "opinions of modes of worship."

> But although a difference in opinions or modes of worship may prevent an entire external union, yet need it prevent our union in affection? Though we can't think alike, may we not love alike? May we not be of one heart, though we are not of one opinion? Without all doubt we may. Herein all the children of God may unite, notwithstanding these smaller differences. These remaining as they are, they may forward one another in love and in good works.[1]

Wesley was adamant that all Christians participate in worship as part of a local congregation, even though the modes of worship are open to the opinions of people. However, even under the banner of opinion, Wesley is clear in this sermon and other writings about the importance of certain elements that should be included, most specifically the Lord's Supper.[2] Clearly under worship there are multiple practices that can be labeled Christian. However, *everything* cannot be properly labeled as *Christian* worship.

Within this generous catholicity of spirit, let me offer a quip from the world of liturgical theology. "What is the difference between a terrorist and a liturgical theologian?" (Pause) "You can negotiate with a terrorist." Within this playful joke, there is also a sense of seriousness to which liturgical theologians hold fast. Liturgical theologians do not desire a blind copying of past practices but an awareness of what Christian worship has been so as to faithfully connect the present to the past and the past to the present. hmm. . .

Section II of this book draws upon a theology of worship explored in section I. Within this move from the theoretical to the practical, there are many places for faithful improvisation and contextual flavoring. However, paying attention to the history of Christian worship can offer a wonderful beginning from which to nuance and extemporize. Improvisation is only possible with a solid awareness of what has been.

## Word and Table

With this background in mind, I will now offer an *ordo* (order) of worship and a rationale for why the rhythms of such worship are faithfully Christian. This is not the only ordo that can be properly Christian even as it is faithful to the history of Christian worship. A basic ordo of Christian worship is the service of Word and Table.

|  |  |
|---|---|
|  | Call to Worship |
|  | Collect |
|  | Song of Praise |
|  | Prayer of Illumination (or earlier) |
| Service of the Word { | Old Testament Reading |
|  | Sing the Psalm |
|  | Epistle Lesson |
|  | Hymn of Thanksgiving |
|  | Gospel Reading |
|  | Sermon |
|  | Confession and Pardon |
|  | Peace of Christ |
|  | Creed |

|                         | Prayers of the People |
|                         | Offering |
|                         | Doxology |
| Service of the Table {  | Lord's Supper |
|                         | Benediction: Sending Forth |

These are not two separate services, but two aspects of worship united into one full service. A Christian worship service celebrates the church being gathered by God's Spirit and then sent out *by* and *with* God's Spirit to continue in worship through doxological mission, participating in God's movement and ministry in the world.

The next four chapters explore the service of the Word by looking at the call of God and the church's response to God's call empowered by the Spirit. The call of God focuses on the role of Scripture and the sermon. The response to God's call considers spoken and sung prayers (including the role of music), the creeds, and offerings.

## Questions for Discussion and Reflection

1. What are your church's greatest strengths and weaknesses in regard to the order and flow of worship?

2. What is the regular order of worship in your local church?

3. What is the rationale for what is done and when?

4. What guides the communal worship team in helping to make sure what is being done is Christian?

## THIRTEEN
# SERVICE OF THE WORD: SCRIPTURE AND SERMON

*Planning worship well begins with giving attention to the worship team, the process for planning worship, the people in a local community, the worship space, and the season of the Christian year; it also means planning worship services that are Christian. **The service of Word and Table emphasizes God's gathering and calling while also empowering humanity's response.** . . .*

The service of the Word is about Scripture, but it also goes beyond Scripture. In the New Testament the Scriptures are named "the word" on several occasions (e.g., Eph. 6:17 and Heb. 4:12). However, the prologue at the beginning of John's gospel observes that another name for the eternal Son is the *Logos*, "Word" (John 1:1-5). Properly speaking, the *Word of God* is not the Bible, which contains the sacred Scriptures, but Jesus Christ. Revelation 19:13 also proclaims, "He is clothed in a robe dipped in blood, and his name is called The Word of God." However, the Scriptures are God's gift to the church by revealing who God is and thus opening up ways for people to be healed to become more fully human. The Holy Scriptures reveal and through reading provide an encounter with Jesus Christ, *the Word of God.*

The service of the Word offers some distinct rhythms that guide the ordo. The basic structure of the service of the Word is God's call and creation's response empowered by the Spirit. Paying attention to this rhythm of call and response provides a helpful backdrop for understanding what function each element serves. In too many cases when worship leaders are pressed into answering questions such as, "Why are you doing that?" "And why are you doing this now?" There is often little awareness of this emphasis on call and response. Let's consider this concept more closely by looking at the rhythms in the service of the Word from the perspective of *God's call* and *creation's response*. We will first explore God's call and then, in the next chapter, creation's response.

# God's Call

God's calling in the service of the Word emphasizes God's gathering of the believers to communal worship and the proclamation of Scripture. As stated earlier, life flows within the rhythms of God's gathering (breathing in) and sending out (exhaling).

The church is gathered by the Spirit to encounter God, and in the service of the Word, this encounter happens most profoundly through the reading of Scripture and the prophetic proclamation of the Word through the sermon.

## Encounter Through Scripture

In order to fully appreciate the significance of Scripture in communal worship some definitions and history will be helpful as we consider the power of the encounter of God through the reading of Scripture. The following definitions offer clarity in understanding the full imagination of Scripture.

**Scripture**—This is based on a Hebrew word meaning "writings." As a technical term it came to be known as religious writings. In its early cultural contexts many religious cults had their own set of Scriptures.

**Bible**—This term early on meant "written pages." Its later use transitioned to mean a "book." Still later the Bible came to be understood as a *book containing our Scriptures.* As a matter of unity and apostolicity, Christians later canonized the sacred writings in the Bible to affirm which books were held to be the most authoritative and helpful for salvation.

**Special Revelation**—Jews and Christians have consistently believed by faith that God has self-disclosed Godself in and through the sacred Scriptures gathered in the Bible. In this self-disclosure, Jews and Christians affirm that God is making known things that had been hidden and obscure. The revelation of God through Scripture is also known as special revelation and is distinct from the general revelation that God has made to all people.[1]

## Scripture and Communal Worship

The reading of Scripture and the proclamation of the Word in the sermon are divine encounters with God. In this encounter God reorients or displaces misguided desires that are too focused on "me" and what "I" want. Smith rightly notes how communal worship provides a practice whereby the church encounters God to renew and refashion our hearts and desires to better reflect God's image in our lives.[2] This renewal of the church is both reuniting the church and healing the church to better "desire what God desires, and seek what God seeks."[3] As part of this dynamic encounter with God, the church often prays *a prayer of illumination.* While this will be discussed more fully below, this prayer of illumination asks God by the Spirit to help the church to be present and attentive to God's presence encountered in Scripture.

*The Problem with "My" Bible*

One of my New Testament colleagues, with over thirty years in Christian higher education, has often pointed out an interesting irony. Those people or congregations who would tell you in person or in their official doctrines that they "believe in the full authority of Scriptures" are often those who rarely read Scripture in worship. Clearly what people really believe can be discerned by what they do. Despite all the verbal declarations about the importance of exercise, if I am not exercising (and I physically could do so), then I really do not believe exercise is that important. Why is there such a paucity of Scripture in Christian communal worship, most specifically among congregations who openly affirm the importance and centrality of Scripture? Part of the problem can be traced both to the invention of the Gutenberg press coupled with a strident individualism that emerged within the modern era.

There was a time when the nearest Bible was stored and locked safely in the local church. The church would break open the texts in the presence of the congregants, many of whom were illiterate, and they would hear and encounter God's prophetic Word through the Scriptures. Without romanticizing the early and medieval church's worship, one can imagine how hearing the words of Scripture in communal worship would be holy moments. With the invention of the printing press and an increase in literacy, families began to have "their own" Bibles.

While the benefits of these changes cannot be overstated, the new possibilities and opportunities also yielded some dangerous pitfalls. People no longer needed to attend communal worship to hear and encounter Scripture; they could read it in the privacy of their own homes. Further, not only could they read the text in the privacy of their homes, but they could also interpret the text according to however they believe God was speaking to them; hence, the birth of "personal Bible studies" and "personal devotions." Now let me be clear. I am not suggesting that individuals or families should stop reading Scripture throughout the week in their homes, schools, or workplaces. However, with these great opportunities afforded by technology and education, several disciplines need attending to.

*Educating People on How to Read Scripture*

Clearly giving a person a Bible and saying, "Go for it," is not ideal. Remember how important is was for Philip to be directed to the Ethiopian Eunuch who needed guidance and instruction about understanding Scripture.[4] Most people would not agree that my reading and interpretation of Hamlet would be as insightful or helpful as a Shakespearean scholar. As the local congregation is inviting people to be daily shaped by prayer and Scripture, it should also offer instruction on how to best encounter and be formed through the texts.

*Take Insights Back to Church*

When God offers illumination through the reading of Scripture, both in communal worship and in reading during the week, a person must share these insights with his or her local congregation both for the edification of the local body and to ensure that what he or she is *hearing* is actually from God. For those who have been trained and habituated to the Scriptures, ninety-nine times out of a hundred, the illumination a person receives can be a blessing and benefit of the local congregation. But all people, including ordained pastors and priests, do not always perfectly interpret the Scriptures. The local community can assist as a sort of gatekeeper to guard against poor readings of Scripture. For example, the nation was shocked to hear about Andrea Yates. *Time Magazine* recounted the tragedy of a family cut off from a local church.

Andrea and her husband, Rusty, chose to consider their own family a home church. Andrea struggled with postpartum depression, and often her isolated reading of the Bible made her depression worse. As she read certain passages from the Bible, she recognized the importance of raising her children well and she felt that if she failed, death was the proper punishment. Because her standards were not being met by her children, she felt she was failing. "She later told the jail psychiatrist, 'the kids were destined to perish in the fires of hell.'"[5]

Andrea was a mother of five young children. She read her Bible one morning and felt that God told her she was a bad mother and that God was commanding her to drown her children in the bathtub, which she did. The family was cut off from a local congregation and thus were relying on their own interpretations.

Clearly such an example comes from the far extreme. Yet too many people read the Bible and then what they claim God is telling them is not from God. Furthermore, people have also taken Bible verses and used them as proof texts to prove whatever they want. Recall that this is called eisegesis and does violence to Scripture. Often this type of proof-texting is done to rationalize behavior or prove "God agrees with me." Even local congregations are not free from making mistakes. It is not enough to say, "Does my local congregation agree?" Many churches in the Southern United States in the nineteenth century were certain that God approved and ordained slavery. Yet the church universal discerned otherwise and many Christians were at the center of the abolitionist movement.

## *The Scriptures and Clergy for Communal Worship*

The Bible is not mine, but the church's. The relationship between Scripture and communal worship is interdependent. The Scriptures were inspired and collected (canonized) for communal worship. "Worship is Scripture's home, its native soil, its most congenial habitat."[6] Furthermore, the importance of the ordained clergy cannot be overlooked. Just as my interpretation and analysis of *Hamlet* is not necessarily wrong, it needs to be set alongside that of the Shakespearean scholars. As noted above, this is not claiming that ordained pastors will never make errors or offer incorrect interpretations, but the church affirms the importance of the clergy. The clergy have been gifted and called by God, affirmed and given authority by the local congregation (and denomination), and empowered by the Holy Spirit to proclaim the Scriptures. The wisdom of the church is placed within each minister both through training and instruction and through the divine empowerment of the Holy Spirit. Reflecting on the past, present, and future of Scripture brings to mind that the Scriptures came about from God for communal worship. The chief place for reading the Scriptures is thus the church's communal worship under the authority of the ordained.

### The Performance of Scripture in Worship

With the importance of God being encountered through the reading of Scripture in communal worship, local churches also need to raise the level of excellence in the performance of the Scripture reading. Local churches would do well to teach and perform with sacred care the reading of Scripture.

I have attended many Christian conferences and rallies throughout my life in the United States and around the world. Often in some of those gatherings greetings are brought from dignitaries and local civic officials welcoming the attendees to their city or state. I will not forget one conference I attended as a youth when a letter was read offering greetings and thanks for what this conference would do in training and service in that local city. Then the conference reader performed a dramatic pause and said, "Signed George H. W. Bush, president of the United States of America." You would have thought Bono, Bon Jovi, or Elvis (for you more seasoned readers) had just entered the room. There was immediate exaltation, clapping, and shouting. Yet I was struck how later in that same service a gospel text was read and was received with as much enthusiasm as receiving spam email.

Do we really believe that when the Scriptures are broken open, by the Spirit, God will speak a powerful word? I imagine if I did receive an email from God, I would probably not just throw it in my junk file. I imagine I would frame it or put it in a special place to read later (I know the analogy has many problems). I want to invite and encourage local congregations to take great care through education and practice to prepare their people to dynamically encounter God in the reading of Scripture.

In celebration of the reading of Scripture, the church has often responded in thanksgiving and praise for God's precious presence encountered through Scripture. When the Old Testament or New Testament lessons were read, the reader often proclaimed, "This is the word of the Lord," and the congregation would respond, "Thanks be to God!" Similarly, after the gospel lesson was read (which was often taken down from the pulpit and read among the standing congregation as a reminder of Christ's continual incarnation) the reader would proclaim, "This is the gospel of our Lord," and the congregation would say in turn, "Praise to you, Lord Christ."

As Scriptures are read, they are enacted; the reading is an event, an encounter that does something in the congregation and the world. One can simply recall the young King Josiah. When the Scriptures were read, they moved the king and Israel to penitence and renewal (2 Kings 22:11-13). Through the reading of

Scriptures God breaks forth across the body offering a powerful word of hope and challenge.

## Good Practices in Scripture Reading

Several of the challenges have now been named that marginalize the importance of reading Scripture in worship. One not mentioned but perhaps the most significant is the poor reading of Scripture in communal worship. How many times has the reader stumbled and fumbled through difficult names of biblical cities or people? How often have they laughed it off as if such names are funny because they are so uncommon today? How often have people skipped lines or lost their place on the page? How often have people read in a monotone voice that would make reading the dictionary more exciting? The point here is that for the sake of quality and the holiness of the Scriptures, local churches should read with excellence. Here are some recommendations and suggestions for lectors (the people who read Scripture):

Scriptural Reading Team

This team would be a collection of people both gifted and dedicated to the ministry of Scripture reading. While some people's voices naturally have a stronger "radio quality," the qualities for reading Scripture well can be learned in community. This team should consist of a wide variety of people in the congregation, including teens and children when possible.

Practice, Practice, Practice

Like quality musicians and dynamic preachers, practicing is crucial. Too many aspects of communal worship that are seen as "less important" are often not given adequate preparation. Readers practicing in a community and when possible with a speech or diction instructor can learn to hone and sharpen public speaking skills. Practicing also breeds confidence and reading with expression and authority. Through such practice difficult words or challenging phrases can be mastered. Of course for this practice to happen, people need to know in advance (at least one week ahead) *when* and *what* they are reading. Here is another instance where planning ahead, even with such small and easy details, opens up new possibilities of liturgical excellence.

The Congregation's Bodily Posture

There is no uniformity in practice both currently or throughout Christian history for whether the congregation stands or sits during the reading of Scripture. Standing tends to be a more engaged posture than sitting, which can suggest an attitude of entertainment. It is largely the practice to stand when the gospel text is read. Moreover, when the gospel text is read, the Bible is brought down among the people and the liturgist reads from the congregation. As mentioned earlier, theologically this emphasizes that Jesus Christ did become and is

Emmanuel—God with Us. Thus the Gospels are a proclamation and revelation of Jesus Christ, who is present within the body gathered by the Spirit.

### Appearance of Reader

The reader should dress in a manner that does not draw undue attention away from Scripture.

### The "Perfect" Performance

Whether readers have practiced or not, they should not dwell on mistakes in reading. This is no time for silly jokes. When a mistake is made, reread the verse and move forward.[7] The performance of Scripture is no less significant than any other element of worship. Most congregations would be bothered by disorganized music or sermons that are thrown together, and they should expect and plan to have a higher quality of performance in the reading of Scripture. Some people may be balking at this performance imagery. More will be said about this later when discussing excellence in leading worship, but performance is an appropriate image. Some may resist this way of looking at Scripture reading because they are equating the idea of performance with actions that are phony or fake. But the concept of performance resists such a reduction. All aspects of communal worship are performed both on the stage and in the chairs and pews. Roy Rappaport notes that only rituals that are performed can have a transformative effect.[8] The issue is rather simple. A worship service on PowerPoint slides or a Word document is not a worship service unless there are people *performing* it.

Along with these general recommendations are several practices that can further add to the excellence of the performance:

1. Announce the passage being read.

2. Announce the version of the Bible. It's helpful for the congregation to know which translation of the Scriptures is being read.

3. Provide some background and a summary of the text. Before the actual reading, offering the congregation a two- to five-sentence background on the text is a good practice. This background can include what has just preceded the passage and other events or themes that are contained in the chapter. On many occasions it will also be helpful to offer a brief summary of the main idea and passion of the passage. The idea is not for the reader to merely say, "The following passage means . . . ," but to open the congregation up to the main points of emphasis in the passage.

4. Pay attention to pace, diction, and expression. A reader will want to read with a steady pace, neither too fast nor too slow. Proper enunciation will help words to be heard without being slurred. Pay attention to articulating clearly the beginnings and endings of words. Reading with passion and expression helps to draw people into the passage. An overly dramatic reading will be a distraction, even though that is generally not the extreme toward which most readings lean.[9]

With all of these aspects, reading in a community can help provide formative feedback.

5. End with a response of doxology. As noted earlier, allow people to respond immediately in thanksgiving to the gift of God's revelation through Scripture. Prompt their response by saying, "This is the Word of the Lord" or "Here is the gospel of the Lord." These phrases permit the congregation to participate in the reading and its gift to the church.

### Creative Options for Scripture Performance

Instead of having just one liturgist read the texts, there is room for some creativity. The local worship team should explore imaginative ways for presenting the Scriptures. For example, many churches sing the Psalms to a familiar hymn melody or follow the leading of a cantor. Scriptures can also be read and sung antiphonally between a leader and the congregants from a variety of places in the worship space. The main thing is to be creative without becoming inappropriate.

## *What Texts? How Many? Where in the Ordo?*

### The Lectionary

The danger for any preacher is only preaching texts that he or she is comfortable with. One of the benefits of following the lectionary is that it opens up the congregation and the pastor to texts that are tough as well as parts of the Old Testament that are rarely addressed. The lectionary is a three-year cycle that is followed by Roman Catholics and Protestants alike. The three years are designated A, B, and C. Each of these years follows a rhythm. The Synoptic Gospels are each given a year of emphasis (A-Matthew, B-Mark, C-Luke). The gospel of John is given primary emphasis in Lent A, in Easter all three years, and for a month in year B. The lectionary has four texts for each Sunday and holy day: an Old Testament lesson, a psalm, a New Testament epistle, and a gospel text. These texts mostly follow themes depending on the season of the church year. Not only is this wide exposure to the Bible helpful, but also there are many benefits in knowing that Christians throughout the world are being encountered by God through the same texts. The lectionary may not work for every congregation, pastor, or worship team, but it is a helpful resource to consider.

### How Many Texts?

The number of texts is open to the worship team. Curiously, most Protestants generally create more space for the pastor's reflections or singing than Scripture. At the minimum, at least two texts would be recommended. The emphasis here is not on a scriptural legalism or fake piety, "Hey, look at us—we read five Scripture passages! Clearly we are more holy than you." Such an approach misunderstands that reading Scripture is not simply a task to be accomplished but an invitation to us for God to transform us.

For those following the lectionary, texts are usually read in this order: Old Testament, psalm (spoken or sung), epistle, and gospel. The emphasis theologically is that all services center around who Jesus Christ is. This does not mean that the main sermon text always needs to be from the Gospels. Furthermore, there are some preachers who work hard to incorporate all four lectionary texts into the sermon. This is a skill that can be learned but is not necessary. On some weeks the common thread between the texts is so thin that it is extremely difficult to find. Moreover, it is not necessary that the preacher "comment" or "tell you what each passage means."

Call to Worship
Collect
Song of Praise
**Prayer of
  Illumination
  (or earlier)**
Old Testament
  Reading
Sing the Psalm
Epistle Lesson
Hymn of
  Thanksgiving
Gospel Reading
Sermon
Confession and
  Pardon
Peace of Christ
Creed
Prayers of the
  People
Offering
Doxology
Lord's Supper
Benediction:
  Sending
  Forth

This is the beauty and power of Scripture. Both in the Scriptures read and sermon proclaimed the Holy Spirit will be at work providing many words of hope, comfort, challenge, and transformation that the minister or music leader may not have intended or planned. This point will be discussed later in the "creation's response," but it is always wise to offer some prayer spoken or sung that seeks the Spirit to open up the congregation's eyes, ears, minds, and hearts. This is often called the prayer for the illumination of Scripture. This prayer should fall prior to the Scriptures being read.

*Sermon: The Prophetic Proclamation of the Word*

One of the main emphases from the Protestant Reformation is the preaching of the Word. I will never forget my first sermon. It was on Rom. 12:1-2. As first sermons go, it was okay. But during my preaching I was struck by the fact that I worshiped in a culture that was more primed to hear my musings on the Bible than the words of Scripture itself. With that said, in many ways the sermon is an extension of the Scriptures being proclaimed. The ordained minister is called and ordained to weekly offer a prophetic word that reaches into the precise context of that local congregation.

Both the reading of Scripture and the proclamation of the Word move the congregation to recognize the ways in which God has brought healing while also recognizing that more healing is needed. The dynamic encounter with God moves the church to confess with the hope and imagination that while the kingdom is present in part, there is a not-yet of the kingdom that is coming and we are invited to live into that hope now through further healing.

Walter Brueggemann's classic text *Finally Comes the Poet* highlights the need for bold and prophetic expositors of the Scriptures. Sadly, our proclamation often falls short. The gospel has been softened when "we depart having heard, but without noticing the urge to transformation that is not readily compatible with our comfortable believing that asks little and receives less."[10] The gospel upsets the comfortable and settled. The gospel needs to be proclaimed through the poet. "The poet/prophet is a voice that shatters settled reality and evokes new possibility in the listening assembly."[11] This prophetic proclamation is not fulfilled by a tone of harsh condemnation or easy, soft grace. The poetic/prophetic proclamation opens the church to respond to God in praise. The conversation that occurs in the dynamic of worship "permits us to become who we are formed by God to be and yearn to become."[12] The poetic proclamation of Scripture breaks open the texts and thus breaks open the congregation to encounter the God who cannot be tamed and demands and hopes that we will find the fullness into which God created and is creating. The church has been gathered by the Spirit and further encounters God through the dynamic event of Scripture's reading and prophetic imagination of proclamation. As God speaks, creation is called to respond.

### Where in the Ordo?

While there are many places for creativity in the service of the Word, the sermon liturgically falls after all the Scriptures have been read.

## Questions for Discussion and Reflection

1. What ideas were the most helpful in this chapter?

2. What ideas are the most difficult or causing the greatest amount of tension?

3. What is our practice for reading Scripture in worship?

4. How well is Scripture being performed in our communal worship?

5. What function does the sermon play in our communal worship?

6. What is the theological and practical emphasis of God's call in communal worship?

7. How may that impact creation's response?

Call to Worship
Collect
Song of Praise
Prayer of
   Illumination
   (or earlier)
Old Testament
   Reading
Sing the Psalm
Epistle Lesson
Hymn of
   Thanksgiving
Gospel Reading
**Sermon**
Confession and
   Pardon
Peace of Christ
Creed
Prayers of the
   People
Offering
Doxology
Lord's Supper
Benediction:
   Sending
   Forth

## FOURTEEN

# SERVICE OF THE WORD: SPOKEN PRAYER AS HUMANITY'S RESPONSE

*Planning worship well begins with giving attention to the worship team, the process for planning worship, the people in a local community, the worship space, and the season of the Christian year; it also means planning worship services that are Christian. **The service of Word and Table emphasizes God's gathering and calling while also empowering humanity's response.** . . .*

---

Being gathered by the Spirit is an invitation to be healed and transformed in order to become more fully human. This healing God offers properly embodies what it is healing people to do—worship God. God created humanity for worship, not to build up God's weak self-esteem, but as a primary way for creatures to reflect God's image and glory in all creation. In communal worship, people are doing what God created them to do, specifically loving God, loving themselves, loving others, being loved, and offering creation back to God as its stewards. This is the purpose and invitation to life God offers humanity.

When creation responds to God in worship, it is properly called work. At the bare minimum this invitation to work can be imagined as duty. Certainly creation is obligated to praise the One who created and sustains it. However, people can be just like the older son, who, in the story of the prodigal son, had performed his actions out of duty and obligation and had missed out on the abundance of the Father's love and thus had missed out on life; in many ways the older son was perhaps just as *far away* from the Father as his younger brother (see Luke 15:11-32). Since humans are created for worship, the invitation is to respond to God in worship as an act of thanksgiving both for who God is and what God has done. Hence, the liturgy, the work of One (Christ) for the sake of the many who become the work of Christ, hopes to move beyond duty to thanksgiving and love.

Moreover, in this attitude of thanksgiving and joy, the church also recognizes that humans cannot offer any response to God if it is not empowered by the Holy Spirit. As seen in the life of Jesus Christ in the Gospels, and after Pentecost, the Holy Spirit is the power that makes possible creation's response to God. In too many areas within Christianity, the power and work of the Spirit is neglected. This neglect disillusions the church to believe it is acting solely on its own power and often blinds the church to all the Spirit is doing in the world and wants to do through Christians. The role of the Spirit as the empowerment of all the church's responses to God cannot be underestimated.

The elements of response to God's gathering of the believers include prayers (invocation, praise, lament, confession and pardon, and prayers of the people), songs, creeds, and offerings. Songs, creeds, and offerings can be broadly understood as prayers bodily spoken and performed to God. It is important to state that communal worship service is a dialogical encounter in which humans encounter God and respond back to God. Within this call and response between God and the local church, there is also a place for brothers and sisters to respond to, engage, and be reconciled to each other.

## Prayer

In some sense all of the church's response to God's dynamic presence in communal worship is prayer. Prayer is a dynamic gift of responding to God by offering oneself back to God in all the times and places one finds oneself. Prayers as response also seek God to help make the congregation present to God's presence in the flow and rhythm of communal worship. Among the kinds of prayers I will consider here are prayers that are spoken, prayers that are sung, prayers that are embodied through offerings, and prayers that are declared through confessions of faith and creeds. These categories are not hard and fast, nor exhaustive, but seek to explore the depth and beauty of encountering and responding to God in communal worship.

Unfortunately, in many areas of Protestant and evangelical worship intentional care is not taken concerning the different types of prayers. Most prayers in communal worship lack creativity because they are committed to a kind of last-minute spontaneity. Too often in communal worship, prayer becomes filler or a sort of transition to assist in the movement of people on or off the platform. If pressed, most people do not have a plan or intention in their praying. Prayers should be created that pay attention to what type of response or petition is called for in light of the rhythms of the liturgy. hmm...

## The Practice of Praying

The Gospels and New Testament are clear, God invites people to prayer that honors, adores, praises, laments, petitions, and intercedes. There is a width and breadth to prayer. Prayer is to be much more than simply offering our requests and supplications, as if prayer becomes a weekly or daily "Santa Claus" wish list:

"God, please do this, then do this, then please do this." While making such requests is appropriate, this is not all that the practice of prayer imagines. Prayer in Christian communal worship is to be a means of transforming communion with God and fellow brothers and sisters.

## Spoken and Sung Prayer

This section explores a variety of the prayers that can be spoken or sung in communal worship. The order in which these prayers are discussed will roughly follow the general ordo suggested.

### Collect for Purity

This is often an opening prayer beseeching God to offer healing and cleansing at the beginning of a worship service so that Christians may more faithfully engage in the work and encounter of worship. While there are a number of variations, a common collect for purity is as follows:

> Almighty God, to Whom all hearts are open, all desires known, and from Whom no secrets are hidden: cleanse the thoughts of our hearts by the inspiration of Your Holy Spirit, that we may perfectly love You, and worthily magnify Your holy name; through Christ our Lord. Amen.[1]

This prayer seeks for cleansing so that the congregants can more fully and faithfully be *present* to God and each other in this communal worship.

Call to Worship
**Collect**
Song of Praise
Prayer of
    Illumination
    (or earlier)
Old Testament
    Reading
Sing the Psalm
Epistle Lesson
Hymn of
    Thanksgiving
Gospel Reading
Sermon
Confession and
    Pardon
Peace of Christ
Creed
Prayers of the
    People
Offering
Doxology
Lord's Supper
Benediction:
    Sending
    Forth

### Where in the Ordo?

This prayer is often spoken at the very beginning of a service of Word and Table. While such a prayer could be used anywhere in response to a Scripture in the service of the Word, it seems advisable that the first response of the church being gathered by the Spirit is a prayer that seeks to have God's Holy Spirit offer healing so Christians can best be at the glorious work and encounter to which they have been gathered.

### Praise or Adoration

A prayer of praise is a response to who God is and arises out of a recognition of creaturely dependence upon God, who is the Creator of all things, the Alpha and Omega. Susan White notes, "The prayer of adoration is not the time for anxiety or for expressing our feelings of inadequacy in the presence of God's majesty, nor to focus on our own needs or desires. It is rather the time to turn our entire attention to the God who has called us to worship."[2]

The primary theme of this conversation emphasizes that humans are created to worship. Earlier it was noted that God created people to worship. The question is not *if* people will worship but *what* they will worship. Being *created to worship* reminds us that to worship ourselves or any other creature not only is idolatry but also misses out on the fullness of what God intends for humanity. It must also be recalled that while God created humans for worship, this was not done because God was codependent and needed humans to worship God as if God was lacking something that humans could fill. The worship of God, both individually during the week and then primarily in communal worship, is God's gift to creatures to help them be more fully human by recognizing that they are not to be the center of the universe.

### Where in the Ordo?

Such prayers of praise and adoration are encouraged early in the service but can also be performed throughout worship where appropriate. While such prayers can be verbally spoken, they are often put to music and sung in hymns and choruses. A prayer of praise early in the service embodies the belief that communal worship and all of life are first and foremost about God. This humble awareness opens people to the full humanity into which God created and is creating.

*Prayer of Illumination*

Similar to the collect for purity, seeking God's healing to be present in worship, is the prayer of illumination. This prayer of illumination requests the assistance of the Holy Spirit to prepare Christians to more fully be *present to* and *encounter* God through Scripture: "Give us ears to hear and eyes to see." The practice of praying the prayer of illumination reminds the church of the necessity of the Spirit not only for opening it to God's prophetic presence but also for guiding how it sees, lives, and encounters God and other people in the world. This prayer of illumination prepares and opens Christians to a posture that more fully imagines and participates in the present and coming kingdom of God. This posture of dependence and reception embodied in the prayer of illumination celebrates the need of and gift from the Spirit to help us better see and imagine the kingdom.[3] As will be noted later, there is an important connection between the church's prayer for illumination of the texts and the prayer at the Lord's Table that the Father would make "us" and Christ present to each other by the Spirit.[4]

### Where in the Ordo?

This prayer should come early in the service of the Word, preceding all Scriptures being read.

*Prayer of Thanksgiving*

While the prayer of praise celebrated and honored who God is, the prayer of thankfulness or thanksgiving expresses gratitude for

Call to Worship
Collect
**Song of Praise**
Prayer of
    Illumination
    (or earlier)
Old Testament
    Reading
Sing the Psalm
Epistle Lesson
Hymn of
    Thanksgiving
Gospel Reading
Sermon
Confession and
    Pardon
Peace of Christ
Creed
Prayers of the
    People
Offering
Doxology
Lord's Supper
Benediction:
    Sending
    Forth

Call to Worship
Collect
Song of Praise
**Prayer of
    Illumination
    (or earlier)**
Old Testament
    Reading
Sing the Psalm
Epistle Lesson
Hymn of
    Thanksgiving
Gospel Reading
Sermon
Confession and
    Pardon
Peace of Christ
Creed
Prayers of the
    People
Offering
Doxology
Lord's Supper
Benediction:
    Sending
    Forth

what God has done. Henry Knight illumines the similarity and distinction between thanksgiving and praise.

> Thanksgiving is when we have gratitude for something which is done on our behalf—an act of compassion, the giving of a gift, an enduring friendship. Praise is an acknowledgment of excellence in another, a recognition of qualities which we deem praise-worthy. In terms of worship, thanksgiving is a response to God's gracious and loving activity in creation and redemption; praise is elicited by who God is. Together, they are linked to such related responses as awe before the mystery and majesty of God and delight as the sheer enjoyment of God.[5]

The prayer of thanksgiving begins with remembering what God has done, not in abstract, but in specific historical situations. For Israel every historical event was a theophany, a manifestation of God's love. This celebration for what God has done is the foundation from which the church moves forward into a challenging present. The importance of memory and remembrance cannot be overlooked. To remember in thanksgiving is not a matter of sentimental nostalgia.[6] To remember is to be present to the God who was and is moving. To remember is to see how one's present is connected to people who have come before and a people who will come after. For the people of Israel, to forget was to die. To forget who God *was* and what God *did* was to become lost, to cease to exist, to move toward death (see Pss. 9:15-17; 78:5-8; 119:93).

The primary historical event for which Christians give thanks is the life, death, resurrection, and ascension of Jesus Christ. This is the lens through which all other events are interpreted. As Christians focus on Christ, thanksgiving is also offered for creation, the blessings of the old covenant, the community of the church, gifts of friends and family, and so on. Similar to prayers of praise, these thanksgivings are often sung as a corporate remembrance that God is the source of all life.

### Where in the Ordo?

A natural location is in response to the reading and proclamation of the Word of God, which reminds the church what God has done and thus what God is doing presently.

### *Prayers of Confession and Pardon*

I am a preacher. I have been called, gifted, and ordained to preach. Currently I am not pastoring a local congregation but have the privilege of attending a church with a wonderful pastor who is a great preacher. At the end of many sermons I am often left mute. I am moved to praise with the kingdom imagination of these sermons. I also recognize that my community and I have a long way to go to be who God desires us to be, not only in our personal piety but also in our calling to help a world in despair and brokenness. From the sermon the church is moved to confession.

As the church encounters God through the proclaimed Scriptures, it recognizes places of growth, along with places still in need of formation, correction, training, and healing. Confession of sins is offered both for personal and corporate sins, all of which continue to hamper and hinder God's redeeming of the entire creation. The church confesses voluntary sins (those we did knowingly and willingly) and involuntary sins (actions that were not meant to harm but did).

Sin is not simply personal or individual; it becomes institutionalized in the cultural imagination. For example, where does consumerism come from? Who is responsible? Who are the victims? It is one thing to consider how my spending habits fail to honor God or trust that God will provide what I need for happiness. However, my consumeristic tendencies provide fuel to a global machine of ongoing producing and consuming, often harming and doing violence to many people I have never known, either by name or face. Confession then becomes much more than a matter of seeking absolution; it seeks to transform habits, desires, actions, and thus cultural institutions that continue to marginalize, exploit, and deny resources to those who truly need them.

With confession the church is always then moved to receive the gift of the assurance of pardon. As God brings to light the desires, hopes, and ambitions that are contrary to life, contrary to love, and contrary to being human, and as we penitently confess and seek to change (repent), God's word of pardon and forgiveness comes like a glass of water on a parched tongue. Smith notes a dangerous tendency in Christian worship to offer assurance without confession. Too often Christian worship can become a place for self-help. By this we understand communal worship to be helping people cope and navigate a stress-filled life, a life where ironically "I" am always the victim. This "salvation" encourages people to look at their internal goodness and believe. Sadly such a model that refuses the role of guilt and shame actually makes it more toxic. Therefore, Christian communal worship offers the gift of confession and assurance of pardon, not simply a pep talk to "make us feel better about ourselves." Yet the imagination does not end there but hopes and seeks to transform thoughts, habits, and desires so that cultural institutions established and fueled by sinful desires may be no more.

The transformation and encounter God offers in communal worship with the church is to more fully redeem, reconcile, and heal the church to better reflect God's glory as those who bear God's image. In this sense, to be fully free is to be fully human, to have one's will and desires aligned with what God wills and desires for creation. Similarly, John Wesley discussed the importance of God's healing of a person's tempers (thoughts, attitudes, and actions) as a primary means of growth in sanctifying grace.[7] As Christians are encountered by God through Scripture and the sermon, they recognize how far short they fall from the life, hope, and joy God is inviting them into. People offer their confessions, not only as avenues to release guilt but also as acts of repentance (James 5:15-16).

Moreover, prayers of confession and pardon are not simply individual prayers but often corporate prayers; they are not just for things I have personally done but also for things my community and world have done. The church confesses as one body. While some may scoff and say, "That is not my sin. Why should I confess to that?" the gift of a corporate confession reminds the church that it is not just one person but, as Paul describes in 1 Cor. 12, one body. Thus the one body rejoices, praises, confesses, and receives pardon together. The parts of the body that are strong are called to help out the weak. This is done through corporate confession. Jesus' baptism can illumine this unity in the body.

The scandal of Jesus' baptism is often lost on Christians today. Who gets baptized and why? Sinners for repentance. Yet the Scriptures declare that Jesus was tempted but did not sin (Heb. 4:15). Why was Jesus baptized? There are several ways the church has understood the significance of Jesus' baptism. One view is that Jesus was baptized by John to offer the church an example to follow. Another perspective is that Jesus' baptism serves as a kind of inauguration to his ministry in which he receives the words of blessing and commendation from the Father and the dynamic presence of the Spirit. Jesus' baptism was also understood as an alignment with his fellow Jews, the people of God, who were in desperate need of God's healing, forgiveness, and transformation. As will soon be discussed, baptism is not simply a sign of personal forgiveness but also an entrance into a people. Jesus' baptism in many ways offers a visible, embodied act of corporate confession and pardon.

---

As a youth pastor, I often had young people who could not get to the prayer altar fast enough on Sunday morning. They had participated in some behaviors on Friday and Saturday night that they now regretted. The guilt was overwhelming and they needed release. Unfortunately, on some occasions this was all they sought—guilt relief, not transformation. The prayer of confession, "I am sorry," must also be accompanied by the prayer of repentance, "I want to change."

Confession is always set within the promise of God to forgive sins embodied in the life, death, and resurrection of Jesus. This is why a prayer of confession must always be followed by a declaration of pardon and assurance of God's forgiveness. Below is an example of a confession and pardon based on Matt. 11:28-30 that I created for a college retreat worship setting:

**All:** O holy and merciful God, we confess that we have not always taken upon ourselves the yoke of obedience. All too often we have made our life, our own.

We confess that we fill our lives with empty calories of entertainment and video games that leave us unsatisfied with a stomachache.

We confess that we have filled our sense of loneliness and isolation with business in order to escape the pain that we work hard to keep suppressed.

We confess that we are afraid of silence, peace, and rest because of the need to rationalize why we cannot complete the tasks at hand.

We confess that we have been so busy we have not faithfully listened to and loved our neighbor.

We confess that we have not loved ourselves and given adequate time to rest, exercise, and a proper diet.

We confess that we have not loved you, gracious God; we have not entered the rest you offer and have attempted to find identity in the building of our own personal kingdoms.

**Leader:** Hear the good news: Jesus Christ invites all the weary and heavy laden to find rest, forgiveness, and healing in him. So in the name of Jesus Christ, you are forgiven.

**Congregation:** In the name of Jesus Christ, you are forgiven.

Corporate confessions such as this one serve as prophetic reminders of areas of sin in our lives that perhaps we have been blind to. Naming sins that my community and I have committed reminds and encourages the community that the invitation to life God is offering by the Spirit should not be seductively misplaced. Confessions name and expose the darkness and shortcomings and illumines practices and patterns to be avoided for the full embrace of *becoming more fully human.*

So where can we find confessions and pardons? Surveying Christian prayer books will yield a wealth of beautiful confessions and pardons. Each worship team should also be encouraged to create confessions and pardons that are contextually appropriate.

Another important issue that warrants attention beyond this conversation is the concern about a "rush to pardon." While confession and repentance are to be met with forgiveness, harm can be done when victims and oppressors are forced to rush the reconciliation process. Thoughtfulness, care, and education for the congregation are essential as these elements are used in a communal worship setting.

## Prayers of Petition and Complaint

As the church lives in thankful remembrance, where the past and future invade an uncertain present, the church can then offer its petitions and complaints. Out of the trust and thanksgiving for who God is (praise) and what God has done and is doing (thanksgiving) the church is invited to present its requests and complaints to God. Prayers of petition can be traced back through Jewish prayers of blessings at meals and other occasions in Jewish worship. While these prayers are vital to the church, too often the center of most prayers is only petition, asking God for something. As any relationship can testify, if the bulk of the communication and dialogue is about requests for what one party can do for the other, such a relationship is both immature and will likely not endure or ever become healthy. Furthermore, these prayers are grounded in a covenantal relationship that has been renewed earlier in worship through the Scripture reading and proclamation and the church's prayers of praise and thanksgiving. Without the proper liturgical rhythms such requests and complaints become misguided.

### Prayers of the People: Intercessory Prayer

The prayers of petition include the prayers of intercession. Normally this is the church crying out especially for those who have no voice. Such prayers intentionally think about the needs of others. Prayers for people in the world facing suffering, violence, and oppression can be lifted along with prayers for leaders of nations needing wisdom and discernment from God.

The intercessory prayer, often called the prayers of the people, is usually practiced as the pastoral prayer. Intercessory prayer imagines much more than a laundry list of people in the hospital, serving in places of conflict, or under terrible suffering. These prayers imagine more than simply the alleviation from the current pain, difficulty, challenge, disease, or struggle. These prayers imagine God's shalom, or peace and well-being, falling into all areas of creation. Intercessory prayer, like the Lord's Prayer, reminds the church of what the covenant given to Abraham declared in Gen. 12:3*b*: "And in you all the families of the earth shall be blessed." The church is a royal priesthood on behalf of all of creation.[8] The imagination of the kingdom of God coming is far beyond "me having a good day" or even "me getting to heaven"; as in the Lord's Prayer, it's about God's will coming to earth and fully redeeming and re-creating it. Intercessory prayers are not only for those in my church, in my community, or in my country, but for the entire world. The church is praying against all the places of oppression and injustice and for all parts of creation still groaning, longing for redemption (Rom. 8:21-23).

### Structure of the Prayers of Petition

The prayers of petition (similar to the prayers of lament described later in this chapter) include the following structural elements:

A. Ascription—offer to God praise, not primarily for what God had done but for who God is.

B. Recall the ways God has answered prayers in the past. In many ways this is a prayer of thanksgiving. The God who has been faithful in the past will be petitioned.

C. Asks God to act on this occasion with the same power and mercy that has been experienced before.

D. The prayer concludes with a Trinitarian doxology: "Hear the cries of our heart, Father, in the name of Jesus Christ, by the power of the Holy Spirit, one God who is praised forevermore. Amen!" This doxology affirms and ends the way the prayer begins, recognizing who God is, and thus reminds the praying people that such prayers are offered in thanksgiving and in trust to God come what may.

Time and again Scripture calls for the church to pray for the sick and present the requests to God (James 5:13-16). This includes any desire in the church's imagination needing God's attention. The challenge, however, is that all prayer, and specifically prayers of petition, are not magical manipulations of the divine. Within these requests is a recognition that God may not answer *how*, *when*, and *where* people desire. Within a covenant relationship, this acknowledgment does not dissuade the petitioner or intercessor but affirms in hope that God is faithful and trustworthy.

Part of the formation and healing that occurs in communal worship is a local church's desires to more closely mimic and reflect (glorify) God's desires for that local church and the world. As people experience further healing and renewal into the image of God, and as the church begins to take on the mind of Christ,[9] the church prays, lives, and breathes that it might more thoroughly have its mind transformed so that God's good will may be known and embodied in all the world, and specifically in the body of Christ (see Rom. 12:1-2).

Although God desires for all people to come and present their requests, there is a sense that Christians should learn both *how* and *what* to pray for. This is not a type of liturgical legalism but the difference between praying, "God, help me on the test I did not study for," and praying, "God, may you use your church and others in the world to alleviate the suffering of those under famine in the Horn of Africa." In the giving of the Lord's Prayer, Jesus clearly intended this as an act of instruction/formation (see Matt. 6:9-13 and Luke 11:2-4). While God hears all prayers, clearly some prayers are closer to the prayers of God than others.

## Practical Suggestions for Petitions

What follows are several practical suggestions for the prayers of the people:

A. Leader may stand amid the people. Similar to the reading of the gospel text, the placement of the leader in the congregation or at a prayer altar celebrates the belief that this is not a prayer by the pastor but a prayer of the entire congregation.

B. A member of the congregation could possibly lead. This is a wonderful opportunity to celebrate the ministerial role of the laity. Having laity lead in this prayer is a physical embodiment of the concept that all Christians can be used by the Spirit to intercede and minister to people in their world.

C. These prayers can be offered in the form of a litany (call and response). Below is an example (words in italics are those prayed by the congregation):

Gracious God, we come into your presence this morning very much aware of your great love for us. We praise you for raising your Son from the dead and loving us though we were unworthy of your love. Lord, though you are rich and we are poor, you call us by name and call us Son or Daughter. We call and proclaim, hallowed be your name. Accept the worship and adoration we lift to you now.

(The leader leaves about fifteen to thirty seconds of silence for individuals to voice their prayers either silently or verbally after each prayer invitation. Please note below the specific encouragement for people to verbally speak the names of those they are interceding for.)

Father, you hear our prayers. *Gracious Lord, grant us the prayers of our hearts.*

Realizing how much you love, O God, reminds us how far short we fall of loving you. We seek today to confess our failures to love, and we ask both your forgiveness and empowerment. We confess that we have not used the resources you have given us for your kingdom and for your glory. Transform us with your love as we wait and listen before you.

Father, you hear our prayers. *Gracious Lord, grant us the prayers of our hearts.*

You came to us when we had turned away from you. You are the God who keeps the covenant when we failed. You offer to us freely your banquet hall of grace, nourishment, and life. How we thank you for Christ, for your Holy Spirit, for the church that has been faithful to bring the gospel to us. We thank you for loving us, the marginalized, and giving us hope and purpose.

Father, you hear our prayers. *Gracious Lord, grant us the prayers of our hearts.*

Some of us come into your presence, loving Father, carrying burdens that are too great to manage. We have reached the end of our ability to cope. Some of us come into your presence with hearts full of joy and blessing. Hear us as we pour out our hearts to you now.

Father, you hear our prayers. *Gracious Lord, grant us the prayers of our hearts.*

God of mercy and compassion, we pray for those in need who are part of our extended church family. We pray your comfort and grace for those who have lost loved ones and grieve today. We pray for those today who need your direction and protection. We also pray for those who are sick and suffering and are facing recovery from surgery. We call out the names of these whom we love asking that you would meet the need of their lives just now.

Father, you hear our prayers. *Gracious Lord, grant us the prayers of our hearts.*

Loving God, we rejoice in your presence. Even the sense of conviction from you is better than soothing of our own consciences that we so often do. We do love you and we want to love you more. We are ready for you to quench our thirst for you. Teach us to pray. Equip us to be good stewards today to serve you faithfully this week, living out the faith we confess even now. In Christ's name we pray. Amen.[10]

In the congregation where this form of prayer was used, it followed the homily (sermon) in the service of the Word. Notice how this prayer incorporates several types of praying: praise, adoration, thanksgiving, confession, and intercession. One of the shortcomings of this prayer is that the pardon following the confession is not robust. This one prayer often incorporated similar types of praying each week; however, each week this prayer changed depending on the church year, the scriptural texts, sermon, and current events in the life of the church and world. There are advantages and disadvantages of doing so many things in one prayer.

Each worship team should consider the appropriate way to respond to the Scriptures and homily. I would recommend that the response of confession and pardon along with intercessions for the local church, community, and world be used every week. Such rhythms allow for transformation both at the personal and corporate level, which then opens up the church to minister by the Spirit to the needs of those in the world. Such a rhythm helps to emphasize personal transformation that aims not simply at "my individual growth" but, like those healed by Christ in the New Testament, at the healing of individuals to become disciple-servants. Moreover, all the church is transformed corporately as the body of Christ and as a further coming of the kingdom of God.

## Where in the Ordo?

This prayer can be located in several appropriate places. Typically this prayer would follow after the sermon and before the offering. It makes the most sense after the confession and pardon, the peace of Christ, and the creed. These acts of healing and renewal of unity then open the church to offer to God the needs of the congregation and the world. With intentionality this element provides an important reminder to the church. Prayers of petition are not simply the church giving God the laundry list of requests into which God alone is now charged to work and act. Within these prayers of petition, the church is also reminded of the ways in which, by the Spirit, they can participate in the answer to which they are praying.[11]

## Lament: Prayer of Complaint

One of the most important aspects of communal worship that is largely absent is prayers of lament. While similar to prayers of petition, asking God to act, these are also prayers of complaint. It is noteworthy that the Psalms have more laments than any other type of prayer. Numerous theological and liturgical reasons likely have caused laments to be lost. The issue of lament is also tied to theodicies that attempt to justify God when bad things happen to good

Call to Worship
Collect
Song of Praise
Prayer of
    Illumination
    (or earlier)
Old Testament
    Reading
Sing the Psalm
Epistle Lesson
Hymn of
    Thanksgiving
Gospel Reading
Sermon
Confession and
    Pardon
Peace of Christ
Creed
**Prayers of the
    People**
Offering
Doxology
Lord's Supper
Benediction:
    Sending
    Forth

or innocent people. Theologically, laments become unnecessary if God wills all things, being a God of total sovereignty, power, and control, or if God could not prevent the evil from occurring. While some find these solutions to the problem of evil helpful, such options appear to abandon the revelation of God through Scripture and the larger Christian tradition.

---

### The Problem of Evil

The problem of evil consists of three premises and a possible conclusion.
1. God is all-powerful.
2. God is all-loving.
3. Genuine evil actions occur in the world.
Conclusion: There is no God. (This is only one possible conclusion; many others can be drawn.)
Theodicies (literally *making God just*) attempt to solve this theological problem. Generally, a solution is attempted by dismissing or altering one of the three main premises.

---

Two of the most famous laments are found in Job 29–31 and Ps. 22. Job is a crucial voice, along with Psalms and Proverbs, in the Wisdom Literature of the Old Testament. Despite the counsel from Job's wife and friends, Job refuses to confess that his sin is the source of his devastation. In maintaining his innocence, Job cries out to God. In this lament Job recalls his previous happiness and present wretchedness. Job asserts his integrity and claims that God has failed to be just. In some sense Job is assaulting God for being morally indifferent and unreliable: "Does not calamity befall the unrighteous, and disaster the workers of iniquity?" (31:3). This is the right teaching of Psalms and Proverbs and is true, but it does not guarantee that a life of obedience will lead to a life that always goes as we want it, with no conflicts coming our way.

Finally, Job asks for God to answer and respond to his pleas and cries: "O, that I had one to hear me! (Here is my signature! Let the Almighty answer me!)" (v. 35). God, graciously and powerfully, answers Job in the whirlwind speech in Job 38. God reminds Job that God is God and Job is not, but God does not rebuke Job for making the complaint. Although God never lets Job in on the cosmic bet with Satan over Job's faithfulness (1:6–2:7), God affirms that the suffering came to Job through no fault of Job's. Job does not offer a theodicy (solution to the problem of evil) but provides a case where authentic worship includes coming to God in our pain, despair, and complaint when God appears absent.[12] Such worship is good and true.

Another famous lament is Ps. 22. From the cross, Jesus cries out to God, "My God, my God, why have you forsaken me?" (see Matt. 27:46 and Mark 15:34). Jews would immediately connect Jesus' cry to the full force of the entire psalm. Most psalms of lament have three parties: the speaker, God, and the enemy. Psalm 22 is a psalm with a theme similar to that of Job, affirming present pain and devastation. It is important to note that laments are not simply immature spiritual whining. People who love God and are in covenant with God approach God in their despair and plead for God to act. Yet the emphasis of lament is not simply on crying out in complaint to God but also on moving to a statement of faith and trust in God. Out of the depths of misery, pain, and frustration at the circumstances and with God comes a declaration of praise: "I will tell of your name to my brothers and sisters; in the midst of the congregation I will praise you: You who fear the LORD, praise him! All you offspring of Jacob, glorify him; stand in awe of him, all you offspring of Israel! For he did not despise or abhor the affliction of the afflicted; he did not hide his face from me, but heard when I cried to him" (vv. 22-24).

When Jesus speaks the beginning of Ps. 22, Jews would know that the full scope of that cry includes an affirmation of praise and trust. Laments, while offering their plea and complaint, move toward a declaration of faith and trust in God, despite the present circumstance. This trust in God is embodied in Christ's declaration from the cross: "Father, into your hands I commend my spirit" (Luke 23:46).

Sadly, the use of laments is rare in many communal worship services. It seems that there are unwritten rules at work here. The notion of being angry or complaining to God feels unholy or sacrilegious. While understandable, recall that laments are not simply prayers of whining but ultimately prayers for God to be at work in the present. That is why they really fall into the category of petition. Too often silent victims are given little space to cry out to God in their anger, pain, and desperation.

An example of laments worship teams should explore would be for Mother's Day and Father's Day. Such days are difficult for the church on many levels. Not only are the origins of these days outside the Christian context, but these days are also very painful for many people, such as those who have recently lost parents, children, or spouses and those who either have no relationship with parents or whose relationship is broken. Another group often overlooked on these days consists of the men and women who have never had the opportunity to have children. Either they are single or they are a couple who are unable to have children. Consideration should also be given to creating worship space for the lament of those families who have lost children not only after birth but before birth.

The pain of Mother's Day and Father's Day can be so thick for people that I have met many who refuse to go to worship on these days. These days can become intentional days to make space and room for those who carry heartaches, pain, and anger toward God. Many other occasions and days in the Christian year can also be used, but these days in particular provide an important opportunity for healing. As laments are used, education will also help to nurture an acceptance of lament as faithful worship.

*Peace of Christ*

Call to Worship
Collect
Song of Praise
Prayer of
   Illumination
   (or earlier)
Old Testament
   Reading
Sing the Psalm
Epistle Lesson
Hymn of
   Thanksgiving
Gospel Reading
Sermon
Confession and
   Pardon
**Peace of Christ**
Creed
Prayers of the
   People
Offering
Doxology
Lord's Supper
Benediction:
   Sending
   Forth

The confession and pardon move liturgically into a beautiful rhythm where church members are to greet each other with the peace of Christ. As people find healing and reconciliation with God individually and ecclesially, they are then moved to offer reconciliation with each other by the power of the Spirit. One of the challenges for many congregations who are being introduced to the exchange of peace is that it may inadvertently be confused with a "meet and greet" time. While this time is for reuniting and connecting, the church is doing much more than simply saying, "Hey, how's it goin'?" or "Glad you are here today." All of these cordial gestures are fine but are aiming at less than the church has imagined in this liturgical element. This is to be a moment of hope, peace, and reconciliation. Education will help your local congregation embrace the power of this moment, which can include "meeting and greeting" but does not limit the imagination at that point. Below is an example of education leading into the peace:

**Leader:** Friends, as those who are being made whole, God has gathered us together for such a time as this. There were times and places in the past, as there are today, in which Christians gathered under the very threat of death. All Christians face trials, temptations, and difficulties as we gather. Furthermore, just as it was then, some of us now in our local body have relationships that are strained. We will now offer the peace of Christ to each other, both as a means of reconciliation and as a prayer that God's peace may reign in all our future situations and circumstances. This prayer and blessing of peace is much more than saying, "I hope your life is free from challenge," or "I hope your dreams come true." This is the peace we receive from God through Christ by the Spirit. This is God's shalom, which grounds all joy, hope, and peace that not only transforms our situations but also overwhelms us in the love of God.

So as those who have been and are being redeemed, may the peace of Christ be with you.

**Congregation:** And also with you.

**Leader:** Let us greet each other in this peace through a handshake or hug.

---

## Education About Communal Worship

One of the great needs in the church today is catechesis. Catechesis (instruction and formation) is much more than learning about church doctrines and covenants of Christian conduct. Those are important. One of the important needs for many evangelical Protestants (and perhaps others) is education about communal worship. The emphasis for education is not only for those who are new to the faith or a local church but even for those who have been cradle Christians. Education is not simply about making people "smarter" but also about facilitating their formation and imagination.

## *Lord's Prayer*

Although the Lord's Prayer is often prayed at the conclusion of the eucharistic liturgy, it needs some attention here. It is curious that Scriptures hand down a prayer Jesus teaches his disciples to pray. It is likely that the practice of praying the Lord's Prayer goes back to the very beginning of the church. Many have written well on the rhythms and imagination of the Lord's Prayer.[13] In our space here I want to consider the importance of praying this prayer.

The Lord's Prayer recognizes and embodies the holiness of God while also imagining the kingdom of God coming on earth "as it is in heaven" (Matt. 6:10). This prayer request for the coming of God's kingdom is further illumined by prayers for the daily sustenance of people. Not only does this prayer move to thankfulness for those who have bread, but it also reminds those who have an abundance to find ways to provide for those who do not. Yet the imagination of the kingdom's coming encompasses not only care for physical needs but also reconciliation between people whose relationships have been ruptured. Moreover, this imagination appeals to God's power and guidance for healing and deliverance from all the evil that would influence us to refuse loving God, loving ourselves, loving others, and being loved. Finally, this imagination ends with the affirmation that the One who is holy, "hallowed," is the One who is above all.

Praying this prayer regularly is not a mindless routine; it is the church's ongoing response to God's call to be healed and renewed. This is a habit, a ritual, that moves the church to remember all that was and is to come. The practice of praying exhibits the imagination of the church, who through this prayer continues to be and become a people captivated by the vision of the present and coming kingdom of God. Such a vision refuses to settle for the present as the only possibility. This prayer not only is about a hopeful imagination but also can, as the church aligns itself in it with the will of God through the Holy Spirit, participate in the further coming of the kingdom of God.

One of the big ideas for this entire conversation is the emphasis on education. While liturgical elements have a transformative aspect of their own, transformation and full embodiment in worship is strengthened immensely with education that introduces people to the encounter and work of communal worship. I recommend including this brief education at least once every other week for the first six months and then perhaps once a month after that as the local congregation begins to "get it."

Consider again the liturgical movement of passing the peace. Congregations should come to understand that it is one of the most embodied movements of worship. One of the Protestant challenges in worship is that the brain, eyes, and tongue are generally the only parts of the body engaged and participating in worship. Passing the peace not only gets bodies moving but also is one of the key elements for being present to one another in worship, loving and being loved. Moreover, the service of Word and Table imagines many hopes and gifts from God. Congregations should realize that the peace offers opportunities of reconciliation and that a thoughtful Christian ordo will then move into prayers of petition and lament for the community and the world. Not only does the passing of the peace embody God's unity and shalom in the community, but it also creates an opportunity to engage people, hear of their needs, and then present those needs in prayers of petition following the peace.

I want to emphasize again that my hope is not for people to receive from this discussion some legalistic order of worship that everyone must rigidly follow. Rather, my desire is for people to understand that the Christian church has developed with great thought and intention a regular pattern of worship.

## Questions for Discussion and Reflection

1. What ideas were the most helpful in this chapter?

2. What ideas are the most difficult or causing the greatest amount of tension?

3. What prayers do you use in your service?

4. What are the strengths of the prayers that you pray?

5. How does the concept of prayers as response impact what prayers you use?

6. What are prayers you may like to incorporate?

7. What education is needed to help your congregation appreciate different types of praying?

# FIFTEEN
# SUNG PRAYERS:
# MUSIC IN COMMUNAL WORSHIP

*Planning worship well begins with giving attention to the worship team,*
*the process for planning worship, the people in a local community, the*
*worship space, and the season of the Christian year; it also means*
*planning worship services that are Christian.* **The service of Word**
**and Table emphasizes God's gathering and calling while**
**also empowering humanity's response.** . . .

What is worship? If I were to ask this question of Christians, I would assume about 93.2 percent would say music. Keeping in mind the earlier rejection of reducing all worship to music, music is still a vital gift from God and a component of worship. The importance of music in worship cannot be underestimated. Why is it the case that many people who leave worship on Sunday celebrating the power of the sermon cannot recall precisely on Thursday the main point of the sermon but have been consistently humming several of the worship songs? In this chapter we will *first* consider the power of singing as a more fully embodied act of response to God. *Second*, we will explore what songs are appropriate responses to God's call. *Third*, we will examine some practices of excellence in the performance of these songs.

## Singing as Embodied Response

Too often the responses of the congregation in the service of the Word involve only the mind, ears, and mouth. Music and singing offer the congregants an opportunity to move and include more of the body, such as the physical and emotional aspects. Singing is an embodied event that invites the whole person to offer himself or herself in love, adoration, and confession to God. Singing is a bodily practice immersed in and expressing one's imagination.[1]

With tempo, rhythm, and beat, music gets bodily into us and captures us in a way that spoken discourse does not. Songs can usher us to past times, places, and people with distinct fragrances and emotions. The making and use of music is a very basic language and shapes how humans communicate and understand themselves to be in the world (*sitz im leben*). John Witvliet draws upon the Psalms as an example of the language training school for worship. Praying/Singing the Psalter expresses with words what we could only utter in groans, as well as shaping congregants into the language and grammar of the kingdom. Song becomes a primary way people learn to speak the language of the kingdom.[2] While spoken prayers are certainly emotive, the power of music and singing as an expression of emotions is unparalleled. Music and singing moves and shapes people in dynamic, powerful, and personal ways. Music is one of God's greatest gifts to creation.

## Music Shapes Theology: Lyrics and Musicality Matters

While the staying power of music has already been mentioned, another by-product of the power of music is the significance of the lyrics. Martin Luther observed, "I place music next to theology and give it the highest praise."[3] I have not met a song leader who would say that lyrics do not matter. Although, on occasion I have heard some song leaders put together song sets based solely on a certain key they were more adept at. Furthermore, often those with expertise in musical leadership and performance have not been trained in theology. On a worship team it is vital that those trained in theology help guide the song selection. Many people who select songs are often quite surprised to learn what type of theological claims are being made in the lyrics. One of the sad battles of the worship wars noted earlier was the fight over hymns vs. choruses. In the end the "hymns vs. choruses" discussion is the wrong question. There are great hymns and poor hymns. There are great choruses and poor choruses. Here are some suggested questions that can guide the discernment process in selecting songs.[4]

## Songs Worthy of Worship

### A. Is the Specific Song Theologically Appropriate?

One of the critiques leveled against choruses written over the past fifteen years is that they are very self-focused, speaking about "what God can do for me," "what I can do for God," "what I want from God," or "Jesus is my buddy." Some of these petitions have an appropriate place, but care must be taken to guard against songs that are simply about "my feelings, hopes, and desires." Furthermore, one small and easy change that can assist in working against such selfishness or individualism in worship is transitioning songs sung in the first person *I* or *me* to *we* and *us*. "Jesus and me" is a reduction that has caused much trouble in Christianity. Switching to the plural is not denying the importance of individuals offering themselves to God but celebrates how the church journeys together.

People wanting to celebrate individualism often remark, "Well, a person cannot ride on the coattails of others." This is true in some sense, but in another sense it is incredibly false. Clearly my response to God and desire to offer my life back to God must be from me; my dad cannot be my proxy. However, there are many moments in the life of a local congregation where one person is strong and full of faith while others are very weak and cannot even pray. Those who are strong are to assist and help the weak, to pray for them when they cannot pray for themselves. Furthermore, as noted in corporate confessions, we are being made Christian together. The apostle Paul's imagery of the church as a body is an imagination that must never be lost.

This Christian journey, we do together. Since people are *created to worship as an invitation to become more fully human,* being more fully human as renewed in the image of God encompasses a love for God, a love for oneself, a love for others, and being loved. One of the main hopes and healings offered by God in communal worship is the renewal of people with each other as the body of Christ. The goal of creation is that "I's" will become "we's." Paying attention to pronouns, along with some education, can assist and facilitate a more Christian worship service as well as a more mature understanding of what it means to be Christian (and thus human).

### B. Is the Song a Fitting Response to God's Call in That Space in the Ordo of the Service?

What type of prayer is this song? How is it responding to God's call in the service of the Word or Table? Is it a response of praise or adoration? Is it a lament or confession in light of a scripture being read? Recognizing each song should be a response to God's call must guide the selection and discernment process.

### C. Is This Song Appropriate for the Main Theme of the Day?

How is this song pushing forward the primary themes of the day found in Scripture and sermon? I have had the privilege of working with many full-time and volunteer music leaders in communal worship. I continue to be amazed how God can guide the song selection of a worship service around certain themes that really can flow with the theme of the service. I have also had moments when songs were chosen without any idea what the sermon was about. While God certainly assists services where there is minimal intentional planning, this is a case of worship leaders hindering the Spirit by not exercising care and attention.

### D. Is This Song Right for the Season of the Church Year?

As noted in the conversation earlier about singing Christmas carols in Advent, the church year should guide the song selection not consumerism. As noted above, the season of Advent is to be a time of waiting, a time of recognizing the church's sinfulness and need for God. This is a season of waiting and expectation. Similarly, the hope and joy of "Christ the Lord Is Risen Today" does not have a place in Lent. Or to sing "Christ Arose" can perhaps miss the imagination of Lent. I know many of you are probably thinking, "What is the big deal?" Part of the problem is that this feeds a cultural addiction that is enslaved to immediate gratification. In our overindulgent culture, the discipline of waiting and longing needs to be nurtured in the seasons of Lent and Advent in order to mark out the distinct joy of Christmas and Easter. hmm.... almost seems forced

### E. Is the Song Singable?

One of the challenges of our present culture and the movement away from hymnals is that more and more of the culture is unable to read music and thus has a difficult time harmonizing. Many times the primary melodies are in a key that has a range beyond what the average person in the pew feels comfortable singing. Often songs chosen can "show off" the voices of the worship team, but when songs are too high or too low, people will vote just to listen, which is not desirable. Furthermore, melodies often modulate so quickly that congregants cannot keep up.

The power and importance of music must not be underestimated. Music either draws members of the congregation deeper into the communion of worship or it can distract and misdirect them. God and good planning can use music to be a powerful medium in the transformative fellowship with God and one another. Curiously, many evangelical services have moved from centering a service around the sermon toward an emphasis on worship through music.

### F. Create a Database of Songs

Technology offers many ways to catalog and organize songs. Such a database will assist in the categorization of songs for their appropriateness as songs of response. Songs can be organized for certain seasons of the Christian year, certain types of prayers (praise, thanksgiving, lament, confession, etc.), certain scriptural texts, and certain emotional tenors. A database with multiple criteria can assist and facilitate the creative process. A database can also help track new songs introduced that should not be lost. Having a database not only is a great resource for song ideas but can also assist in creating a list of songs with appropriate theology. Some might be surprised to find that one of the functions hymnals served was to regulate acceptable tunes and lyrics for the church to use. While the day for musical "control" has past, it is advisable that congregations work to establish a list of songs that are theologically and contextually appropriate. (See appendix 2, "Song Review Worksheet," to assist in creating such a database.)

## Good Practices for Introducing New Songs

Technology not only facilitates the creation of new choruses but also widespread distribution. One of the blessings of recent days is a plethora of new worship songs created for Christian communal worship. However, with these new opportunities some challenges have been presented with the deluge of new choruses available. Below are some recommendations and suggestions that are necessary for proper and faithful leadership of a congregation.

## A. *Only Introduce One New Song Per Month*

I am a firm believer that people can only worship through songs they know. While some songs are easier to learn than others, a barrage of new songs often will transition a congregation from participation to passive entertainment. Worship leaders would be well advised to appreciate how exhausting and frustrating it is for congregants to keep learning new songs that may never be sung again.

## B. *Tell the Congregation It Is New*

Telling the congregation a song is new releases some pressure from the congregants who may not know the song. It also provides the worship leader space for teaching the song to the congregation. Many people often feel embarrassed because they do not know certain songs. This brief announcement simply provides a space for learning.

## C. *Summarize the Song*

Offer the congregation a summary of the song, give its emphasis, and explain why the song is being sung today at this point in the service. While the reason and purpose of the song is obvious to the worship leaders, when the congregation is busy learning the tune and the words, the meaning and import early on can often be missed.

## D. *Sing It Once and Invite the Congregation to Join When Ready*

It may prove helpful for many people to hear a verse and chorus so the musicality of the song can be heard before the congregation follows the leader. This is especially important when songs are used that are very new or written by someone in the congregation. Often worship leaders introduce new songs that are popular on the radio. While it is true that some people may already *know* such songs, giving the congregation permission to hear them first will facilitate their reception. Furthermore, offering a listening moment allows the leader to call the congregation to sing a new song, instead of providing an excuse for nonparticipation.

## E. *Sing as a Prelude or Repeat Later in the Service*

Along with the previous suggestion, it can be helpful to sing the song during the prelude. This will provide more exposure to the song for later participation in the service. It can also be helpful to repeat a song later in the *ordo*. Often a new song is brought into the service specifically as a response to the Scriptures and sermon. When appropriate, that song can be learned earlier and then recalled later after the sermon for a richer worship opportunity.

## F. *If It Is Good, Keep Singing It; If It Is Bad, Get Rid of It.*

Before a song ever finds its way into a service, the appropriateness of its theology for the season of the church year should have been vetted. However, some songs that have been imagined to work well on paper fail in communal worship. The evaluation of the music should be included in the overall service evaluation.

The evaluation of the song must take into consideration many factors. Questions must be asked, such as, "Why did this song not work?" Perhaps extenuating circumstances led to a song "not working."

If a song does work and fit, then keep singing it when appropriate. If new songs are continually introduced and never sung again, the congregation is going to have little incentive to learn new songs. Furthermore, a new song can be learned through repetition. Curiously, many worship leaders feel guilty when they use the same song several weeks in a row, as if somehow they are breaking a creativity law. While repeating every song from week to week would not be advisable, some songs, particularly new songs, can and should be sung often while they are being learned, especially for a season of the church year. As a new song enters into the communal memory of the congregation, it moves from songs that are simply sung to songs that can be used for worship.

## Excellence in Instrumentality

As part of the conversation about music, another important dimension is the use of instruments in worship. Like the power of worship space, lighting, and smell, the importance of instrumentality and sound dynamics demands attention. Dynamic theological statements and worship atmospheres are shaped by what instruments are used. On this issue there is no *right* or *wrong*. Each worship leadership team has probably been using a similar instrumental scheme for many years. The reason can simply be the "rut" of tradition and/or what is being done is working well. The emphasis here is not to change what is being done but to question it and be intentional about it. When looking at instrumentality, paying attention to *who we are* and *what skilled musicians we have* begins with hard pragmatics. Who can do what?

While each local context will find its faithful and beautiful tones for worship, paying attention to the seasons of the church year should impact instrumentation. The seasons of both Advent and Lent lend themselves to a more reserved and muted instrumentality. These are not seasons for boisterous celebration. Often during these seasons, many churches reduce the instrumentality as much as possible. Some congregations move to a minimalist acoustic atmosphere. Such a change will be off-putting to several who are used to "normal," and this would be precisely the point. Again, the tension between the pageantry surrounding December and the minimalism of Advent need to be carefully thought through. Moreover, the seasons of Christmas and Easter are to be seasons of joyful, loud celebration. These are seasons to use musicality to create an atmosphere of unreserved hope and joy. almost like trying to manipulate the Spirit, not a big fan

## Volume of Worship

Another important matter is the volume (decibel level) of the worship leaders and instruments. One of sad arguments in the wars over worship was a battle over the organ or drums. One of the issues underlying the "organ and drum" debate that needs attention is the volume of the sound system and instruments. Some churches have followed the model of rock concerts and assume louder is always more powerful and hence more spiritual. That is poor logic. Each context and worship space will need to find the appropriate acoustic sound level. When the sound is too soft (this is now rarely the problem) or too loud, it can be a devastating distraction for the worshippers. Not only can loud worship be physically painful, but it can also encourage people to fall into the entertainment posture of just watching. Something powerful occurs when every congregant recognizes the need for his or her voice. This is best demonstrated when a worship leader calls for *voices only* (acapella). Often in those contexts the singing by the congregation becomes more robust.

## Worship Teams, Choirs, and Specials

Who leads the worship in song? Answers to this question must be considered for each local context. There are many positives to a worship team approach and many positives to having just one leader. Whoever is leading worship must understand that their primary task is to authentically worship God and in so doing encourage the congregation to participate in worshipping God. Those leading in worship either through song or instrument must be dressed in a way that is not distracting and must perform with both sincerity and enthusiasm. Too often those who are at the front leading the congregation in worship look as though they are in pain or would rather be any other place.

When discerning who should serve on the vocal worship team, it is paramount to find people who are gifted and recognize the importance of this calling. All worship leaders recognize that on some days team members are just not in the mood. When possible in such cases, team members should excuse themselves. If this is not possible, worship team members need to perform with excitement, joy, and enthusiasm. Worship leadership both on the stage and in the pew is a type of performance. While authenticity should not be ignored, sometimes we are called to do what we are not in the mood to do. This is the work to which we are called, and many days we accomplish it in joy and some days through determination. Those leading in worship must pay attention to their faces and postures. Lead well, with passion, joy, and enthusiasm, even when you do not feel like it.

Furthermore, when selecting people to lead in worship vocally, the excellence desired may not always be from those who have the best voices but from those who have the best presence in leading on stage. I know of several churches who have people who are not the strongest vocally, but the spirit in which they worship is dynamic and contagious and moves people to join them. While the volume of their microphones is lower than those of others, their leadership remains powerful.

What about choirs and "special" music? This is another place where each local context will guide how choirs or specials are used. Growing up in the church, I have been encountered powerfully by God through choirs, individuals, and groups who have sung songs as testimonies to *who God is* and *what God is doing*. Choirs have historically been used to help guide and call the larger congregation to worship. A soloist is not necessarily showing off his or her musical prowess but is testifying as one of the community about the glory of God. As such, a solo becomes an offering and thus can be sung as an offertory. Along with the wonderful and important reasons for including choirs and specials, the danger exists that those elements could be viewed in the service as entertainment pieces. Care should be taken to guard against such a misperception. Each of these elements should be properly imagined to draw people into the work of worship. As they do so, they can be faithful elements used weekly. However, attention must be paid to the pitfalls of any worship element that becomes more about appealing to those seated and less about worshipping God or inviting people to offer themselves to God.

## Questions for Discussion and Reflection

1. What ideas were the most helpful in this chapter?

2. What ideas are the most difficult or causing the greatest amount of tension?

3. On a scale of one to ten, how well are you doing in the use of music in communal worship?

4. How are you doing with the introduction of new songs?

5. What are some ways you can improve the use of music in worship?

# SIXTEEN

# SERVICE OF THE WORD: RESPONSE THROUGH THE CREEDS AND TITHES AND OFFERINGS

*Planning worship well begins with giving attention to the worship team, the process for planning worship, the people in a local community, the worship space, and the season of the Christian year; it also means planning worship services that are Christian. **The service of Word and Table emphasizes God's gathering and calling while also empowering humanity's response.** . . .*

Along with the response through music, the congregation is also called to respond to God's call through the confession of the creeds and the giving of tithes and offerings. These responses imagine a full-bodied response to God as well as a renewed union with Christians who have gone before as well as those who are present. This chapter will consider the importance of the creeds in worship and the physical giving of tithes and offerings as responses to God's call to be more fully human.

## Creeds: Confessions of Praise

What does it mean to be Christian? What are the bare essentials? The creeds serve as one place for uniting Christians today with those who have gone before them. The creeds provide a picture of the church at work wrestling through the union of theology and worship. Too often the creeds are considered to be simply doctrinal statements. What is missed is the early church's concern about idolatry and worship. Consider what is perhaps the most famous church council and the creed that emerged from it—the Nicene Creed. At stake was not simply declaring the Arians as heretical or those following Athanasius as orthodox. At stake was not simply deciding if Jesus was fully God and fully human, nor was it simply a matter of "believing" rightly. As the Old Testament affirms, only God is worthy of worship because only God is uncreated. So should Jesus Christ be considered worthy of worship? At stake was worshipping in fullness and truth.

Creeds are not merely statements to which mental assent is to be given, which is often how the term "belief" is imagined. They are not statements merely to be recited. Creeds are to be confessed and professed. As the church confesses the creeds, it acknowledges the triune God. The church's profession is a public declaration of allegiance to the One in whom all authority is placed. The political power in the declaration "Jesus is Lord" directly challenges the notion that "Caesar is Lord." It is largely affirmed that the Apostles' Creed was developed as a declaration for baptismal candidates before baptism. Furthermore, these creeds can and should be recited weekly as both a summary and a confession of the central affirmation of Christian faith.

Creeds are not simply concepts for our heads but frames of reference that shape our bodily living in the world. What does it mean to live daily under the affirmation that it is not I but "God the Father almighty, maker and creator of heaven and earth" who is the center of creation? What does it mean to seek healing and forgiveness during times of despair through the name of Jesus Christ, "who suffered under Pontius Pilate, was crucified, died and was buried, on the third day he rose again"? What does it mean to recognize that I am not the source of my power and life, but "the Holy Spirit is the Lord and giver of all life"? What does it mean to be a people of hope who have been and are being healed to participate in the present and coming kingdom of God, "who look for the resurrection of the dead, and the life of the world to come"?[1]

The weekly confession and profession of the creeds is an embodied declaration of praise of who God is and, in light of this, who God is calling the church to become. This declaration of who God is, is also an affirmation that God has anointed the church to participate in the imagination of the kingdom of God. As observed earlier, an affirmation in praise of who God is, is also a prayer that God would transform and heal creation to properly reflect God's glory in all the earth so that God may be all in all.

Moreover, the creed must be imagined as a communal and hence political pledge of allegiance, rightly understood as an act of liturgy. "The original sense of *leitourgia* was an action by which a group of people become something corporately which they had not been as a collection of individuals."[2] Therefore, "Christian worship is where individuals are made a communion of people in the church—the eschatological *polis.*"[3] Smith notes that the very act of confessing the creed is a further participation not only in forming people into kingdom people but also in celebrating the kingdom's further coming. Through the creeds "what we believe is not a matter of intellectualizing salvation but rather a matter of knowing what to love, knowing to whom we pledge allegiance, and knowing what is at stake for us as people of the 'baptismal city.'"[4] The creed is a prayer of affirmation to be lived. The creeds are a response to God's presence, revelation, and invitation *to become more fully human.*

Professing and confessing the creed also embodies an *apostolicity* to each communal worship service. The creed's recitation is more than simply regurgitating a sentimental slogan or blind subservience to tradition. The connection to the past is vital for its faithfulness in the present and movement into the coming future. This is also a place where the emphasis and imagination of *anamnēsis* bears weight. The creeds serve as a liturgical and apostolic memory of who God has revealed Godself to be to the church. The apostolicity of the creeds also form an important aspect of the liturgical initiation of people in the church at baptism.

### Where in the Ordo?

There are several places in the ordo where the creed could fit. In the suggested order of worship I have placed the creed immediately after the peace of Christ. Recall that the peace of Christ was a place for reconciliation and renewal in the local body. Confessing the creed is an embodied event that both celebrates and further renews the local body of believers, not only with each other but with all other believers present, past, and future. This confession is also a political charge and prayer that rightly moves the church into offering itself back to God in light of confessing this kenotic God.[5] As God has poured out love upon the world, so, too, as people respond to the *invitation to be fully human*, will they offer themselves in love, for love. While the creed placed after the peace of Christ makes theological and liturgical sense, there are several other places and moments where the creed could be placed.

| |
|---|
| Call to Worship |
| Collect |
| Song of Praise |
| Prayer of Illumination (or earlier) |
| Old Testament Reading |
| Sing the Psalm |
| Epistle Lesson |
| Hymn of Thanksgiving |
| Gospel Reading |
| Sermon |
| Confession and Pardon |
| Peace of Christ |
| **Creed** |
| Prayers of the People |
| Offering |
| Doxology |
| Lord's Supper |
| Benediction: Sending Forth |

## Announcements: Necessary and Always a Challenge

Those who plan worship recognize the necessity of communicating information about upcoming events or important details for the church body. Sadly, announcements are often a worship killer. Regularly they are not well rehearsed, so they become a distraction and break the flow of worship. In every organization I have participated in as a leader or follower, one of the critiques of the leadership is a failure to communicate.

Refusing to do verbal announcements in the service may not be possible. However, many churches have explored creative ways of getting the information to the congregants outside of the communal worship service. Some churches run announcements on big screens before and after services, as well as using paper bulletins. Some churches send announcements out by way of email and on the podcasts of the weekly sermons.

Because announcements help to facilitate the fellowship and building up of the community and provide opportunities for service in the community, doing announcements well in communal worship is appropriate. One of the challenges of announcements is that often so many are given that people do not really hear any of them. Worship leaders should discern and choose carefully what announcements are worthy of attention. This is not easy, since people whose events are not given verbal space in the communal worship space often feel slighted. Conversely, when announcements become long and laborious (or silly), they distract and work against the overall flow of communal worship. If verbal announcements must be given in communal worship, three liturgical spaces seem to be optimal.

1. Prior to the prelude: The announcements can serve as a gathering of the body to important information before worship begins.
2. After the peace and before the offering: As people are offered a significant time to greet and exchange the peace, the announcements can help gather the congregation together to celebrate and inform about important ministry and service events.
3. After the Lord's Supper and before the benediction: At the very end of the service people can be sent out with some announcements on their minds.

Worship teams should work with diligence, discernment, and excellence in dealing with important items needing the attention of the congregation. In all matters care must be taken to not detract from the primary emphasis and focus of communal worship.

## Offering Oneself Back to God

I was six or seven years old. It was Sunday night. Just like every other Sunday of my life, we had been to church that morning and that evening. I liked church, but I did doodle quite a bit during the sermons to help pass the time. My Christian imagination was boldly naive and precious. My dad was on the counting team, and that day I asked him how counting the offering worked. I knew that these were God's tithes and offerings, but I was not sure exactly how God got them. The best I could imagine is that after Sunday night and after all the money had been counted, the ushers would put the money on top of the church and God would "zap" (perhaps like a lightning bolt) the money back to heaven. So I tried out my hypothesis the next evening with my dad, who informed me what it meant to understand they were God's.

Fast-forward to a precocious twelve. My dad and I were having a passionate "discussion" on the way to church. He was extolling me on why I must use a tithing envelope when putting in my tithe each week. I retorted, "But God knows it was from me. Isn't this just showing off to others when I put my name on it?" My dad then informed me about the role of accountability the church plays by reminding us how much we have given.[6] "But, Dad, if I put my name on it, it feels like I am paying off God. Aren't we saved by grace and not works?" Another teaching lesson ensued.

Several surveys seem to suggest that only 15 percent of people who attend church actually participate in giving their tithes and offerings. Part of the problem surrounds ignorance concerning the role of tithes and offerings. I wonder how many churched people have a base knowledge that the tithe is to be 10 percent of all that God has blessed us with. Offerings can be given to a variety of people and places as a gift back to God over and above "what is required."[7] While many are very nervous (or downright appalled) about the "health and wealth" gospel that turns tithes and offering into a divine lottery ticket, hoping for a return 10 to 100 percent on the original "investment." It is true that God honors those who are faithful to the tithe. Tithing, like prayer, is to be a spiritual discipline.

Giving tithes and offerings encompasses two important ideas that are linked to the giving of manna to the Israelites in Egypt and the command to observe the Sabbath. God provided manna to the Israelites as they wandered in the desert. The manna was to be collected daily (I hope the Lord's Prayer is ringing in your ears here). If the Israelites tried to hoard or store more than one day's manna, it would spoil, except for the day before the Sabbath. Only on the day before the Sabbath could they collect two days' worth and it would not spoil (see Exod. 16). This narrative is grounded in the liberation that the Israelites experienced from Pharaoh's brick quota. In Egypt under Pharoah there were no days off, no days for worship, bricks every day. The exodus was liberation from the need to work every day. There was a temptation to return to a seven-day workweek for survival. God offered the Israelites the command/gift of the Sabbath as a way to remind them that all good things come from God and that God can be trusted to take care of them.

Let us consider some theological imaginations of the tithe.

## A. All of What I Have Is God's

One of my great pastor friends offered a prophetic word often during the receiving of tithes. "The question is not, 'How much of my money am I going to give to God?' but rather, 'How much of God's am I going to keep for myself?'"[8]

## B. Trust for God to Provide

Commanding the Israelites to take a Sabbath was not simply to provide rest and health to their physical bodies but also to remind the Israelites that God was the One who provided all they worked so hard for. To offer a tithe to God is to trust that God will be faithful. The Scriptures, which speak about money more than any topic, record God as saying in Malachi, "Test me in this" (3:10, NIV). As noted earlier, this testing has parameters that should not be violated or manipulated. Furthermore, this does not mean that those who love God will never go hungry. Yet when people go hungry, it is not so much an indictment against God as an indictment against the church that it is not helping people find their daily bread. ouch...

## C. Offering Is Placing Oneself on the Altar

A third crucial component largely missed among many in the church is the connection of the offering with self-sacrifice. As an embodied extension of all the congregations' praises, confessions, and laments, the church is invited to bring forward tithes and offerings as an embodied sacrifice, thereby fulfilling Paul's challenge in Rom. 12:1.

---

### What About Electronic Tithing?

With new technology many banks are encouraging their customers to stop using paper checks and use electronic transfers exclusively. This method is more secure and helps to prevent identity theft. Studies also show that churches that provide electronic methods for paying tithes see an increase in the number of givers. Some of the rationale has to do with resolving the problem of people forgetting to bring their tithe checks to church. With electronic banking people can now include the church when paying other bills electronically. Is electronic tithing a faithful way to tithe? Yes. While churches should not encourage people to pay their tithes with credit cards for a number of reasons, electronic transfers can be appropriate. People who pay by way of electronic transfer should also put some note in the offering, representing this gift. In many ways this is all a written check is. Along with the appropriateness of electronic transfer, the importance of putting something material that represents oneself in the offering plate should not be lost.

At communal worship and specifically in the giving of tithes and offerings, a mother's check or cash that goes into the offering plate is literally her offering herself on the altar. Offering ourselves as a living sacrifice means that *all that we are and all we hope to be are God's*. This offering is not a payment to God for forgiveness. Much like Christ, Christians offer themselves to God as a thank offering for all that God has done and as a response to the *invitation to become fully human*. Baptism declares that people die to sin and selfishness so that they may be raised with Christ to new life (Rom. 6:5-11). The offerings are collected as an embodied practice where Christians weekly offer all of themselves to God so that God may do with them what God desires in their further healing and the further coming of the kingdom in creation. This is why the church collects these offerings and puts them on the Eucharist Table where the church will offer itself with Christ as a thank offering to God.

### D. Doxology in Response

Often a doxology is sung as offering plates and eucharistic emblems are brought forward and put on the Communion Table. This doxology is an important reminder that all of God's provisions, not only the body and blood of Christ but also all of the physical offerings the congregation has offered (re-presenting themselves), are only possible because of God. The church's attitude is not about displaying how generous it is. Rather, as the offerings are combined with the eucharistic gifts, the church recognizes that God has made every offering possible, and thus the church is moved to thanksgiving for God's provision for it in all ways: spiritually, physically, and emotionally.

## Where in the Ordo?

As noted in section I, the physical collection of tithes and offerings is a culmination of all that has been occurring throughout the church's response in the service of the Word. The practice of spoken and sung prayers and creedal confessions are all different kinds of offerings, different ways of presenting oneself (collectively) before God in praise, humility, complaint, submission, and supplication. The taking of the physical offering is a fitting culmination of these responses to God encountered in the service of the Word.

Since all of these responses are tied to the physical taking of the offering, we find here another reason to encourage people to put something material in the offering every week. The amount is not significant, but the materiality of the gift celebrates the offering of our material bodies and lives to God for God to use and transform us in our material world. Again, offerings are a response to God's *invitation to become fully human*. The full and proper response to God's invitation to life is to offer all of oneself back to God.

Call to Worship
Collect
Song of Praise
Prayer of
    Illumination
    (or earlier)
Old Testament
    Reading
Sing the Psalm
Epistle Lesson
Hymn of
    Thanksgiving
Gospel Reading
Sermon
Confession and
    Pardon
Peace of Christ
Creed
Prayers of the
    People
**Offering**
**Doxology**
Lord's Supper
Benediction:
    Sending
    Forth

## Questions for Discussion and Reflection

1. What ideas were the most helpful in this chapter?

2. What ideas are the most difficult or causing the greatest amount of tension?

3. How and when are creeds being used in communal worship? How could this be improved?

4. How well does your community understand the theology of tithes and offerings?

# SEVENTEEN

# THE WORSHIP EVENT: EXCELLENCE AND PERFECTION IN WORSHIP LEADING

*Planning worship well begins with giving attention to the worship team, the process for planning worship, the people in a local community, the worship space, and the season of the Christian year; it also means planning worship services that are Christian. The service of Word and Table emphasizes God's gathering and calling while also empowering humanity's response. **Planning worship well further includes paying attention to the final details and leading with excellence.***

---

To further improve worship planning this chapter includes several suggestions for excellence in leading during the worship event and some advice on how to imagine what is *perfect worship*. First, here are some suggestions for the final preparations of worship leaders.

## Final Checklist

The days, hours, and minutes before a communal worship service often include a bit of anxiety and stress for worship leaders (some of you may find this the biggest understatement of this entire discussion). As the stress and pressure intensify, these are the moments when caring for worship team members and parishioners often gets lost under the stress of *getting it done*. What follows are some ideas to help ease some of the anxiety as things come down the stretch.

### Excellence in the Details

The quality of preparation and planning one does often will be inversely proportional to the amount of last-minute stress. In other words, better planning leads to less stress. In worship, excellence is often found in paying attention to the details. The goal is to create a system of worship planning that remains consistent and flexible enough to make room for each week. Mistakes and laziness are distinct and yet often result in similar problems. While a person can be mistaken without laziness, laziness rarely can occur without mistakes. Laziness is more difficult to correct than mistakes.

## Final Order of Service

Try to get the final order of service to every person in leadership or with responsibility in the worship service by the Thursday before the Sunday service. This amount of time allows people involved a chance to ask any clarifying questions. On most weeks some part of the order will have to be tweaked, but with three days' notice nearly all the people will know their jobs and will be able to envision them in light of the whole.

The service order should include not only *who* is doing *what* but also *when* and *where* people and liturgical elements are to appear. Transitions between liturgical elements are often neglected during planning and are thus not attended to during the performance in communal worship. Most transitions between elements involving new people occur slowly, often with great hesitation. Many times this tardiness is a result of people not knowing exactly when their leadership begins. While this detail may seem insignificant, consider the way theatrical productions intentionally use blocking and timing to gain precision for performances. Moreover, most worship spaces can be used creatively, but often little thought or attention is given to where people are to lead from. Most worship spaces are not creatively imagined and are thus underused.

Another issue that needs attention in the final order of worship pertains to the bodily movements of congregation members and the instructions given to them. In college my wife and I attended a service where we literally stood and sat, up and down, over eight times in a twenty-minute span. We were young and able-bodied at the time, so it was simply comical. People in the congregation for whom standing and sitting requires great physical effort must be considered. Bodily posture is theologically significant. Directing people to sit or stand should be discussed and treated with intentionality. Furthermore, once those decisions are made, worship leaders must direct the congregation at the appropriate times into the requested or invited posture. Clearly, this is not about controlling people's bodies but about inviting the physical bodies into communal participation.

## Precision with Media

One of the most important and challenging areas demanding excellence is the use of print and digital media. Those working with the media should be among the first to receive a detailed order of service. I often tell my students that some people are looking for things to distract them. The most common distractions occur frequently on the big digital screens. Song slides not in the order the worship team sings them and misspellings are common mistakes that distract worshippers. Some fonts are too big; some too small. Some images or backgrounds are distracting. Some of these stylistic and design issues can be corrected in time, other issues, such as spelling errors and out-of-sync slides, require constant vigilance. If videos or other special media are being used, performing a test run with sound levels before the service begins is strongly encouraged.

Media technology can be a wonderful aid to worship; however, it must never become central or distracting to worship, and thus great care should be taken in its use.

### Sound Check

Another component that is never noticed if handled with excellence is the sound system. Here are some tips: *Always* put new batteries into wireless microphones for each use. Just as with other media, it is wise to put all microphones and instruments through a microphone check for balance and sound levels.

### Not If, But What Disasters

With all the planning and preparation it is normal for something to arise at the last minute that requires adjustment to the order or changes among the people leading the liturgical elements. Worship leaders who have planned well are able to adjust at the last minute, while worship leaders who are planning at the last minute have a more difficult time adjusting. Worship planning is not simply a means to an end but an act of worship: either to God, pragmatics, or pride. With God's assistance and diligence we can lead the church in hearing God's call and responding with all that we are.

## Excellence in Worship Leading

The planning is done, all the media has been checked, and the people are in their places with their assignments. Now, how do we lead worship? Here are some general considerations to keep in mind for imagining worship leading.

### Worship Is for God and Not People

One of the terrible pitfalls exposed in the worship wars is that people thought communal worship was for them. So the goal of worship was simply, "How can we keep our people happy?" Rejecting this question does not neglect the importance for contextualization, but the worship leader must always be mindful that all that is done is done for God. Clearly everyone knows this and will proclaim it aloud, but too often that is not what is practiced in all phases of worship.

### Worship Leaders vs. Entertainers

Care must be taken by all worship leaders, including the preaching pastor, to aim the congregation members' attention away from themselves and toward God. This is another point that is so obvious and "known" that occasionally worship leaders overlook it. For my young students, this also implies that they are not to be comedians on stage. There are appropriate times for fun and humor, but silliness and seriousness must not be confused. Worship leaders serve as priests and prophets, and such a calling demands respect and maturity.

Within the importance of this leadership role in the church, it is also crucial that worship leaders allow their own personalities to come through. There is a tension here. In what follows I am going to recommend that worship leaders lead in a way that is more exuberant and extroverted than they are comfortable with, while all the time intent that such leading will move people to worship God. This should be another point to consider during the service evaluation each week.

## Worship Leaders Worshipping

With all the work put into planning, and all the details that must be remembered during the event, it can be difficult for members of the worship team to actually find a space to worship in the service. While it is a joyous work, often the worship event itself demands so much attention and focus that relaxing just to *be present* to God and others is difficult. But try! In my experience, it is much more difficult to worship when you are planning the service while it is happening. Good planning allows for more emotional and mental time to worship and reduces the time spent worrying about what is coming next. This is especially important for those who are leading the congregation in worship through song (choruses or hymns) or spoken prayers. For those worship leaders, in those moments, authenticity, passionate enthusiasm, and intensity must all come together (whether or not you feel like it).

## Minimize Distractions

As a *live* event, a worship service is subject to a variety of distractions that fall completely outside the control of the worship leaders: babies screaming; audio problems with microphones, such as feedback or buzzing; lights going out; things falling over; people having medical emergencies; fire alarms; birds or other animals in the sanctuary; people standing, running, and shouting, both appropriately and inappropriately—the list could go on. If you can think it, it can and will happen. Then watch out for the things you have never imagined. The basic goal is to keep facilitating a spirit of worship. With minor distractions, ignoring the nuisance may prove best. With other distractions, simply naming the distraction (microphone buzzing, feedback, bird, etc.) can assist in deflating it. There will be some incidents that will require putting the service on hold: fire alarms, some medical emergencies, and so on. Worship leaders should work with the sound and tech team, as well as having ushers ready to respond as crises or disturbances arise.

Let me offer another suggestion on sound, audio, and media technology issues. When something goes awry and causes such a disturbance that the situation must be acknowledged, this would be a great time for the worship leader to offer a word of thanks for all that sound and media people do every week that often goes unnoticed until something malfunctions. Sound and media teams work diligently and tirelessly, often with little recognition. Taking time to honor them during such moments can be a way to both alleviate the tension and express gratitude to those who are serving.

### Education in Worship

Many people who are new to the faith or have been cradle Christians may not be very educated about the elements of worship. While many long-term Christians can describe what physically happens, they often do not have an underlying understanding of *why* some things are done. Education in the worship service is necessary and needed in all Christian congregations. While the communal worship service is not the place for a twenty-minute lecture on a certain liturgical element, teaching moments sprinkled in communal worship services can assist people in worship. The emphasis on education about worship is aimed not at making people *smarter* but at making them, in the work and response of worship, more *present* to God, others, and themselves. Congregations would benefit by having classes on worship that offer some history and rationale for *why we do what we do*. Planned teaching moments in communal worship can be as short as twenty seconds or as long as three to five minutes when appropriate. Although these teaching moments will not be exhaustive, they can open up people to a greater participation in worship.

### Open to the Spirit

The importance of planning ahead cannot be stated strongly enough. It is a poor theology of worship to think that *worship is more spiritual if it is unplanned*. As noted earlier, a lack of planning makes the Spirit's job more difficult. With that said, worship leaders who plan well must be open to having the Spirit change or alter their plans. It is the prayer and hope that the Spirit has been guiding and empowering the entire planning process. However, the power of God's call and the people's response may become so dynamic that adjusting the order of service is both appropriate and necessary. This is one of the main skills that worship leaders need to hone and develop. Problems can occur if such adjustments are not made. Too often the Spirit has moved and the worship leader (the person leading in music or delivering the sermon) is not prepared to adjust and just ignores the movement, leaving many in the congregation who have or are wanting to respond confused and frustrated. For example, most of the churches I have attended announce that the prayer altars are open any time during the service. However, when people respond by spontaneously coming forward during a song or musical number, I have seen some pastors just plow ahead with the order of service and, when the song is over, launch into the announcements about the pizza feed that night for the teenagers.

Sensitivity and discernment along with experience can help guide the worship leader in how best to respond to the Spirit. There is a dark side to being open to the Spirit. Often worship leaders have been conditioned (and thus have conditioned the congregation) that a service is only "Spirit-filled" if the worship order gets changed. In these contexts, rather than being *open* to the Spirit, there are attempts to manipulate the emotions of the people and claim the results as spiritual.

## Invitations to the Altar

Not all local churches have prayer altars as part of their liturgical furniture, nor are the altars used with great frequency. Altars or prayer rails have a dynamic history in many parts of Christian history. When altars are opened, a couple suggestions can help facilitate people coming forward. First, invite all people to stand. If people are in rows or pews, it is more physically difficult and awkward to get to an aisle if fellow congregants are sitting. Second, people will generally move with music rather than silence. While many congregations will come forward when the worship leader invites them, it is likely more people will come if a song or a chorus can be sung, giving the people time to make it to the altar. Inviting people to the altar and then beginning to pray four seconds later is not conducive to encouraging people to come forward. In the evangelical and holiness traditions people are often invited to come to the altar to respond to God's call. A local congregation should have trained altar workers who can assist people in prayer at the altar. Discernment again is important, since some people would prefer to pray alone, yet many can often be assisted by friends and mentors. The following point about safety is imperative for the helpful use of altars.

## Creating an Atmosphere of Safety

Educators will tell you that one of the essential ingredients to a healthy learning environment is safety. The same is crucial for local churches in communal worship. Creating a safe environment in worship means that people begin to trust the worship leaders to not manipulate them, to not exploit or psychologically and emotionally abuse them. As people feel safe in trusting the worship leaders, they will then be able to more freely express themselves in worship. When people are given permission to worship in freedom, this spirit of freedom becomes contagious and people become more vulnerable and open to the Spirit's leading and moving in their lives. In this spirit of safety and freedom, worship leaders should call and invite people to worship. Although scolding is not recommended, calling on the congregation to be more present is appropriate.

Along with this goal, worship leaders must vigilantly guard their people from outsider abuse. On too many occasions outside speakers have caused considerable psychological harm through what they said and suggested. Special guests should be used carefully and sparingly. It may even be appropriate for a worship leader (perhaps the lead pastor) to interrupt and stop a speaker who is going down a harmful road. Those who do harm rarely intend to do so and often believe they are following the Spirit's voice; however, the Holy Spirit is not one of confusion, and worship leaders must discern when abuse (even unintended) is occurring.

## Perfect Worship

What is perfect worship? Is there such a thing? Despite all the planning and care, the wrong Scripture reference is put on the screen, the pastor goes to the platform too soon, the drummer misses the bridge transition, and the slides to the third hymn do not have the same words as the worship team has. What is *perfect* worship? I suggest we think about the Greek understanding of "perfect" instead of the Latin.

The Latin understanding of "perfect" is the concept of something without error, flaw, blemish, or mistake. If this is our idea of perfection, then there probably has never been perfect worship. However, the Greek notion of "perfect" is found in the word *telos*—the goal, aim, or purpose of an object. Recall from section I that communal worship seeks to move, by the Spirit, to the glorification of God and the sanctification of the people of God. Perfect worship is not about everything going as planned but about the local church responding well to God's call in the work God has called it to do. Worship events are live and anything can happen. Worship leaders should not be overly discouraged when some things do not go as planned. Perfection of worship comes in the planning, not in the execution. When God is glorified and God further heals and sanctifies creation, worship is moving toward God's purpose for it.

## A Diversity of Gifts

Many skills are needed for excellence in communal worship planning and leading. This is why a worship team should be made up of people with a diversity of gifts and abilities. Some people are fabulous at imagining, planning, creating, and organizing but are poor at leading the congregation in the communal worship event. Although many of these qualities of excellence can be learned and God can use people humble and willing to learn, there are people who are especially gifted for leading in worship but who may not be as talented at organizing—and vice versa. In most cases worship leaders need to do their best either to improve in areas they are weak in or to surround themselves with people who have strengths that complement their areas of weakness.

Imagining, planning, creating, and then leading communal worship are all demanding tasks but not impossible to do. Proper preparation—attention to details, understanding the goal of worship, recognizing personal weaknesses, appreciating and relying on the strengths of others, and so on—can help keep communal worship moving toward the purpose God intended for it.

## Questions for Discussion and Reflection

1. What ideas were the most helpful in this chapter?

2. What ideas are the most difficult or causing the greatest amount of tension?

3. What is going well with your worship leadership in the service? What areas need attention?

4. How is your congregation doing with getting all the final details together for a communal worship service? What is going well? What could be improved?

5. What level of spontaneity does your local worship team allow for each week?

6. Does your congregation feel safe in worship? How do you know?

# SECTION III
## Sacraments: God's Healing Making Individuals More Fully Human

Sacraments are healing encounters with God, occasions when people respond to God's invitation to become more fully human and when God's transformation and healing occur to make it so. In other words, sacraments are divine-human events and encounters in which God heals individuals to *become more fully human.*

### Command and Promise

Sacraments are God's gift to the church for communal worship that serves as a *command* and *promise.* Protestants have largely considered baptism and the Lord's Supper as the two primary sacraments. The rationale for the elevation of these two is that in Scripture followers are explicitly commanded by Christ *to do* them as they participate in salvation.[1] Christian tradition recognized the importance of following these commands of Christ. John Wesley, in his sermon "The Duty of Constant Communion," challenges those who are not taking Communion because of their unworthiness:

> Fear it not for eating and drinking unworthily; for that, in St. Paul's sense, ye cannot do. But I will tell you for what you shall fear damnation: for not eating and drinking at all; for not obeying your Maker and Redeemer; for disobeying his plain command; for thus setting at nought both his mercy and authority. Fear ye this; for hear what his Apostle saith: "Whosoever shall keep the whole law, and yet offend in one point, is guilty of all."[2]

Wesley is clear that disobeying God's command to partake should cause one to quiver before God. This emphasis on commands is not to create a system of legalism or blind obedience. The emphasis is not a rule simply to follow but a command grounded and saturated in God's promise to heal, renew, and transform.

James White observes that one of the most significant Protestant documents on the sacraments is Martin Luther's *The Babylonian Captivity.* Luther's emphasis was to name sacraments as promises that have signs attached to them.[3] Just as the commands come from Scripture, Scripture also provides promises from God in these actions. These promises from God in Scripture are central to what Luther believed could properly be called sacraments. A promise moves the church to belief, and vice versa. "For is it not possible to believe unless there is a promise, and the promise is not established unless it is believed. But where these two meet, they give a real and most certain efficacy to the sacraments."[4] This prompts James White to affirm, "Sacraments are scriptural promises to which Christ has given a sign."[5] Moreover, as these signs are connected to Scripture they *effect what they signify*. That is to say, God's promises of healing, renewal, and forgiveness come through the signs God has established. This is not to say that God's healing and transformation only occur in these two proper sacraments.

Part of what is needed for many areas of the Protestant church is a larger and grander sacramental imagination. Because God is present to all parts of creation, so, too, is God healing, renewing, and redeeming creation both within and outside Christian communal worship. A sacramental imagination celebrates the pouring out of God's love over the entire world for the world's redemption. Moreover, the church affirms that in the *command* and *promise* of Christ in the sacraments of baptism and the Lord's Supper, God heals and renews people to *become more fully human*.

## Human Empowered Response

While the power of the Holy Spirit, in the name of Christ, by the will of the Father is the operative power of the sacraments, the importance of people believing, confessing, and offering their very bodies to God plays an important role in their healing. There is often a misunderstanding by Protestants about the Roman Catholic sacramental theology of *ex opere operato* (literally "by the very fact of the action's being performed"). Often Protestants believe that Roman Catholics teach that a person's response is irrelevant in the sacraments. This is incorrect.[6] The grace offered at baptism and at the Lord's Supper must always be connected to the *ex opere operantis*, the work and proper disposition of the church to receive the gift of Christ's presence.

This cooperation in the Spirit between Christ and the church resonates strongly with the Wesleyan understanding of divine-human synergism.[7] Lawrence Mick notes that Thomas Aquinas's teaching of *ex opere operato* emphasizes the "permanent availability of God's salvation in Christ."[8] Wesleyans recognize that God is the power of healing, forgiveness, and reconciliation, and yet a human response (empowered by God) is necessary for the sacraments to be fully fruitful. "While [God] made you without you, [God] doesn't justify you without you."[9] This fruitfulness celebrates the renewal of individuals into the image of God (becoming more fully human). Yet the imagination of redemption does not end with the individual. Recall that being renewed into the *imago Dei*, becoming more fully human, celebrates also the re-*membering* of the church as the body of Christ, called to love the world as a further participation in God's redemption of all creation.

## Transformed Bathing, Eating, Drinking

The signs through which God *commanded* and *promised* to offer healing and forgiveness draw upon very ordinary and common practices humans do every day: bathing, eating, and drinking. Not only are these practices common, but so are the very material elements involved: water, bread, and wine—the fruit of the vine. The theology of the sacraments is powerful and breathtaking. God uses very common (profane) and average actions and materials and transforms them so that they become sacred, holy, set apart for God's purposes of healing and redemption. The sacraments are God's love made visible in the world, in people, through the ordinary actions of bathing, eating, and drinking.

This section will consider the theology and practice of baptism and the Lord's Supper as divine-human healing events.

### Questions for Discussion and Reflection

1. What ideas were the most helpful in this section introduction?

2. What ideas are the most difficult or causing the greatest amount of tension?

3. What sacraments are being celebrated in communal worship?

4. What are the strengths and weaknesses in the sacramental celebration of your local worship service?

5. What are some liturgical changes that are needed?

6. What education is needed to help offer your local congregation a fuller imagination of the sacraments?

## EIGHTEEN
# BAPTISM: THE WATERS THROUGH DEATH TO NEW LIFE

———————

The sacrament of baptism celebrates the healing of believers who are brought into the church. This chapter explores the relationship of baptism, ecclesiology (doctrine of the church), and salvation. Furthermore, special attention will be given to the theological distinctives of infant baptism, adult (believers') baptism, and infant dedication.

The baptism of Jesus and Jesus' command to baptize has been received by the church as a command and promise inviting *individuals to become fully human*. However, many who celebrate the sacrament of baptism may be missing out on the full promise and practice of new life offered through the gift of baptism. Before describing the main focus of baptism, some secondary matters, often treated as primary, must be addressed.

## Baptism Is Not Primarily . . .

### A Personal Testimony of What God Has Already Done in Your Life

In many places where adolescent and adult (believers') baptisms are performed, the candidate for baptism offers a testimony declaring what God has already done in his or her life. The understanding is that a person is baptized "to make a public declaration that God has already saved me." The emphasis of a public declaration is appropriate for believers' baptism, and it is certainly true that God has been healing and renewing a person before baptism. However, when the emphasis is solely on what has already happened, little space is given for the healing God will *do* in baptism. In such cases, God is often vacated from the baptism. The event becomes more about an individual's decision to get wet, rather than about a person being drowned and God birthing him or her to new life.

### Centered on the Person Baptized

During many baptisms the emphasis is reduced to the spiritual life of the believer. While this divine work is significant, attention should also be placed on

God's gift to the church, the community of faith. Baptisms are God's continual gift and promise for the further becoming of the church. Baptism is "how God grows the church."[1] While each person's baptism is cause for celebration and joy, the imagination of baptism is more than what is happening to *that* person; it is about what God is doing in the entire life of the body of Christ. Baptism is about God's sustaining gift to the church as the ongoing incorporation of people into the body. Baptism is a celebration and a participation in God's continual re-creating of a people.

Now with these clarifications in mind, let us consider some theological imaginations for Christian baptism.

## Baptism Celebrates . . .

As the blessing and healing of baptism is explored, each of the aspects considered below should be seen as part of the whole and in harmony with each other.

### *Healing from Sin Through Union with Christ's Death and Resurrection*

Baptism is a healing and cleansing from sin through union with Christ's death and resurrection. Wesley celebrated the healing offered at baptism through the ministry of Christ's life and death:

> And the virtue of this free gift, the merits of Christ's life and death, are applied to us in baptism. "He gave himself for the Church, that he might sanctify and cleanse it with the washing of water by the word;" (Eph. v. 25, 26;) namely, in baptism, the ordinary instrument of our justification. Agreeably to this, our Church prays in the baptismal office, that the person to be baptized may be "washed and sanctified by the Holy Ghost, and, being delivered from God's wrath, receive remission of sins, and enjoy the everlasting benediction of his heavenly washing."[2]

In baptism God offers the healing, cleansing, and restoration of people from the disease of sin.

This healing described in the New Testament by God invites and joins together a person's need to confess, repent, and be baptized. "Peter said to them, 'Repent, and be baptized every one of you in the name of Jesus Christ so that your sins may be forgiven; and you will receive the gift of the Holy Spirit'" (Acts 2:38). At baptism, sins are forgiven as an invitation to reconciliation between God and fellow humans. At baptism, this reconciliation is the beginning of the healing from the disease of sin, inviting and empowering people to love. The healing benefits offered at baptism are ongoing and continue to offer healing as people grow and mature. For example, the full measure of healing in baptism is not exhausted in the moments of infant or believer's baptism.

Furthermore, as an act of entrance into a covenant with Christ, people find healing by joining Christ in his death and resurrection. One of the baptismal images throughout Christianity follows the theology of Rom. 6, in which those who die with Christ will be raised (see vv. 1-11). Hence, baptism becomes this immersion and union *with* and *into* Christ's life, death, and resurrection. While the emphasis of baptism is on what God is doing, within God's invitation and healing to life, people are called to live into the baptism they receive. The good news is that they are not required to remain faithful based on their own power, but the Holy Spirit offers encouragement and empowerment to assist people in living into the fullness of life God invites and makes available.

## Initiation into the Church

Baptism is a person's initiation into the church by God. Baptism is the church's bold declaration of God's healing available to all people. Baptism celebrates people being marked by God and brought into the church. "By baptism we are admitted into the Church, and consequently made members of Christ, its Head."[3] Baptism replaces circumcision as the sacrament through which people are brought into God's covenant with God's people. John Wesley affirmed that baptism is "the initiatory sacrament, which enters us into covenant with God."[4] John Wesley further noted that baptism is a sign and seal of God's covenant:

By baptism we enter into covenant with God; into that everlasting covenant, which he hath commanded forever; (Psalm cxi. 9;) that new covenant, which he promised to make with the spiritual Israel; even to "give them a new heart and a new spirit, to sprinkle clean water upon them,"—(of which the baptismal is only a figure,) "and to remember their sins and iniquities no more;" in a word, to be their God, as he promised to Abraham, in the evangelical covenant which he made with him and all his spiritual offspring. (Gen. xvii. 7, 8.) And as circumcision was then the way of entering into this covenant, so baptism is now; which is therefore styled by the Apostle, (so many good interpreters render his words,) "the stipulation, contract, or covenant of a good conscience with God."[5]

It is crucial to note that God is the primary actor offering the healing of forgiveness for a "new heart and new spirit." A person's entrance into the covenant with God is entrance into the covenant already established with God's people. Baptism not only incorporates new believers but also helps to renew and remake the church as the body of Christ. At each baptism the church family grows and expands to encompass more people who have been adopted as daughters and sons.

Baptism offers a fuller imagination of becoming human by proclaiming that ongoing healing occurs in the church. There is no biblical concept about being a solitary covenant member. The Scriptures never envision a simply "Jesus and me" lifestyle. It is always "Jesus and we." In a Western culture that idolizes individual freedoms, liberties, and rights, the Scriptures offer a bigger imagination of what being fully human really means—being a member of the body of Christ. Thus the church affirms, "For in the one Spirit we were all baptized into one body— Jews or Greeks, slaves or free—and we were all made to drink of one Spirit" (1 Cor. 12:13). This one Spirit offers the one church one baptism for the redemption of the world (see Eph. 4:4-6). This unity imagines a world relationally reconciled into one body: "'There is one baptism,' which is the outward sign our one Lord has been pleased to appoint of all that inward and spiritual grace which he is continually bestowing upon his church. It is likewise a precious means whereby this faith and hope are given to those that diligently seek him."[6]

This illumines one of the major ideas of celebrating *communal worship as God's invitation to become more fully human*: God created people to be united with each other in God, the communion of creation in God and God in creation. This is not the erasure of the beauty and uniqueness of each creature, but actually makes possible each person's beautiful peculiarity. God created people in diversity for the beauty of the whole.[7] Unity is not about uniformity, but about being one in Christ. John D. Zizioulas notes that being human is indispensably about being in communion with God and others. This possibility of communion occurs first through baptism.[8] This calls for the church to become the body of Christ without fighting, discord, or fissure. Members of the body must never work against the Spirit of unity, lest they become agents of destructive division.

## A Covenant Renewal of the Entire Church

Similar to every Lord's Supper, each baptismal celebration is not simply about what is happening to the person in front getting wet but also about inviting the entire congregation to remember and reaffirm the covenants they made at baptism. The baptismal liturgy in the *Book of Common Prayer* provides space for people who have previously been baptized to stand and give testimony to publically reaffirm their baptisms.[9] This testimony of reaffirmation can include standing during the pledge of faith and offering a personal testimony. This remembrance of one's baptism is also celebrated through the use of baptismal fonts at the back of sanctuaries in some traditions. As people come or leave communal worship, they are invited to dip their hands into the waters and place their dripping fingers on their heads with an attitude of prayer, "By the power of the Holy Spirit may I remember and be thankful by living into the baptism that heals, transforms, and is making me more fully human." Because baptism is a renewal of the church and since people do not belong to a generic church, but to a particular local congregation, the taking in of members is a proper concluding part of a baptismal service.

## The Ordination of Laity to Become God's Priests to the World

Every baptism is a celebration not only of God's healing of people in the church but also of a Christian's ordination into the ministry and mission of the church, Christ's body in the world.[10] In section I the ordination of pastors and priests for leadership in the church was discussed. Yet all Christians are called and ordained to become ministers to the world, offering and proclaiming the good news. This ordination of the laity occurs at baptism and celebrates the priesthood of all believers. All Christians are being healed so that through them

God's healing ministry of reconciliation may spread like an epidemic throughout all the earth. As Christian baptism is a healing and incorporation into the body of Christ, God also offers empowerment and vocation to continue the ministry of Christ in the world.

## Pastoral and Theological Issues Concerning Baptism

Within the beauty of baptism, there are some pastoral and theological issues needing attention. First, the church has strongly encouraged the inclusion of education, discipleship, and mentoring as part of this healing sacrament of initiation. Second, there is much confusion between infant baptism and infant dedication. Third, there must be a proper response to people who have been baptized previously and who (for a variety of reasons) want to be baptized again. Finally, it is essential to understand the process of initiating people into the community of faith from catechism to the actual communal worship event of baptism. The chapter will explore each of these issues, beginning first with education and catechism and continuing with the similarities and distinctions between infant baptism and dedication.

### Formal and Ongoing Catechism (Discipleship)

The importance of education is vital for the continual formation of Christians. The word *katēchēsis* literally means "instruction by word of mouth often through questioning and answering." Catechism is the church's process of teaching, habituating, and forming people into the Christian faith. What has been called catechism is similar to what others call discipleship. There is often a formal catechism for people preparing for baptism or membership. This formal catechism is often organized within a set time frame with a sponsor, mentor, or godparent. People preparing for baptism are often named catechumens (literally, those who are receiving instruction) and this time of training, forming, and nurturing is called the catechumenate.

### Catechumenate

In the early third through fifth centuries church leaders developed a period of preparing for baptism called the catechumenate. The teaching during the catechumenate was not simply about learning information but about receiving a fuller and richer immersion into the Christian narrative. In some parts of the church this catechumenate lasted over three years. The length of the catechumenate depended not so much on the amount of training material as it did discerning how serious the catechumens were about their commitment to God. The catechumenate regularly included times of prayer, instruction, and communal worship with a sponsor or mentor. When people were deemed ready for baptism, they would be enrolled in an intensive forty-day period of spiritual preparation for the proper reception of the sacrament offered at Easter.

Catechism has an intention similar to that of Sunday school and Bible studies. The goal of catechism/discipleship is not to pass a written test but to help form the imagination and habituate people who are being and becoming more fully human in the Christian narrative.

What about today? There should be an intentional catechism/discipleship for children and adults seeking baptism and for children/adolescents who have been baptized as infants. Education and formation is about being further formed into the people of God. While catechism will lead to the baptism of adults, teens, and children, people who were baptized as infants can find the culmination of their initiation into the church at confirmation after their formal catechism.

We live in a culture that has lost the discipline of patience. "I want to be baptized right now." Pastors must resist altering practices simply to appease the wishes of sincere believers. The church must remember that people do not get to decide when they are ready; rather, the church must come alongside people with training, guidance, and mentoring to help them more fully embrace the gift and commitments of the Christian covenant, including the healing that comes with being initiated into the church. No one would recommend to a couple that they should get married spontaneously, without preparation or time to consider the blessings, costs, and commitments of the covenant they were entering. Similarly, catechism, Sunday school, Bible studies, and accountability groups all assist in training and habituating people into the Christian covenant.

## Ongoing Catechism

For all Christians catechism/discipleship never ceases. The Christian journey is one of continual learning, formation, and renewal into the image of God. In this way catechism and being trained up in the faith is ongoing. This ongoing catechism celebrates how fellowship and training in the church become the dynamic way Christians continue to grow and mature in the faith. Baptism is not an isolated event but part of the process of initiation that participates in the ongoing healing of people who are becoming more fully human in the body of Christ.

### Infant Baptism

The church has a long history of baptizing infants, even though there has not been uniformity in thought and practice. Although infant baptism has not been universally practiced by Protestants, the practice of baptizing infants draws upon a rich theology of healing. As a Wesleyan, I want to consider what infant baptism is by first suggesting what it is not.

## Infant Baptism Is Not . . .

### Protecting Young Children from Hell

Within the beautiful tradition of infant baptism there were some motivations that have been employed by Christians that Wesleyans should avoid. Some Christians who affirmed with conviction the pervasive and total disease of original sin (that all people are born into and have inherited the guilt and penalty of sin) were fearful that if babies died before being baptized, they would suffer eternal damnation.

In Christian tradition a number of people affirmed that baptism "cancels the guilt of original sin."[11] While it was believed the guilt of original sin was cancelled, the propensity to sin was not.[12] It was thought that if infants died with the guilt of original sin, they would be condemned to hell. Baptizing to ensure infants would not go to hell aided the reduction of the baptismal imagination to the remission of the guilt of original sin.[13]

John Wesley is not entirely consistent on this issue. In a "Treatise on Baptism" (1758) he affirms that the guilt of original sin is washed away at baptism.[14] Later in Wesley's career while debating with Calvinist predestinarians about the universality of the atonement, he "ultimately declared that any inherited human guilt was universally cancelled *at birth*, as one benefit of Christ's redemption. In effect, his concession of inherited guilt was now annulled by the invocation of Prevenient Grace."[15] In other words, Wesley felt it was not baptism but prevenient grace that cancelled the guilt of original sin at birth. It is crucial to clarify that while prevenient grace cancels the inherited guilt of original sin for Wesley, prevenient grace is not *offered* at baptism but *proclaimed* most powerfully in infant baptism.

---

Prevenient grace is God's *coming before* to all people that *all* may find life.[16] Prevenient grace affirms that God reaches out to all people to woo and draw them to God before any person acts on his or her own accord. God always seeks and initiates healing and redemption. Any response people offer to God is only possible because God has made the first move and has also empowered that response. Prevenient grace is offered to all people and empowers any and all responses to God's initiatives to healing and life.

Thus Wesleyans do not baptize people, especially infants, out of the fear that if they die unbaptized, they will go to hell. Wesleyans have long affirmed that people who have not reached accountability are not morally responsible and that if they die, God will not condemn such people to hell. "Therefore no infant [baptized or not] ever was, or ever will be, 'sent to hell for the guilt of Adam's sin;' seeing it is cancelled by the righteousness of Christ, as soon as they are sent into the world."[17]

Guaranteeing People Will Go to Heaven

Within the blessing of baptism, being baptized as an adult or infant does not guarantee that a person has secured his or her eternal destiny. In fact, John Wesley recalled that as a child, his poor behavior chipped away at the grace extended at baptism.[18] For a Wesleyan then, baptism is not to be considered some human work achieving or securing an eternal destiny. The work of God in Christ by the Spirit is the only means of salvation. However, people must respond continually to the Spirit's healing work as they journey in life.

Denying the "Choice" of the Person

Wesleyans, in affirming infant baptism, are not denying the importance of each person's response of faith to God. For Protestants this is perhaps one of the greatest theological challenges to infant baptism. The Anabaptists strongly affirmed God's healing in baptism but did not allow infants to be baptized because they felt that infants could not fully confess and repent. In the Anabaptist tradition, people could only be baptized if they had been catechized (trained in the Christian history and doctrines) and professed repentance.[19] For Wesleyans, although the infant is not choosing on his or her own to be in the covenant, the church and parents are choosing on his or her behalf. Meanwhile, each infant must be trained and raised in the church.

For Christians baptized as infants, the importance of catechism and confirmation offers them at some point in their lives an opportunity to affirm the baptismal covenant into which the church ushered them and for the church to *confirm* their training and testimony.[20] For the baptized infant, "repentance is necessary in this development all along the way."[21] All parents make choices for their children early on regardless of the will of the child; this is called parenting. However, all parents realize that their influence over the formation of their children begins to lessen and lessen as the child grows and hopefully matures. Infant baptism does not deny the importance of each person responding to God's call just as people baptized as adults must continue to respond to God's invitation to healing throughout their lives.

Some people also believe that the sacraments are only "valid" if they are received by faith. Rob Staples notes that "*Faith does not constitute baptism but receives it.* Baptism summons us to faith."[22] Remember, baptism celebrates what God is doing and inviting the church to be and become. At baptism God is offering infants and adults the faith to respond to God's continual healing as they grow and mature from this birth. However, this does not deny the importance of faith that God has already offered to the church. At child, teen, and adult baptisms, the person comes already having responded to God's saving initiatives in his or her life, seeking God's further healing and faith. In infant baptism, the church (including parents and godparents) brings the infant in faith to God. This distinction of faith is worthy of attention to guard against confusion. In this way, the full benefits and healing of baptism are not realized in the infant until he or she responds in faith to God's healing initiatives.

## Infant Baptism Celebrates . . .

God Makes the First Move

God moving toward us first is the emphasis and celebration of prevenient grace. In many ways this is the greatest strength of the practice of infant baptism. When infants are baptized, the entire congregation is reminded that we did not choose God but that God first chose us. In this way, infant baptism embodies and celebrates *prevenient grace*, that God has made the first move of love, the first move of healing, the first move of reconciliation. Infant baptism is thus a sacrament of healing for the entire congregation. Note again, prevenient grace is offered to all at birth and is therefore not offered at baptism, but fully proclaimed in infant baptism for all the church to remember, celebrate, and live into. In this manner adult and infant baptism are the same—God makes the first moves of healing. Infant baptism, in many ways better than believer's baptism, leaves no room for the idea that by works one is saved. However, despite the strength of emphasizing salvation through grace alone that infant baptism brings, there will still be those who want to emphasize and celebrate the active faith of the baptized and who therefore prefer adult (believers') baptism.

God Desires to Be in Covenant with Children

When the disciples tried to keep the children away, Jesus commanded the disciples to let the children come to him (Luke 18:16). Not only does Jesus desire relationship but he also warns those who lead children astray and holds a child up as the model of faith.[23]

I do not recall ever being outside the church. My "choice" was not to join the church but to remain within the church. Infant baptism celebrates that children can begin their lives only knowing life in the body of Christ. What a great beginning. Such a beginning does not guarantee a child will not leave; however, countless sociological studies mention the importance of children coming to faith early as a strong factor in their faith as adults. Infant baptism celebrates that from the child's first days on the earth he or she is loved and included as a part of the body of Christ.

God Offers Healing to Infants

As Wesleyans, the healing and forgiveness God offers to infants in baptism needs further discussion. Because God offers prevenient grace to all, Wesleyans affirm that God is wooing and loving all people, baptized and unbaptized. Since infants cannot respond properly to all the benefits of salvation, how can the church imagine the healing offered to infants at baptism? Just as for adults, infants are marked as God's and brought into the body of Christ, a place of healing, formation, and nurture. These infants are initiated into God's covenant people. What a tremendous gift! As God offers healing to the infants at baptism, they are empowered to keep responding to God's initiatives of healing as they grow and mature. Moreover, it must not be lost that infant baptism is also a crucial event for the local church in affirming that God makes the first move.

Wesley's Encouragement of Infant Baptism

John Wesley encouraged the baptizing of infants even as the motivations for doing so were nuanced throughout his life.[24] In arguing the case for infant baptism Wesley drew upon Deut. 29:10-13:

You stand assembled today, all of you, before the LORD your God—the leaders of your tribes, your elders, and your officials, all the men of Israel, your children, your women, and the aliens who are in your camp, both those who cut your wood and those who draw your water—to enter into the covenant of the LORD your God, sworn by an oath, which the LORD your God is making with you today; in order that he may establish you today as his people, and that he may be your God, as he promised you and as he swore to your ancestors, to Abraham, to Isaac, and to Jacob.

Baptism replaces circumcision for Christians. Circumcision was practiced on infant males and would have been seen appropriate for children as their entrance into the covenant with God as a member of God's people. Moreover, several New Testament passages indicate that *households* were baptized and thus would have included children.[25] Church tradition offers a compelling case for the practice of infant baptism, including an imagination of being Christian as a part of the body of Christ and not some isolated pilgrimage. Infant baptism proclaims God's initiative in salvation that seeks and empowers any person's response *to God's invitation to become fully human.*

Along with this compelling case, there are many within the Christian tradition who assert that baptism is most properly only for those who can respond themselves to God's initiatives of faith and healing. While such logic is reasonable, such an emphasis on "my choosing" tends to reinforce an individualistic Christianity outside the church. Believers' baptisms certainly do not need to do so, but care and caution must be given.

## Challenges and Requirements for Infant Baptism

Importance of Church and Family

The church has a long tradition of not baptizing infants of families who are not actively participating in the life of the church. This practice is not elitist (although church history is full of sad stories where restricting sacraments was abused for unholy reasons) but an affirmation that children are to be nurtured and educated in the faith into which they have been initiated.

The role of godparents in the Roman Catholic tradition is comparable to the part played by Sunday school teachers, mentors, children, and youth pastors. Such people are those outside a child's biological family who join the family in taking up the calling to help raise the child in the ways of the Lord (see Prov. 22:6). This training and nurturing by parents, godparents, teachers, mentors, and pastors should be seen as the church's calling and commitment to the vow made at the infant's baptism. In many infant baptismal liturgies the parents, godparents, and congregation are invited to vow, "Will you be responsible for seeing that the child you present is brought up in the Christian faith and life?"

All baptisms require commitment. For an infant, the church and parents are making a commitment to raise this child in an environment of faith. Rob Staples observes, "Baptism is always an act that demands commitment, either from the candidates themselves or from someone who assumes responsibility for leading them toward maturity in faith."[26] Staples is emphasizing that just as in adult baptism, commitment is also required at infant baptism. Although the celebration of God's healing at baptism continues for a lifetime, the church recognizes one of its callings is the training, nurturing, and disciplining of those whom God has brought to each local congregation, no matter the age at their entrance. James White notes that in some sense "the entire church is a sponsor."[27]

The Confirmation of Baptism vs. Rebaptism

In infant baptism, the child's will is taken up by the parents and church. The child does not choose to be in the covenant of the community of faith any more than the child chooses first to be loved by God or his or her parents. As mentioned earlier, infant baptism does not replace the significance of the child repenting of his or her sins and seeking God's continual healing and forgiveness. The infant's will is not simply being overrun but being formed and powerfully shaped by God. Furthermore, a person baptized as an infant does not choose to join the church in those moments but eventually will choose to stay or leave. One profound event of choosing to remain in covenant with God in the church occurs during confirmation.

"Confirmation," according to one church, "includes three aspects: a) God confirms the divine promise to those who were too young to grasp what God was doing in their baptism, b) they respond by professing their own acceptance of the grace they have received and their own faith in Christ, c) the Church, as represented by [the local] congregation, confirms the commitments they make."[28] At confirmation people declare their desire to accept in thanksgiving the gift of being brought into the community of faith, recognize their need for God's continual healing and forgiveness, and make a commitment to continue to live into the covenant with God and the body of Christ. Furthermore, confirmation names and celebrates the faithfulness of God's presence in a person's life in the past, present, and future. The local church also bears witness and can testify to the truthfulness of this person's profession of faith.

Confirmation of those baptized as infants is often a process that includes a specific period of catechism along with a mentor, such as a parent, godparent, or sponsor. Infant baptism, catechism, confirmation, and the celebration of the Lord's Supper, while separated by the calendar, are all seen together as the way by which people are initiated into the church. While most Protestants have not joined the Roman Catholic Church in naming confirmation as a sacrament, certainly confirmation should be viewed as an event of further healing by God and growth of people becoming more fully human as part of the body of Christ. The emphasis of all the practices of Christian initiation is quite simple: *Christians are not born; they are made. God, by the power of the Spirit, through the life, death, and resurrection of Jesus, in the church makes Christians.*

Unfortunately, many parts of evangelical Protestantism are not practicing confirmation. Often people who were baptized as infants do not "remember" the actual event of baptism. This lack of memory is not the fault of the person baptized, but local churches must be more intentional in the ongoing formation and discipleship of their children and youth by assisting their memories. This lack of memory is not about a person failing to recall events during his or her first year but failing to appreciate the full story into which infant baptism brought him or her in. This failure of memory often leads to a limited baptismal imagination for those who have been baptized as infants.

A young woman who was baptized as an infant came into my office with a question that was really more of a request. "Pastor, I was baptized as an infant. I do not remember it. I had many years away from God, but now that I have decided to really live for God, I want to be baptized again to tell everyone that I am now really committed to loving God passionately for the first time in my life." Many pastors have faced this issue. Most evangelical churches offer a simple response: "Absolutely, we will baptize you again, since this time you mean it." Many who rebaptize are often local churches that do not celebrate or really appreciate infant baptism and so have little caution about rebaptizing.

People should not be baptized again, since at baptism God has already marked those people as part of the covenant, the body of Christ. God does not need to mark them a second time, and God will always be faithful to the covenant. Sadly, rebaptizing demonstrates a level of ignorance about the full imagination of Christian baptism. The issue, like most in pastoral ministry, is more than simply theological. A sincere and devoted follower of Christ desires to celebrate what God is doing in her life. She is wanting and perhaps needing to make a bold public declaration to celebrate the *new* life she is experiencing in God. This desire for a public profession and testimony is right and true. The desire for an event of "memory" to profess her faith and trust in God should be honored. The good news is that the church can provide such a worship event without rebaptizing. She can confirm or reaffirm her baptism.

While there is often one formal confirmation of people who have been baptized as infants, usually performed during a person's adolescence, every baptism is an opportunity for all people who have been previously baptized to *reaffirm* their baptisms. A *reaffirmation* is similar to the practice of people married for many years who renew their vows at an anniversary celebration. Every baptism should thus provide space for people in the congregation to stand and publically proclaim the goodness and grace of God and their desire to remain in God's covenant.

Again, people should not and do not need to be rebaptized. Remember, baptism is a celebration of what God is doing, not what I am doing. Essentially to rebaptize is to tell God, "I am sorry you were not quite good enough the first time, so I need you to really make sure your healing sticks this time." No pastor or believer is explicitly intending this, but this is precisely what rebaptism is saying. Moreover, rebaptisms tend to deemphasize the divine activity in baptism and make the person who wants to be baptized the main actor.

Pastors must refrain from always doing what people think they want. It is likely the young woman requesting rebaptism had never heard or seen a dynamic confirmation of baptism and thus could only imagine a baptism where she could testify to God's great work already done. In some cases, those baptized as infants also went through confirmation in their youth but often do not find that memory satisfying. If a person has already been confirmed, the church would have to provide space for that person to stand before the congregation and reaffirm his or her baptism as a testimony of God's faithfulness and his or her desire to remain in the covenant he or she was initiated into so long ago.

In the case of the young woman, through her reaffirmation she would become a living testimony to the power of the baptism of infants. God's healing presence (grace) had remained constant, always seeking after and wooing her even during seasons of her life when she intentionally was saying no to God. God never gives up on us. Through it all, God had kept on saying yes to her. God had continued to affirm her in love, wooing and calling her back. Yet since she most properly said yes to this covenant, new healing has been made possible in her life. This woman's story is an example of the power, hope, and healing of God in infant baptism. The other good news is that people can reaffirm their baptisms often. The reaffirmation of baptism is a testimony celebrating both the power of God's healing work from the past to the present along with a person's commitment and openness to offer himself or herself to God through confession, surrender, and repentance.

I cannot urge churches strongly enough to stop the practice of rebaptizing and instead embrace the practice of offering confirmation for people baptized as infants as the completion of their initiation into the church. Furthermore, there should be space in every baptismal liturgy for any in the congregation who would like to reaffirm their baptism to do so. Every movement of the people by the Spirit, breathing them into worship and then blowing them out, comes in through the waters and leaves by the waters of healing and renewal.

### Infant Dedication

Zwingli suggested that "water-baptism is nothing but an external ceremony, that is, an outward sign that we are incorporated and engrafted into the Lord Jesus Christ and pledged to live to him and follow him."[29] James White notes that "Zwingli's concept of baptism as dedication, as pledge, or as covenant sign, tends to make of it an external matter of record rather than the source of a warm inward relationship."[30] White suggests that Zwingli helped set a trajectory for a rite of dedication.

While the precise history of dedications is a bit murky, eventually water stopped being used and the term "baptism" was replaced by "dedication." The practice of dedication consists of parents who bring children to church and give them back to God, recognizing that each child is a gift from God. Children are dedicated to God. In many ways dedication celebrates a primary Christian conviction that a true reception of life and gifts from God involves giving those gifts back to God. Since children are received from God as gifts, the act of dedication affirms that children are not "ours"; rather, parents and the local church offer them back to God while also assuming the responsibility of stewards to raise God's children in the ways they should go. During a dedication ritual the parents and often the congregation pledge to train, raise, nurture, and habituate the children in the faith so that one day each child might choose to profess faith in Christ. On this point, there is a great deal of similarity between infant baptism and dedication.

A major distinction of dedication from baptism is that the emphasis resides solely on the parents (and perhaps the local church) who are vowing to raise their child in the ways of God. In this sense, dedication is not a sacrament as is infant baptism because God is not being asked or invited to do anything.

## Dedication or Baptism?

So what should people do? Some denominations allow both practices. Pastors would do well in counseling families about the distinctions between the two. In infant baptism God marks children and brings them into God's covenant people, the church. Infants baptized are empowered by God to respond to God's healing initiatives as they grow and mature in the faith as part of the body of Christ. Those who practice infant baptism celebrate how these children have been marked by God and brought into the church by *water and the Spirit*. Dedicating children can also be a powerful step of faith and trust for the family who desires to publically vow to raise their children along with seeking the church's help in doing so.

Every context is different. While infant baptism may be preferable in some contexts, others may find dedication to be a more faithful way of participating in God's "making Christians." In both cases, what must be shared is the recognition that families and churches accept the charge in the raising, nurturing, and training of people so that one day they can publically respond to God's healing by a profession of faith.

Concerning these practices here are some suggestions to help educate congregations in the practices of infant baptism and dedication.

### Avoid the Confusion Between Dedication and Baptism

Some churches that have practiced dedication are now also beginning to practice infant baptism. The dedication and baptismal liturgies offered are often so similar they claim a distinction but are without a difference. While one child gets wet and another gets a rose or Bible, worship leaders need to offer education and liturgies that recognize the distinction between the two. Rob Staples notes the confusion when pastors anoint with oil children who are being dedicated.[31]

Somehow the oil is trying to compete and offset getting wet, and the confusion between the two is further complicated.

Avoid the Confusion Between Baptism and Church Membership

It is proper for worship services that celebrate baptisms to also take in local church members. However, while this practice is recommended, education is essential to guard against confusion. What is the difference? Church membership is a rite where individuals offer a confession of faith and a pledge to uphold and support the doctrines of that denomination and/or local church. Christian baptism is about initiation, but it is not simply initiation into this local church but into the church catholic (universal).

## How Are the Dedicated and Baptized Infants Different?

So what is the difference between an infant that is baptized versus a child dedicated? Since infants who are baptized still need to confess their sins and confirm their baptism, why not have them wait until they can make their own choices?

As just noted, all that dedication imagines is included in the vow by the parents at infant baptism and yet infant baptism also celebrates God's further healing by marking and initiating infants into the church. Theologically and spiritually, infants baptized are more properly a part of the people of God. Moreover, the grace (God's healing presence) offered at baptism is a celebration of the church and not only of the child. Furthermore, for Wesleyans, as is true for all sacraments, the grace God offers at baptism will empower people to better respond to God's healing initiatives as they grow. This does not guarantee anything or speak against the efficacy of God's work in children in the church who are not baptized. The issue is not which children God loves more or is more present to but how the healing grace extended at baptism offers new possibilities to those baptized.

## Recommendations

- Local congregations are often in need of training and education to help imagine the similarities of infant baptism with infant dedication.
- Pastors in the Wesleyan tradition should educate and offer both options of infant baptism and dedication to parents.
- For infants who have been baptized and all other people seeking baptism, there should be an intentional training and discipleship (catechism) along with a mentor or sponsor (godparent).
- People baptized as infants, after catechism, should celebrate confirmation as part of a regular baptismal service, when the church, family, and believer discern the time is right.
- People should never be rebaptized but instead offered an opportunity to be confirmed or, if already confirmed, permitted space to publically reaffirm their baptisms.

- Dedication should be an option for congregations who believe baptism is for people who can respond personally to God's healing initiatives. Along with this, as soon as a child desires to be baptized, the church should baptize only if some form of catechism and sponsor is employed. The caution here has to do with making baptism only available to children who cognitively can "master the meaning of baptism." Such restrictions should be avoided.

Through the waters of baptism, God's healing flows. These healing waters are the initiation into the church God is redeeming and drawing to Godself. Being brought into such a community is a primary means by which people *can become more fully human*. The baptism of infants and adults is a celebration for the church of what God is doing in the community. Baptism is a means by which God continues to offer the gift of new life.

## Questions for Discussion and Reflection

1. What ideas were the most helpful in this chapter?

2. What ideas are the most difficult or causing the greatest amount of tension?

3. If asked, how would your congregation describe the importance of baptism?

4. What are some ways to help educate and guide your local congregation into a richer imagination of baptism?

5. Does your church practice rebaptism? Do you find this chapter's argument against rebaptism compelling or not?

6. Is there a formal catechism for people in the church?

7. Does your church's current baptismal liturgy provide an opportunity for confirmation of a person's baptism?

## NINETEEN
# THE CELEBRATION OF BAPTISM IN WORSHIP

Drawing upon the theology of baptism previously mentioned, this chapter offers some practical suggestions for baptismal celebrations. This chapter will also explore baptismal liturgies that include elements for people who desire to confirm their baptisms. Before looking specifically at the liturgies, attention will be given to when and how baptisms should be celebrated.

## Baptismal Preparation

### When in the Church Year

A survey of early baptismal liturgies and writings indicates that most Christian baptisms occurred during the Easter Vigil.[1] The initiates were baptized and anointed with oil by the bishop, symbolically declaring that they had been signed and sealed by the Holy Spirit. They were then escorted to worship where they were brought to the eucharistic Table for the first time. "The Easter Vigil was the night of nights, the church's annual celebration of the death and resurrection of the Lord, manifested concretely in the new Christians who died and rose in baptism."[2] Following these events the baptized would enter a time of further training and contemplation in the mysteries of the faith called *mystagogias*. This additional formation provided more time to consider the implications of the calling to completely live into the responsibilities of full membership in the body of Christ.

When possible, continuing the tradition of Easter baptisms seems appropriate. However, other traditional days for baptism include Pentecost, the Easter season, All Saints Day, and Baptism of the Lord Sunday. Even taking into consideration the importance of baptism's offering of healing, forgiveness, and initiation into the church, those who do not have the opportunity to be baptized are not automatically condemned to eternal damnation. However, pastoral situations do arise in which baptizing remains faithful to the tradition even though it occurs outside the ordinary scheduled times (e.g., in times of severe illness).[3]

## Components of Baptismal Liturgies

*Public*

There was a season in the medieval church when private baptisms were performed. This practice has largely been condemned. Baptisms are not private individual events but public celebrations for the entire church. Baptisms should be performed within a regular Sunday congregational service. As baptism is a celebration for the entire church, the entire congregation's presence is vital. This does not preclude such services from happening outside sanctuaries, but if river or pool baptisms are chosen, accommodations should be made for the entire congregation to be present.

*Focus on Water*

The Roman Catholic practice of baptism involved many actions in addition to getting wet (being drowned to the sinful nature), including the anointing with oil, offering the sign of the cross, and the giving of a lighted candle. Many Protestants who were committed only to doing what is taught in Scripture began to focus exclusively on pouring, sprinkling, or immersing with water. Because of the liturgical renewal of the past forty to fifty years, some aspects of the baptismal ritual are being recovered. Some cautions at this point are in order. Accompanied with the proper understanding, such recoveries can become extremely meaningful and formative. But care should be taken when classic practices are recovered simply as a "cool" novelty.

Call to Worship
Collect
Song of Praise
Prayer of
     Illumination
     (or earlier)
Old Testament
     Reading
Sing the Psalm
Epistle Lesson
Hymn of
     Thanksgiving
Gospel Reading
Sermon
Confession and
     Pardon
**Baptism**
Creed
Peace of Christ
Prayers of the
     People
Offering
Doxology
Lord's Supper
Benediction:
     Sending
     Forth

*In Service of Word and Table*

Baptism is a culminating act of response to the Word and thus should be included in the service of the Word after the sermon. It also makes liturgical sense that it follows the confession and pardon. Most baptismal liturgies include the Apostles' Creed, which is to be affirmed by the candidates and should be confessed by the entire congregation. Note that it does precede the offering of the peace of Christ. This sequence follows the Christian tradition in which people who were baptized were welcomed into the community through the kiss of peace. The baptismal imagination can affirm those who come out of the water and are then greeted by fellow brothers and sisters with the peace of Christ, a wonderful liturgical space where God is renewing the bonds in the local church community.

*The* Book of Common Prayer *Baptismal Template*

The ritual considered in this section is from the *Book of Common Prayer*, one liturgical resource to draw from if a church's denominational affiliation does not regulate its liturgies. This liturgy provides a template from which theological contextualization is appropriate and necessary.[4] Along with this encouragement for contextualization a caution must also be offered. Contextualization cannot simply be reduced to "what seems cool to us" or "what we want to do." There is a need for the primary theologians and liturgists of a denomination or local church to consider the sacraments and liturgies from the perspective of church history. From such an informed position, discernment and careful theological considerations can become the lens through which liturgical and ritual decisions can be made. Dangers exist on both sides. One is a blind adherence to rituals that have been handed down for generations; the other extreme is a preference for the novel on the basis that it is the most "relevant."

What follows is a full baptismal liturgy that offers a Christian imagination of the healing, cleansing, and birthing of individuals to become *more fully human.*

### A. Presentation of Candidate and Desire to Be Baptized

For adults and children, sponsors first present the adults and older children, which is followed by a response by the candidates (catechumens) acknowledging their desire to be baptized. In cases of infants, parents or godparents present the infant to receive baptism. When presenting the infants for baptism, parents and godparents also vow to bring the child up in the witness of full Christian faith and life.

### B. Renunciations

The candidates (parents and godparents speak on behalf of infants and younger children) are then asked to renounce Satan, evil powers, and sinful desires. This renunciation is followed by asking the candidates if they seek to turn to Jesus Christ as Savior. Such renouncing and pledges should be imagined as political vows of commitment. These vows are political because those seeking baptism are pledging their primary allegiance and loyalty to God and God's kingdom as members of the body of Christ (a body politic). In renouncing evil with the desire to turn toward Christ, people are offering themselves to Christ and the church as a vow to *become more fully human.*

### C. Confirmation and Reaffirmation

At this time people are presented who desire to confirm their baptisms (those baptized as infants) and people who desire to reaffirm their baptismal vows (those previously baptized). Those desiring confirmation are also asked if they renounce evil and seek to renew their commitment to Jesus Christ. While every baptism is an opportunity for all in the local church to reaffirm their baptisms, some may wish to come forward to make their reaffirmation more explicit. For clarification, *confirmation* emphasizes the first public profession of a person who renews the vows, promises, and covenants made on his or her behalf at infant baptism. *Reaffirmation* is a time when a person commits again to live into the grace and covenants promised at baptism. Like baptism, people only need to confirm their baptism once, while people are invited to reaffirm their baptism at every celebration of baptism.

## D. The Congregation's Pledge

Not only is baptism a cleansing, healing, and sealing, but it is also birth into the church. The local congregation is thus invited to join the parents, godparents, and sponsors and pledge to support the people confirming their baptism or being baptized. The overarching emphasis in baptism is a celebration of what God is doing; however, the understanding must not be lost that baptisms occur in the midst of the church and people whom God has been and is continuing to heal and make more fully human. While God's healing grace is offered, the church's role to support, encourage, and nurture the healing extended at baptism must remain in focus. In this way Christianity is never understood as a private, personal spiritual journey. People are becoming more fully human (Christian) in the community of faith, together. By the power of the Holy Spirit, members of the body must support, encourage, and build each other up in the faith (see 1 Thess. 5:11).

## E. Baptismal Covenant

The baptismal covenant is the confession of the Apostles' Creed, along with pledges for continual instruction in the church, participation in the sacrament of the Lord's Supper, and prayer. Moreover, the candidates pledge to persevere in the resistance of evil. When sin occurs, candidates commit to confess, repent, and seek God's further healing. Candidates also pledge a love for God and neighbor in which all people may receive justice and peace. This is a commitment to live into God's healing as renewal in the *image of God*, a renewal and healing to *become more fully human*. Also noteworthy is that the candidate's response is always a divine-human synergy (working together), "I will, with God's help."[5] While God provides the empowerment, people are healed enough so as to respond well to God's healing initiatives.

## F. Prayers for the Candidates

The *Book of Common Prayer* offers a prayer seeking God's continual deliverance and protection.[6] The verbs of the prayer illumines the continual work of God in baptism and beyond: "deliver them," "open their hearts," "fill them with your Spirit," "keep them in the faith," "teach them to love," "send them into the world," "bring them to the fullness of your peace and glory." These verbs highlight the ongoing work of the Holy Spirit to further the healing of becoming more fully human, which includes ministry not only in the world but also in all of creation as it moves toward the full glory of God. This entire conversation is considering the imagination of God's healing of creation through worship—this healing to become more fully human—as a renewal of people into the image of God, which consists of a love for God, oneself, and others, being loved, and a care for creation. This healing and renewal is not for people simply to celebrate their individual humanity. All of God's healing and redemption in the world moves toward the full glory of God, as imagined by Paul, where God will be all in all. The glory of God is an invitation into the very imagination where all of creation more fully glorifies God in the very breath of the triune Godhead.

### G. Thanksgiving over the Water

This thanksgiving begins with a proper *remembrance of* how God has used water to offer freedom to Israel out of their bondage. This remembering also includes the baptism of Jesus by John and the anointing of Jesus by the Holy Spirit.[7] It is through Jesus that the church is invited to be baptized with him into his death so that the church may also be raised with him, released from the bondage of sin to everlasting life (see Rom. 6:3-11). After this thanksgiving, the celebrant (priest or pastor) asks that through the water the Holy Spirit may cleanse people from sin that they may be born again and continue into the resurrected life of Jesus Christ. The *Book of Common Prayer* also makes provision for the consecration of oil called the chrism. This anointing with oil follows a long Christian tradition that symbolically emphasizes that in baptism the Holy Spirit will seal people to share in the priesthood of Jesus Christ. As noted above, every baptism is the ordination of every Christian to become a minister of the gospel to the world, embodying and proclaiming the good news of salvation. This ordination is part of the emphasis on the priesthood of all believers.

### H. A Triune Baptism

Christian baptisms include baptizing in the name of the Father, Son, and the Holy Spirit. The celebrant offers another prayer asking that God may forgive and sustain people by the power of the Holy Spirit.[8]

### I. Pouring, Sprinkling, Immersion

While some parts of Christianity prefer one mode over another, in the Wesleyan tradition all three should be considered as appropriate means of baptism. All three have the rich biblical symbolism of healing, washing, and cleansing.

### J. Postbaptismal Actions

Some liturgies include offering a prayer of thanksgiving for new life, acts of anointing with oil, laying on of hands, and offering the sign of the cross. Such actions should not be considered a backup plan as if the water at baptism is insufficient; rather they name the full implications of the full imagination of Christian baptism. These actions make visible the promise and healing offered at baptism.

### K. Welcoming the Newly Baptized

After all have been baptized, the celebrant welcomes the baptized into the household of God as those confessing Christ, proclaiming the resurrection, and sharing in the priestly ministry the church is called to participate in as the body of Christ.

### L. Peace of Christ

As those who have been brought into the body of Christ, the newly baptized are welcomed by giving and receiving the peace of Christ.

### M. Culminating in the Lord's Supper

Later it will be observed that the Lord's Supper is the *meal of the baptized*. As such it is the *ordinary* practice that one of the first actions the church offers to the baptized is the meal that will sustain them in their Christian journey.[9] In this way the Lord's Supper is the culmination of the acts of initiation into the church.

The sacrament of baptism is both a death and resurrection. It is a death to the power, dominion, and disease of sin in a person as well as a further healing of the world. Along with being a death, a drowning, it is also a time of resurrection and new life as people emerge from the waters healed, cleansed as members in the body of Christ. While there are continual debates among Christians about a variety of matters concerning baptism, emphasis on God's healing activity and a person's entrance into the community of faith should become a proper and shared imagination of the healing of baptism from infants to adults. The baptismal imagination offers a hope, covenant, and promise far beyond an individual's public testimony of what God has already done. Together with the healing and prevenient grace of the Holy Spirit celebrated at baptism, Christian baptism celebrates a dynamic healing offered by God, inviting people to *become more fully human.*

## Questions for Discussion and Reflection

1. What ideas were the most helpful in this chapter?

2. What ideas are the most difficult or causing the greatest amount of tension?

3. What is the current practice of celebrating the sacrament of baptism in your local congregation? Specifically, what liturgy is used?

4. What are some ideas or practices raised in this chapter that may be worth exploring?

# TWENTY

# THE LORD'S SUPPER: THE RENEWAL OF THE CHURCH AS THE BODY OF CHRIST

---

The Lord's Supper, as the service of the Table, is the culmination of the service of the Word. The Lord's Supper is a primary sacrament for people becoming more fully human, for the further healing of creation, and for the further coming of the kingdom of God on earth as in heaven. Similar to baptism, it is a divine-human encounter in which God offers and invites healing and renewal of covenantal relationships. This chapter considers the theological significance of the Lord's Supper as the primary place for Christians to renew their covenant to God and one another. This chapter suggests, first, that the Lord's Supper imagines how God and humans are made present to each other. Second, in this dynamic of *presence* humans are invited to offer themselves as living sacrifices to God as their response of thanksgiving for the offering of Christ for salvation. Third, the Lord's Supper celebrates the renewal of the church with each other and with Christ who is the Head of the body. Fourth, the Lord's Supper heals, transforms, and renews the church as the body of Christ so that the church may be sent out into the world to continue to participate in God's further healing and redemption of creation. The church is sent *by* and *with* the Holy Spirit to continue the doxological ministry of the incarnation. At the Table, the church is renewed as the body of Christ and is sent out to be Christ's broken body and shed blood in the world.

## Presence at the Table

The issue of Christ's *presence* in or around the elements is one of the most intensely debated topics of eucharistic conversation. Unfortunately, the conversation has sadly and ironically caused division and discord in the Christian church. Teams and camps have been pitted against one another. Lost in the conversation is the gift, command, and promise of God to be present. The Roman Catholic Church strongly affirms and celebrates the *real presence of Christ* in the eucharistic gifts of bread and wine. This affirmation is called *transubstantiation*.[1] Many of the

Protestant Reformers were nervous about this position and offered variations of Christ's presence *in* or *around* the elements. Martin Luther strongly affirmed the bodily presence of Christ but did not affirm transubstantiation as the explanation for how Christ was present. Luther asserted that Christ was bodily present *in*, *with*, and *under* the wine and bread, a view that has been named *consubstantiation*.[2]

Ulrich Zwingli strongly challenged Martin Luther and developed what become known as the *memorialist* view. While Zwingli is unfortunately often labeled as having a *doctrine of divine absence*, Zwingli emphasized that as believers remember and commemorate Christ, such a disposition and posture toward Christ offers a kind of spiritual formation in their lives. For Zwingli the emphasis is not on what God is doing but on the response and posture of what humans are to promise and pledge to God. In the memorialist view, the believer is celebrating in faith the importance of Christ's life, death, and resurrection and thus Christ is present in the hearts of the faithful. Staples notes that for Zwingli "Christ is present in the Supper, not in essence or reality, but only by contemplation of faith."[3]

John Calvin, in refuting the Roman Catholic position, also found the views of both Luther and Zwingli incorrect. Calvin emphasized that Christ's physical body was in heaven because it could not be in more than one place and that accordingly the reception of Christ by Christians was that of a spiritual presence. With all of this nuancing, every one of these categories seems to have misplaced the primary emphasis.

### A Wesleyan Doxological Agnosticism

John Wesley's view of Christ's presence is complex and actually takes a few steps back into the realm of mystery. Charles Wesley penned many eucharistic hymns, and with John's approval these hymns were collected in the book *Hymns of the Lord's Supper*. While the Wesleys showed approval for the memorialist view, they go much further, emphasizing that Christ is really present at the Lord's Supper. Through such hymns they affirmed in thanksgiving and praise that Christ is present and worthy of praise (doxological) and, at the same time, remained in wonder and awe (agnostic) as to *how* Christ is present metaphysically. Christ's presence is always a matter of doxology without metaphysical and philosophical definitions. Holding to a doxological agnosticism keeps Christ's presence central without reducing the conversation to how Christ is scientifically present. Christ's presence is a mysterious promise that should not be exhausted by attempting a science of the sacraments.

The Wesleys reflect on this glorious mystery of Christ's presence at the Table in hymn 59 from *Hymns of the Lord's Supper*, which draws on a passage from Daniel Brevint's *The Christian Sacrament and Sacrifice*.[4] Brevint describes the joyful mystery surrounding Christ's eucharistic presence by allegorizing upon the gospel's narrative of Jesus healing the blind man: "Indeed in what manner this is done, I know not; it is enough for me to admire. *One thing I know* (as said the blind man of our Lord), *He laid clay upon mine eyes, and behold I see.*"[5] The Wesleys affirm the following:

> God incomprehensible,
>> Shall man presume to know;
> Fully search him out, or tell
>> His wondrous ways below?
> Him in all his ways we find:
>> *How the means transmit the power;*
> *Here he leaves our thoughts behind,*
>> *And faith inquires no more.*
>
> How he did these creatures raise,
>> And make this bread and wine,
> Organs to convey his grace
>> To this poor soul of mine;
> I cannot the way descry,
>> Need not know the mystery;
> *Only this I know, that I*
>> *Was blind, but now I see.*[6]

This hymn captures well the spirit of doxological agnosticism. While not exhausting the mystery of the manner of Christ's presence, mystery leads to worship—doxology. This hymn proclaims that God reveals all things necessary for healing, namely being seen by and then *seeing* Christ. Somehow the eyes of people are opened so that they are seen by Christ and see Christ, which describes all the illumination needed. Some may find the position of doxological agnosticism as not going far enough in describing *how* Christ is present. While the scholastic categories and the Reformers' conceptions played an important role in history, for today such categories of transubstantiation or consubstantiation are an overreach into what can be discerned and thus doxological agnosticism becomes a most helpful position. The Wesleys strongly affirmed Christ is present at the Lord's Supper.

Doxological agnosticism does not retreat from logic and reason but shows that when responding to the Eucharist, doxology grounds all activity. Christ's presence in this new event always comes as a surprising irruption and yields a doxological joy. Charles writes,

> Sure and real is the grace, the manner be unknown;
> only meet us in thy ways and perfect us in one.
> Let us taste the heavenly powers, Lord, we ask for nothing.
> Thine to bless, 'tis only ours to wonder and adore.[7]

### The Chief Event of Presence

While professing a doxological agnosticism on the metaphysics of Christ's eucharistic presence, the Wesleys argued for the primacy of the eucharistic encounter with Christ by the Spirit. In light of Christ's promise and command, the Eucharist is the *chief* place where Christ may be found.

> If *chiefly* here thou may'st be found,
>> If now, e'en now we find Thee here;
> O let their joys like ours abound!
>> Invite them to the royal cheer;
> Feed with imperishable food,
> And fill their raptur'd souls with God.[8]

The Eucharist is the chief context where Christ and imperishable food will be encountered and offered. Brevint writes, "And thus his Body and Blood have *everywhere*, but *especially* at this Sacrament, a true and Real Presence."[9] Hymn 91 reflects that the imperishable food consumed fills souls with God. Hymn 81 also points out the peculiar and intensified presence at the Table:

> Jesu, we thus obey
>> Thy last and kindest word;
> Here, in thine own appointed way,
>> We come to meet our Lord:
> The way Thou hast enjoin'd,
>> Thou wilt therein appear:
> We come with confidence to find
>> *Thy special presence here.*[10]

The Wesleys affirm the significance and priority of the Eucharist where they encounter "Thy special presence."[11] These two stanzas from hymns 91 and 81 affirm Christ's unique eucharistic presence that offers healing.

The emphasis of Christ's presence is crucial. What is often missed is the emphasis on the Spirit helping the church in being present to Christ. In the Great Thanksgiving (the primary liturgy of the Lord's Supper) a portion of the prayer is called the *epiclesis*. This epiclesis petitions the Father through the power of the Spirit not only that Christ may be present to the church but also that the church may be present to Christ. The eucharistic liturgy in *The United Methodist Hymnal* prays, "Pour out your Holy Spirit on *us* gathered here, and on these gifts of bread and wine. Make them be for us the body and blood of Christ, that we may be for the world the body of Christ, redeemed by his blood."[12] Notice that the prayer is not simply about Christ being present but also about helping to make Christians present. Too often when emphasizing *how* Christ is present, there is great neglect emphasizing *how* the church is to be present. For the church, being present is about humans being fully present to each other and to God. A primary way for Christians to be present to God in the service of Word and Table is through offering themselves as their response of thanksgiving. In this way the Eucharist is a sacrifice.

## The Eucharist as an Oblationary Sacrifice

Along with the Reformers' rejection of the Roman Catholic position on Christ's presence (transubstantiation), most of the Reformers strongly rejected what they understood as the Roman Catholic doctrine of sacrifice in the Lord's Supper. Many Protestants wrongly believe that the Roman position on sacrifice in the Eucharist implies that Christ's sacrifice—his life, death, and resurrection—was insufficient and so God demands more payment. This is not the Roman Catholic position. The Wesleys strongly affirmed that the Lord's Supper is a sacrifice. As a sacrifice, people are not trying to make up for the insufficiency of Christ's sacrifice. Rather, the sacrifice offered at the Lord's Supper is a sacrifice of oblation. An oblation is a thank offering for all that God has done. People, in giving their tithes and offerings, which are placed on the Eucharist Table, are also offering their bodies as living sacrifices. Such an offering is done in thanks and praise to God, not as if it were earning God's mercy or forgiveness. This idea is crucial in understanding God's *invitation to become more fully human*. The only proper way to receive the forgiveness and healing grace offered by God to become fully human is by offering ourselves back to God.

### Sacrifice as Sanctification

Part of the challenge is that when many hear the word "sacrifice," the primary images that come to mind are animals being killed as an attempt to appease, or pay off, a vengeful God. The Latin term for sacrifice is a combination of two words, *sacere facem*. This can literally be translated "to make" (*facem*) "holy" (*sacere*). In this way sacrifice and sanctification are linked. It is intriguing that one of the passages John Wesley used often when talking about sanctification was Rom. 12:1-2, which is a powerful call for Christians to offer themselves as living sacrifices to God. Moreover, John Wesley asserted that the Lord's Supper was a primary means of growth and healing in sanctifying grace.[13] By the Spirit, people are to be present to God and one another through the offering of their very bodies to God as living sacrifices. People can respond to God's healing grace to becoming fully human by offering themselves to God. This opens them to the continual healing of sanctification and healing from the disease of sin.

## Renewal of the Church as the Body of Christ

The healing that occurs through this divine-human encounter of sacrifice also renews the church together as the body of Christ. From the narratives recorded in Acts through the accounts from church history, the healing offering, the invitation to become fully human through the service of Word and Table, not only imagines personal healing but also celebrates the healing and renewal of the church as the body of Christ. Recall that the invitation to become fully human is a healing to love God, love oneself, love others, and be loved. Through the service of Word and Table, the church is renewed again to Christ and to each other. The United Methodist liturgy draws upon this aspect of the Christian tradition by praying in the eucharistic liturgy, "By your Spirit make us one with Christ, One with each other, One in ministry to all the world."[14] This follows from a very early Christian prayer from the *Didache:* "As this broken bread was scattered over the mountains, and when brought together became one, so let your Church be brought together from the ends of the earth into your Kingdom."[15]

While the healing and invitation to become fully human celebrates healing from sin to love God, love myself, love others, and be loved, it also sends the church out in mission to become Christ's broken body and shed blood to further participate in God's healing and redeeming of the world.

## Doxological Mission: Breathed Out to Be Christ's Broken Body and Shed Blood

Recall the rhythm of being "breathed in" to be "breathed out." As the service of Word and Table gathers in (breathes in) the church to be healed and renewed as the body of Christ, this healing and renewal also offers the church an empowerment and vocation to continue the ministry of the incarnation by being breathed out. Recall the request following immediately after the prayer in the United Methodist eucharistic liturgy beseeching God to make the church one—this unity also hopes for a unity in "ministry to all the world." As the church is renewed as the body of Christ, it is sent (massed) out by and with the Spirit to become joyfully and doxologically broken and poured out into the world so that God's healing and hope, God's invitation to become fully human, may reach those in despair and in the shadows. This illumines another crucial element of the invitation to become fully human. Such an invitation finally does not focus on *individual healing* or *individually becoming fully human.* The Christian imagination of creation celebrated in worship in the service of Word and Table anticipates in hope the redemption of all creation so that God may be all in all. This is not a devaluing of the healing God desires to do in each person, but it opens up the invitation of healing and becoming to all of creation.

## Eschatological Vision and Hope

One final component of the Lord's Supper to be addressed is the eschatological hope offered in the celebration. Just as the Lord's Supper celebrates a healing and renewal of the church, so, too, the Lord's Supper is an anticipation and foretaste of the heavenly banquet that is coming. The hope of what will be encourages and shapes the eucharistic imagination in a present where the circumstances may be unsettling.

A powerful expression of an eschatological imagination was a video of a U2 Concert at Slane Castle. When the band begins "Where the Streets Have No Name," the people in the video appear united in hope, joy, and celebration for what is and what will be. I recognize this is a rock concert. But for many who follow U2, especially in Ireland, they are much more than a rock band. "Where the Streets Have No Name" is a song naming a hope and an imagination envisioning Protestants and Catholics walking down any street without fearing death. U2 has played a very influential role in marginalizing the violence occurring between Protestants and Catholics in Ireland and other parts of the United Kingdom.

This imagination of peace has realized great progress, while still affirming there is more work to do. It is a song that casts an imagination of peace that has moved the culture at large to find such senseless fighting and violence absurd.

The assurance and hope of what will be does not move the church to a lazy apathy but compels the church to participate in what God is doing in the world. This participation in the mission of God is *the* vocation of those who are becoming more fully human. Such a calling and vocation is precisely where life is being received as a gift from God. This ministry in the world is a continual act of sacrifice and doxology whereby the church finds continual healing and hope in God. This hope of what will be invites the church to become fully human by refusing fear, enemies, and despair. This hope is not a naive bliss that life will never be challenging. This hope offers a peace that invades circumstances that are daunting and encourages the church to never be captivated by ethics that are grounded in fear.

At the Lord's Supper, Christ is present in a manner that cannot be fully exhausted and controlled. While the manner is not fully known, the church can affirm with doxological agnosticism that Christ continues to offer himself to God, the church, and the world. The church responds to Christ's continual offering of himself by offering itself as a living sacrifice, as its response to God's invitation to become fully human. To accept God's invitation to become fully human, people must offer all of themselves back to God. This sacrifice is the continual sanctification of the church.

The Lord's Supper also imagines the invitation of becoming fully human as a renewal of the church as the body of Christ. This renewal with Christ and each other sends the church out in hope to doxologically become broken and spilled out for the world. As the church is gathered by God to communal worship, it is through this gathering that God continues to renew the church as the body of Christ as both a continuation of what God has been doing and a promise and hope for what God will continue to do, until the kingdom of God comes in its fullness.

Within this encounter of eschatological hope there may be a concern about the distance lying between where the world is (the "already") and where God is bringing the world (the "not yet"). In this tension flanked by the imagination of the kingdom and all that *will be* on one side and the "reality" of the present on the other side, communal worship becomes a bold statement of hope.

The imagination of what will be is both a reminder of how far we are from it and also a hope that it is what God is inviting the church to participate in and live into.

## Questions for Discussion and Reflection

1.  What ideas were the most helpful in this chapter?

2.  What ideas are the most difficult or causing the greatest amount of tension?

3. How can a proper guide to considering presence (Christ's and the church's) shape the theology and practice of the Lord's Supper?

4. How might the affirmation of the Lord's Supper as a sacrifice offer a more dynamic theology and practice of the Lord's Supper?

## TWENTY-ONE
# PASTORAL ISSUES AT THE TABLE

Drawing upon the theology of the Lord's Supper explored in the previous chapter, this chapter will consider pressing pastoral issues related to the celebration of the Lord's Supper.

## Who Can Partake?

On this issue there is not universal agreement. The overall trajectory of Christian history affirms that the Lord's Supper is the meal of the baptized. As noted in the conversation on baptism, the Lord's Supper is a meal for the family of God and is not to be profaned by those who are outside the covenant. Being "outside" is not about denominational lines but about the church as Christ's body. Without the sacrament of baptism, a person has not been fully initiated and brought into the church. Some parts of Christianity continue to assert that if you are not a member of their part of the Christian tradition, you are not allowed to partake of the Lord's Supper.

However, John Wesley affirmed that the Lord's Supper can be a "converting ordinance." Wesley responded directly to those who disallowed the notion of the Lord's Supper as offering converting grace:

> Many have affirmed that the Lord's Supper is not a converting, but a confirming ordinance. And among us it has been diligently taught that none but those who are converted, who "have received the Holy Ghost," who are believers in the full sense, ought to communicate. But experience shows the gross falsehood of that assertion that the Lord's Supper is not a converting ordinance. Ye are the witnesses. For many now present know, the very beginning of your conversion to God (perhaps, in some, the first deep conviction) was wrought at the Lord's Supper. Now one single instance of this kind overthrows that whole assertion.[1]

The Lord's Supper can be both a converting and confirming ordinance.[2] As a converting ordinance, to the person who comes penitently seeking healing, God offers justifying grace, pardon, and forgiveness. Wesley believed the Lord's Supper could be the occasion of a person's faith response and conversion to seeking God's forgiveness. Some Wesleyan scholars will claim that while this was true, this does not mean that Wesley would allow those who were not baptized to partake at the Table. In many ways such a claim is a bit anachronistic. The majority of people were baptized as infants in the Church of England during Wesley's lifetime. So to force this on Wesley is not legitimate. Moreover, Wesley clearly stretched the boundaries of accepted practices of the Church of England concerning who was allowed to partake of the Lord's Supper.

The suggestion is not to lower or remove any fencing of who can partake but to acknowledge that the Gospels portray Christ as continually eating and drinking with those "outside," the sinners and tax collectors. Still, some Christians would claim that such meals should not be considered eucharistic. The evidence seems contrary. The feeding of the five thousand is the only miracle of Jesus found in all four Gospels. It is striking to observe the actions of Jesus in this meal compared to the actions of Jesus in the Last Supper. Jesus *taking, blessing, breaking, and giving* the bread and the wine. These actions are clearly eucharistic. Curiously, the gospel of John does not include the institution of the Lord's Supper on the night before Jesus was betrayed; rather, it records the washing of the disciples' feet and Jesus issuing the new command (recall this is the foundation for the Maundy Thursday service) that the disciples "love one another as I have loved you" (15:12). John 6 serves as the proper institution of the Lord's Supper that occurs around the feeding of the five thousand.

So what should pastors do? For Wesleyans, it is right and proper that the Lord's Supper be proclaimed as the meal of the baptized and as a renewal of the baptismal vows and covenants made. However, for those who are not baptized but who want to respond to God's invitation to become fully human, the Table can become a place for healing and conversion. Such practices should be seen as the exception, and people should be encouraged to soon enter the process for baptism. The invitation to the Table should be made explicit for the baptized and all others who are open to God's healing and invitation to become more fully human.

## What About Children?

When should children be permitted to commune, or communicate? This is another issue where Christians are not in full agreement. Some who emphasize the importance of baptism for partaking also encourage any infants and children who have been baptized to commune, while others who uphold the necessity of baptism believe children should wait until after catechism and confirmation. Still others who are not as cautious about fencing the Table with baptism often do not allow children to partake of the Lord's Supper because their children "do not understand what is happening." Christians of the Wesleyan tradition have a different perspective from which they should approach this matter.

With their emphasis on the Lord's Supper as a means of grace, Wesleyan congregations should offer the Lord's Supper to all infants and children who are a part of the local congregation. While this entire conversation celebrates the importance of education and catechism, fencing the Table based on the sufficiency of cognitive abilities to comprehend what is occurring at the Lord's Supper is wrong. Not only does the gospel celebrate Jesus' invitation to "let the little children come to me" (e.g., Matt. 19:14), but also the invitation to encounter and be present to Jesus should not be based on sacramental mastery. Furthermore, the overwhelming mystery of the Eucharist should be kept in focus. Such a posture does not suggest that education and teaching on the Lord's Supper should be ignored, but within the rich mystery and eucharistic imagination, there is a beautiful simplicity in coming to Christ to be loved, healed, transformed, and sent to love others.

## How Often Should the Lord's Supper Be Celebrated?

The Lord's Supper is the "Table" of the service of Word and Table. The service of the Word has a distinct rhythm and imagination that anticipates and prepares the congregation to the response and encounter of healing at the Table. A service of the Word that does not include a service of the Table misses out on all the healing and transformation God desires to do. Thus the practice of weekly Communion is strongly encouraged in every service of Word and Table. Moreover, John Wesley, along with much of Christian tradition, took very seriously Christ's command to *do this*. In his sermon "The Duty of Constant Communion" Wesley emphasizes the importance of obedience of Christ's command:

> We must neglect no occasion which the good providence of God affords us for this purpose. This is the true rule—so often are we to receive as God gives us opportunity. Whoever therefore does not receive, but goes from the holy Table when all things are prepared, either does not understand his duty or does not care for the dying command of his Saviour, the forgiveness of his sins, the strengthening of his soul, and the refreshing it with the hope of glory.[3]

With his command to commune continually Wesley hoped to foster a new eucharistic zeal within the Church of England. Christ's command provides the primary reason the church should commune as frequently as God gives opportunity. The title of the sermon makes clear that communing continually is not just a good idea but the Christian's (hopefully joyful) "duty." While the emphasis on obedience is important, there is a danger when such an emphasis is seen simply as a rule to be followed.[4]

Many Wesleyans have in their polity an ordinance requiring quarterly Communion. The history of this is striking. In the Americas there were so few ordained priests that Wesley charged his ministers to celebrate the Lord's Supper at least once a quarter in all the churches that were under their jurisdiction (circuit). However, as time went on, what Wesley intended as a bare *minimum* was practiced by many as a *maximum*, and even that was not followed with diligence for almost two centuries.

Some Protestants are quick to resist such weekly frequency by observing that repetition often yields familiarity and that familiarity often leads to boredom and meaningless action. Protestants "think" they are afraid of ritual. What such Protestants fail to be aware of is how deeply ritualized they are, not only in life but in their local expression of communal worship as well.[5] When presented with this concern, I often provide a metaphor to help guide the emphasis behind the *command* to commune weekly.

Using such logic it would be wrong to repeatedly tell my wife, "I love you." If I tell her too frequently, it would eventually come to mean nothing. So I am going to tell her only once on the first Sunday of the month. Doing this will make it a "rare" and "special" occasion, and she will really know I mean it. Furthermore, while there is hesitation about celebrating the Lord's Supper weekly, these same people read Scripture, sing, pray, and drink coffee every week, yet those practices are not categorized as dead ritual.

Clearly anything that is practiced regularly can be done without really being present to it. That temptation is very real for any behaviors and actions that are done routinely. Even saying, "I love you," as personal as that can be, can become a ritual devoid of care and intention. Celebrating the Lord's Supper can become a disembodied routine where people are simply going through the motions. However, a person can make the same case from the opposite direction concerning continuous change. Worship patterns can change so much that people can become so unfamiliar with what is happening that they never really have the space to engage. This can be said about any aspect of worship whether it has to do with routine practices or ongoing change.

The emphasis on Eucharist in this chapter is not meant to be taken as rule but as an invitation. The Lord's Supper is a gift to the church that is also couched in Christ's command, but it is similar to a command to children to open presents at their birthday party. This attention to the Eucharist is not given to demean communal worship services that only include a service of the Word. Rather, this attention is intended to highlight the good things resulting from communing more often. A more frequent celebration of the Lord's Supper provides the sustenance for the Christian life as people encounter God's healing and renewing of the church so it can be doxologically broken and poured out before the world.

## Who Can Lead or Preside at the Table?

On this issue where there is almost uniformity of opinion in the Christian tradition. John Wesley was adamant that only those who have been ordained can officiate and preside at the Lord's Supper. In John Wesley's sermon "Prophets and Priests" he explicitly states that while some who are not ordained may preach, only those who are ordained may administer the Lord's Supper. He notes that this is the same doctrinal teaching of the Anglicans, Presbyterians, and Roman Catholics. Wesley understands this to be central to eucharistic orthodoxy.

> Hence the same person acted as priest and prophet, as pastor and evangelist. And this gradually spread more and more throughout the whole Christian Church. Yet even at this day, although the same person usually discharges both those offices, yet the office of an evangelist or teacher does not imply that of a pastor, to whom peculiarly belongs the administration of the sacraments—neither among the Presbyterians, nor in the Church of England, nor even among the Roman Catholics. All Presbyterian churches, it is well known (that of Scotland in particular), license men to preach before they are ordained, throughout that whole Kingdom. And it is never understood that this appointment to preach gives them any right to administer the sacraments. Likewise in our own Church persons may be authorized to preach— yea, may be Doctors of Divinity (as was Dr. Alwood at Oxford when I resided there)—who are not ordained at all, and consequently have no right to administer the Lord's Supper. Yea, even in the Church of Rome itself, if a lay brother believes he is called to go a mission, as it is termed, he is sent out, though neither priest nor deacon, to execute that office, and not the other.[6]

Wesley is clear; only those ordained may administer the Lord's Supper. In America, the Church of England's priests were leaving in droves because of the Revolutionary War and the disdain for all things "English." Wesley faced a crossroads. There were so few ordained priests and yet the importance of regular participation in the Lord's Supper was becoming more difficult. This issue was so important to Wesley that he went against his lifelong commitment to unity in the Church of England and ordained superintendents for the Americas. Wesley's zeal and persistence on this issue encouraged him to ordain Thomas Coke, who was already an Anglican priest, to the office of superintendent. In turn Coke ordained Francis Asbury as deacon, elder, and joint superintendent.[7] These ordinations gave Coke and Asbury general superintendency over the Methodists in America and allowed them to ordain others. These ordinations were needed for the Methodists in America to celebrate the Lord's Supper. The importance of the Eucharist for the Methodists in America and the necessity that only the ordained could preside at the Table underscores both Wesley's eucharistic passion and theology of ordination.

The necessity of the ordained at the Table confirms his belief in the role of the ordained for sacramental leadership in the church. Those who are ordained have been set apart by the church and have been empowered by the Holy Spirit with charisms (giftings and graces) for leadership in communal worship, specifically preaching and the administration of the sacraments. Specifically, the ordained have been trained in what the church intends to pray at the Lord's Supper and have been empowered to lead the congregation in the Great Thanksgiving, including the epiclesis, which is the prayer that God may send the Spirit on the congregation and on the bread and wine to make Christ present in the eucharistic meal.

This call for the ordained to preside at the Table does not mean that only the ordained can distribute the elements. Local churches can invite a variety of people to lead in the distribution of elements. For example, there is something dynamic and powerful about receiving the body and blood of Christ from a child. It is much more than simply "cute" but a powerful reminder of Jesus' command to receive the kingdom of God following the example of faith of one of these (see Luke 18:15-17).

## Significance of Bread and Wine (Juice)

Does it matter what types of elements are used? The church has followed Christ's use of two very common food items: bread and wine. Some Christian traditions in desiring to do what Jesus did recall that in the gospel of Luke when he instituted the Lord's Supper, it was during the Passover meal. At such a meal, Jesus would have used unleavened bread. Unleavened bread is a reminder that in Egypt the Israelites had nothing. Leaven is what Pharaoh, the oppressor, had. The Israelites ate unleavened bread in the land of milk and honey to remind them that it was the Lord and not Pharaoh who brought about their deliverance.[8] Conversely, while Jesus' meal in the upper room began as a Passover, this Passover meal was transformed into a meal that participates in Christ's death and resurrection as the church anticipates the heavenly banquet that is to come.

As a meal of celebration, a proper bread sign emphasizes how the common becomes sacred. Recall the prayer of the *Didache* offered earlier. The bread and wine are made from the work of God and human hands. While God grows grapes and wheat, the many grains of wheat and the many grapes are crushed by human hands and made into one loaf and one cup of wine. Some in Christendom emphasize the importance of the grapes fermenting into wine as the full and proper symbol of the blood of Christ. For those Christian traditions who feel called by God to abstinence from alcohol, the use of juice rather than wine is an appropriate symbol of Christ's blood. As far as an appropriate bread sign is concerned, there are a variety of opinions. While using yeast is an issue for some Christians, some are also nervous about using breads that are too sweet.

If the local church is considering using something different from bread and wine (or juice), it should discern what would be suitable as a bread-and-wine sign. Although the use of Coke and Doritos is clearly not an appropriate sign, there is room for thoughtful and intentional consideration. It can also become meaningful if people in the congregation can actually bake the bread and in some cases help supply the wine (or juice).

## Questions for Discussion and Reflection

1. What ideas were the most helpful in this chapter?

2. What ideas are the most difficult or causing the greatest amount of tension?

3. What do you think about the importance of baptism for the Eucharist?

4. How often is the Lord's Supper celebrated in your church and why?

# TWENTY-TWO

# SERVICE OF THE TABLE: THE CELEBRATION OF THE LORD'S SUPPER IN WORSHIP

This chapter considers the eucharistic liturgy, often called the Great Thanksgiving. As an example, the Great Thanksgiving as offered in the current *United Methodist Hymnal* will be considered as one model.[1] At its core the Great Thanksgiving is a prayer. In examining the great eucharistic prayers of the Catholic, Orthodox, and Protestant traditions, variations can be found, but there is also a *shared center* that unites all the meals. Also significant is the awareness that the eucharistic prayer, with some common threads, has developed and evolved throughout the history of Christian worship. Worship teams today should work to be faithful to the past while also drawing upon the Spirit's inspiration for appropriate contextualization. Such prayers and liturgies are not magical incantations; yet attention to the history of eucharistic prayers is important when there is a need for improvisation. In looking at the prayer, or Great Thanksgiving, some rubrics (directed actions and movements in the sacrament) will also be suggested.

Before exploring the liturgy it is important to emphasize that the eucharistic prayer is the church's prayer. While the minister has been empowered to lead and pray this prayer, this prayer should be imagined, not as something the minister does *for* the congregation, but as something he or she does *with* the congregation. The ordained minister's charisms (giftings) are a function of the church universal and local. While some priestly prayers are done on behalf of the congregation, the Great Thanksgiving is a prayer of the entire congregation, even as the minister leads and vocalizes more of the prayer.

## A. Procession of the Gifts onto the Eucharist Table

The tithes and offerings collected can be brought forward along with the eucharistic emblems of the bread and wine and put on the Eucharist Table. Those offerings and emblems of the local church and Christ are united into one offering of thanksgiving-oblation (thank offering) and given to God. This action is central for the consideration of the Lord's Supper as a sacrifice.

## B. People Invited to Stand

The entrance of the pew into the sanctuary was a fairly late addition into Christian worship. The posture of standing reinforces that a person is to be physically, spiritually, and emotionally present. In contrast, a posture of sitting embodies an attitude of reception. In the invitation to stand, care should be given for those who are not physically able. So the minister can say something such as, "Those who are able we invite you to stand."

### The Great Thanksgiving
### United Methodist Word and Table I*

(The minister leads the congregation. Words in bold are spoken or sung by the congregation.)

The Lord be with you.
**And also with you.**

Sursum Corda

Lift up your hearts.
**We lift them up to the Lord.**
Let us give thanks to the Lord our God.
**It is right to give our thanks and praise.**
It is right, and a good and joyful thing, always and everywhere to give thanks to you, Father Almighty, creator of heaven and earth. You formed us in your image and breathed into us the breath of life. When we turned away, and our love failed, your love remained steadfast. You delivered us from captivity, made covenant to be our sovereign God, and spoke to us through your prophets. And so, with your people on earth and all the company of heaven, we praise your name and join their unending hymn:

Sanctus

**Holy, holy, holy Lord, God of power and might,**
**heaven and earth are full of your glory,**
**Hosanna in the highest.**
**Blessed is he who comes in the name of the Lord.**
**Hosanna in the highest.**

Thanks-giving for Jesus Christ

Holy are you, and blessed is your Son Jesus Christ. Your Spirit anointed him to preach good news to the poor, to proclaim release to the captives and recovering of sight to the blind, to set at liberty those who are oppressed, and to announce that the time had come when you would save your people. He healed the sick, fed the hungry, and ate with sinners. By the baptism of his suffering, death, and resurrection you gave birth to your Church, delivered us from slavery to sin and death, and made with us a new covenant by water and the spirit. When the Lord Jesus ascended he promised to be with us always, in the power of your Word and Holy Spirit.

---

*From "A Service of Word and Table I" © 1972, 1980, 1985, 1989, The United Methodist Publishing House. Used by permission.

On the night in which he gave himself up for us, Our Lord Jesus took bread, gave thanks to you, broke the bread, gave it to his disciples, and said: "Take, eat; this is my body which is given for you. Do this in remembrance of me."

Likewise, when the supper was over, he took the cup, gave thanks to you, gave it to his disciples, and said: "Drink from this, all of you, this is my blood of the new covenant, poured out for you and for many for the forgiveness of sins. Do this, as often as you drink it, in remembrance of me."

And so, in remembrance of these your mighty acts in Jesus Christ, we offer ourselves in praise and thanksgiving as a holy and living sacrifice, in union with Christ's offering for us, as we proclaim the mystery of faith:
**Christ has died; Christ is risen; Christ will come again.**

*Sacrificial Oblation*

Pour out your Holy Spirit on us gathered here, and on these gifts of bread and wine. Make them be for us the body and blood of Christ, that we may be for the world the body of Christ, redeemed by his blood.

*Epiclesis*

By your Spirit make us one with Christ, one with each other, and one in ministry to all the world, until Christ comes in final victory and we feast at his heavenly banquet.

*Eschatological Imagination*

Through your Son Jesus Christ, with your Holy Spirit in your Holy Church, all honor and glory is yours, Almighty Father, now and forever.

*Triune Doxology*

*The Lord's Prayer*
And now, as our savior Christ has taught us, let us pray:

*Lord's Prayer*

**Our Father, who art in heaven, hallowed by thy name,**
**Thy kingdom come,**
**Thy will be done on earth as it is in heaven.**
**Give us this day our daily bread.**
**And forgive us our trespasses, as we forgive those who trespass against us.**
**And lead us not into temptation, but deliver us from evil.**
**For thine is the kingdom, and the power, and the glory, forever. Amen.**

*The Breaking of the Bread*
*The Sharing of the Cup*
Because there is one loaf, we, though we be many, are one body, for we all partake of the one loaf. The bread which we break, it is a means of sharing in the body of Christ!

*Fraction: Breaking the Bread and Sharing the Cup*

And the cup over which we give thanks, it is a means of sharing in the outpoured blood of Christ![2]

## C. *Sursum Corda*

(Rubric: During the *sursum corda* the minister will lift and raise his or her hands, embodying hearts lifted to God.) The Great Thanksgiving begins with the greeting of unity in Christ and then is followed with what is called the *sursum corda* ("lift up your hearts"). Such an invitation and response by the congregation affirms in this prayer that they are offering their very lives to God in thanksgiving.

## D. Thanksgiving for What God Has Done

Many prayers thank God for creation and God's redemption of creation after people turned away from God.

## E. Sanctus

(Rubric: The church's proclamation of the Sanctus can be sung or spoken.) In response for what God has done and also who God is, the church offers its praise to God who is holy. The Sanctus combines both the praise from Isa. 6:3 and part of Ps. 118, which is the song shouted during Jesus' triumphal entry on Palm Sunday (Matt. 21:9).

## F. Thanksgiving for Jesus Christ

This prayer offers praise for the person and ministry of Jesus Christ. It serves as a proclamation not simply of what Christ did while on the earth but also of the direct impact his ministry will have on the ministry of the church as his body sent from the Table. The liturgy prays,

> Your Spirit anointed him to preach good news to the poor, to proclaim release to the captives and recovering of sight to the blind, to set at liberty those who are oppressed, and to announce that the time had come when you would save your people. He healed the sick, fed the hungry, and ate with sinners.[3]

To remember and be made present to Christ's ministry offers the church a vision for its ministry empowered by the Spirit. Beyond simply recalling what Christ did, in this remembrance (*anamnēsis*) the church will be sent out to continue Christ's ministry as the body of Christ.

## G. Institution Narrative

As part of the proclamation of Christ's life and ministry the church also represents (makes present again) the narrative of the Last Supper meal. For many parts of the Protestant faith this institution narrative is the only liturgy offered in the Lord's Supper. The reason for this is complex. One of the primary reasons is that some of the Reformers felt compelled to only perform in the liturgy what was explicitly scriptural. However, this proclamation of the narrative of the Last Supper is not simply a history lesson but also a new and fresh encounter between the church and Christ, who continues to offer himself to the church for its continual healing. This is the power of *anamnēsis*.

## H. Sacrificial Oblation

In the light of Christ's offering himself again to the church, the church responds by offering itself with Christ back to God. The church prays, "And so, in remembrance of these your mighty acts in Jesus Christ, we offer ourselves in praise and thanksgiving as a holy and living sacrifice, in union with Christ's offering for us, as we proclaim the mystery of our faith. **ALL: Christ has died; Christ is risen; Christ will come again.**"[4] The previous chapter observed that the Lord's Supper is a sacrifice. It is an oblationary sacrifice—a thank offering for all that God has done. The proper response to Christ's offering of healing and redemption is to offer oneself back to God as a living sacrifice. This sacrifice is not *earning* anything, but it is the proper *response* to God's invitation to *become more fully human for the glory of God*. This prayer embodies the command and imagination of Rom. 12:1-2.

Also noteworthy is that the church's offering of itself is joined to Christ's offering into one oblationary sacrifice. The church does not offer itself alone but only does so *with* and *in* Christ's continual offering of himself to the church and to the Father. Along with this prayer of sacrifice, the church can only do so in the mystery of the imagination grounded in what God *has* done, *is* doing, and *will* do in and through Christ by the Spirit. Christ's death, resurrection, and promise of return is the imagination and invitation into which Christians are invited to become more fully human.

## I. Epiclesis

(Rubric: The minister when praying for the Holy Spirit to come on the congregation should raise his or her hands over the congregation and then over the eucharistic elements.) This is the prayer for God to "pour out the Holy Spirit" on the church and eucharistic gifts for the purpose of Christ and the church being dynamically present to each other for a healing encounter. The primary emphasis of this request for the Spirit is that the church may become the body and blood of Christ renewed with Christ as the Head of the body. Recall from the previous chapter that this renewal and unity will send the church out to continue the ministry of the incarnation.

## J. Eschatological Imagination

The Lord's Supper is a foretaste of the heavenly banquet that is coming, and as such the church will keep celebrating it until "Christ comes in final victory." This renewal as the body of Christ and ministry in the world is guided by the hope and promise that one day the kingdom of God will be consummated. The hope of Christ's resurrection is the guide by which all Christians are released from enemies, fear, and hatred.

## K. Triune Doxology

The Great Thanksgiving concludes with praise for the triune God who is the source and power of all that is and will be. This prayer is a very important reminder for this entire conversation about the *invitation to become more fully human*. While each congregant's response to God's invitation is important for each person and the church as a whole, the full redemption of the world, the consummation of the kingdom of God, is all for the glory of God. As creation is being redeemed and restored in God, God becomes more fully "all in all" (1 Cor. 15:27-28).

## L. Lord's Prayer

This prayer offers an imagination of who the church is called to be as a reminder in thanksgiving for who God is.[5]

## M. Fraction: Breaking the Bread, Sharing the Cup

(Rubric: Take bread, lift up, break, and say)

"Christ's body broken for you."

(Rubric: Lift up the cup and say)

"Christ's blood shed for you."

Another option is the following:

(Rubric: Take the bread, lift while proclaiming)

"Because there is one loaf, we, though we be many, are one body, for we all partake of the one loaf. The bread which we break, it is a means of sharing in the body of Christ!"

(Rubric: Break the bread)

(Rubric: Take and lift the cup proclaiming)

"And the cup over which we give thanks, it is a means of sharing in the outpoured blood of Christ!"

(Rubric: When more than one chalice is used, the wine [juice] can be poured into the needed chalices. This act of pouring is also a participation in Christ's blood being poured out.)

(Rubric: Then offer the following invocation)

"The Table is prepared; all who are hungry and thirsty are invited to come and partake of the body and blood of Christ, the very means of life, healing, and hope."

(Rubric: Distribute the elements with the following prayer and promise spoken to each person)

"Here is the body of Christ broken for you." "Here is the blood of Christ broken for you."

## Method of Celebrating the Eucharist

The church has practiced several ways of distributing the eucharistic emblems of the bread and the cup. Intinction is preferable for several reasons. With intinction there is generally only one loaf that can be broken and one cup that can be poured into others. Often when the elements are distributed in the pews there are individual breads and small individual cups. The theological danger is the implicit affirmation that "I get my own personal Jesus." Moreover, when people come to the altar, it is a movement toward God at God's invitation. When those who are physically able are simply allowed to receive Christ in their seats, something can be lost about their commitment and response.

As people come forward, their hands should be together with palms up ready to receive. The servers should break off a piece of bread and place it in a congregant's open hands. What is the difference between a person receiving the bread and each person tearing off and taking his or her own piece? Theologically there is a difference between a person taking and tearing off Christ's body and the church offering a person Christ's body. An individual does not take Christ, but the church offers Christ to that individual.

With intinction the bread can be dipped into the cup and then consumed. Some people who prefer receiving individual cups and breads find it piously meaningful for all to take the bread and the cup at one time. While such a desire is fine, the church has not given importance to taking the elements at the same moment.

# N. Prayer of Thanksgiving

(Rubric: After all have received the elements, the entire congregation prays a thanksgiving prayer. An example is offered below.)

Eternal God, we give you thanks and praise for these most precious gifts of the sacred body and blood of your Son our Lord and Savior Jesus Christ. Renewed as the body of Christ, send us with your Spirit to be joyfully broken and poured out before the world, that the world may continue to find healing, hope, and redemption.

This concludes the celebration of the Lord's Supper. For those who are accustomed to only reading the institution narrative this entire liturgy may seem very overwhelming. Some may be concerned that such a full eucharistic liturgy "takes too long." While it may seem so, it is not necessarily the case; moreover, the Lord's Supper is a powerful climax to the service of Word and Table, where people are encountered by God to be healed, renewed, and sent to be Christ's broken body and shed blood in the world. One of the major ideas of this entire conversation is something very obvious, but essential to remember. The amount of time you spend on something proclaims its importance. Local churches should consider the amount of time given to worship elements and discern if that properly reflects the desired theological and liturgical priority. Local worship teams should consider carefully the eucharistic liturgy celebrated. While contextualization provides some liturgical space for improvisation, whatever is chosen must be guided theologically and not simply based on pragmatics or what seems to be a good idea.

## Questions for Discussion and Reflection

1. What ideas were the most helpful in this chapter?

2. What ideas are the most difficult or causing the greatest amount of tension?

3. What is the current practice of celebrating the Lord's Supper in your church? Specifically what liturgy is used?

4. What are some ideas or practices raised in this chapter that may be worth exploring?

5. What education is needed for your local congregation to encounter a great eucharistic imagination in worship and life?

## TWENTY-THREE

# BENEDICTION: EXHALED BY AND WITH THE SPIRIT TO BE DOXOLOGICALLY BROKEN AND POURED OUT

As the Spirit gathers believers to the divine-human transforming encounter, the Spirit exhales (blows) them out into the world whereby the church continues its vocation as the body of Christ. The church is sent *with* and *by* the Spirit to be broken and poured out into the world. The benediction is not simply a "sweet and comfortable" maxim, but a hopeful charge, calling, and blessing. In a very nonviolent way, it is the church's marching orders. The benediction is literally the church being massed (sent) to participate in God's mission in the world empowered by the Spirit. The benediction is a blessing that is often different from a closing prayer. Some closing prayers often feel as if the church is simply saying good-bye to God. Care and attention must be given here by worship leaders.

The church's worship does not end at the benediction, but the congregation's entire life outside of communal worship is to be a continuation of worship—a life of service, praise, offering, and transformation. The church's calling to be doxologically broken and poured out before the world participates in their continual transformation as the body of Christ and renewal into the full imagination of the *imago Dei*.

Many young Christians disillusioned by the deficiencies, bitterness, hypocrisy, and pettiness in local churches often are eager to serve the world but feel as if participation in communal worship is not necessary to do so. While God is at work in and through people who do not participate in communal Christian worship, God established the church and guided the rhythms of communal worship as part of what it means to be human. Christian communal worship provides a vision and empowerment to continue to participate in God's kingdom more fully coming. When communal Christian worship is imagined as something to check off on a list of rules, much has been lost. Like life, communal worship is God's invitation to become more fully human.

## Communal Worship: God Is Always the End

Along with this invitation to doxologically minister in the world, it is recognized that communal worship, as praise to God, is its own end. The primary function and work of the church is to be encountered by God in communal worship and thus be fully present in praise and offerings that exalt and glorify God for who God is. For Wesleyans, it is critical that while God extends the invitation to people, people must respond, recognizing that God empowers all responses. This is perhaps another way to understand God's invitation in worship as sacramental. God synergistically desires to empower that response both in the call to communal worship and in the embodiment of that worship in the world. Worship has no other pragmatic or institutional hidden agenda. The ministry in the world simply becomes the church's doxological living out and response to who they are invited to become in communal worship.

Communal worship in the church is God's invitation to people to become the church, the gathered community of faith. It is in this event of communal worship where God is sacramentally present that the congregation is invited to be encountered by God, transformed into the body of Christ, and sent into the world to be joyfully Christ's body and blood, broken and spilled out for the world. Coming alongside the poor, lost, and hopeless is the church's continual doxological response of worship to the invitation offered specifically in communal worship. Yet in the course of this invitation to continue the ministry of the incarnation, the church is breathed back in each Sabbath to be breathed out again. It is the assertion that the church is only able to properly be (as Spirit empowered) the body of Christ and have eyes to see and ears to hear as the church is continually breathed into communal worship and breathed out again.

God spoke creation into existence to worship as an invitation to life, love, and joy. People are created to worship God and become more fully human as they love God, love themselves, love other people, are loved, and care for the rest of creation. The question in life is not *if* we will but *what* we will worship. What we worship we will become. Sin is a disease and cancer that moves the congregation away from life into death. Through communal worship, people are being healed, redeemed, and restored to more fully glorify God in the world. In this invitation to life, in this healing to become more fully human, the full imagination does not end with our healed humanity. As blessed as that is, our becoming fully human is a participation in all of creation glorifying God so that God may be all in all. This is the hope of the kingdom of God into which God is redeeming and restoring the world. With this imagination and with this hope, Christian communal worship becomes a gift for the further being and becoming of creation for the glory of God.

# CONCLUSION

In this conversation there is a fine balance that I have attempted to maintain. On the one hand, some of the liturgical and sacramental issues offered are non-negotiable (remember the difference between a terrorist and a liturgist). On the other hand, every communal worship service needs to be contextually appropriate, drawn from the inspiration that God offers to each worship team. So what is command and what is an open suggestion? This is the tension those called and gifted to imagine, plan, and lead communal worship must wrestle with.

In the first section I offered a mosaic theology of worship:

Christian communal worship is the glorification of God and the sanctification of humanity as a divine-human event where God offers transformation and healing to help people become more fully what God created them to be and do. God breathes (inhales) and gathers in individual Christians to heal, transform, and renew them as the body of Christ to breathe (exhale) them out to continue the ministry of the incarnation that participates in the kingdom of God more fully coming. The consummation of the kingdom will come and God will be all in all.

The image of a mosaic rather than a building is intentional. While most worship teams are laser focused on "getting worship done," I am hopeful that taking a few steps back can offer a bigger and richer imagination of the promises and possibilities of communal worship.

While the first section provided a theology of worship, section II offered some suggestions about how worship should be planned:

Planning worship well begins with giving attention to the worship team, the process for planning worship, the people in a local community, the worship space, and the season of the Christian year; it also means planning worship services that are Christian. The service of Word and Table emphasizes God's gathering and calling while also empowering humanity's response. Planning worship well further includes paying attention to the final details and leading with excellence.

The third section explored the beauty and gift of the sacraments of baptism and the Lord's Supper.

Through these suggestions, my hope is that worship teams will continue to wonderfully find their faithfully Christian and contextually appropriate liturgical voice. Some of the suggestions offered will not work in every context. The model offered tried to embody the importance of not simply what is being done but also *how* and *why* it is done. There is always a danger of attempting to explain or exhaust what is happening in worship. Unfortunately, the other extreme often feels closer to the reality for many local churches. Too often people attend communal worship and have a sense of what will happen without a full understanding and imagination of why the church is doing what it is doing in worship.

Here are some of my primary hopes for those who have journeyed through this conversation.

## Fall in Love with Imaging, Planning, and Leading Worship

For pastors, worship teams, and congregations the routine of the rituals can become lifeless. Being aware of the importance of communal worship can inspire new ideas, creativity, and careful planning.

## Imaging, Planning, and Leading Worship Is Important Work

Too often worship is planned by one person alone with a computer and deadlines pressing in from all sides. Too often clergy and parishioners have not celebrated the importance of excellence in communal worship. I am persuaded that Christian communal worship is the main reason the church exists and why humans have been given breath from God. As such, paying attention to communal worship is a worthy task for worship leaders.

## Imaging, Planning, and Leading Worship Is Hard Work

My students, many of whom have been "worship leaders," often finish my course saying, "Planning faithful Christian worship is hard work." This is very true. God hopes, demands, and empowers our very best. Excellence does not come accidentally.

## Imaging, Planning, and Leading Worship Is Simple Work

By the Spirit, the work God has called worship leaders to can be accomplished with excellence when creativity, organization, and care are given to the entire process. While some may find rocket science easier than imagining and leading worship that is Christian, it is not impossible.

We have been created to worship. As such we have been created as humans to love God, love ourselves, love our fellow people, be loved, and care for creation as an extension of the first four. As the preceding chapters have emphasized, worship is an invitation to become more fully human. The imagination of Christian communal worship is a divine-human healing encounter where God continues to redeem creation and sends the body of Christ from communal worship to participate in the kingdom of God's further coming so that one day the kingdom will be consummated and God will be all in all.

# APPENDIX 1
# QUESTIONS FOR INTERVIEWING A CONGREGATION

## Worship at First Community Church

1. Describe a typical Sunday morning in this congregation.
2. What are distinctive characteristics about worship at First Community?
3. What is the atmosphere of worship at First Community?

## Personal Questions About Worship

1. Why do you come to corporate worship?
2. Describe important elements in worship. Why are they important?
3. Describe the right attitude of the worshipper as he or she approaches corporate worship.
4. Describe a recent worship service that was specifically meaningful or inspirational.
   - In what way was it meaningful?
   - If it is possible, explain whether it was a moment during the service or your attitude to that service?
5. What would you describe to be the purpose of a corporate worship service?
   - In what ways does a service meet or not meet that purpose? Give an example.
6. Think of the last worship service you attended. What has remained with you from that service?
7. How does our corporate worship enhance your spiritual life throughout the week?
8. What are things that disengage you from worship?

## Other Questions

1. Is there something missing from Sunday morning worship that you wish were present?
2. Is there something that is present in Sunday morning worship that is a distraction, unhelpful, or uncomfortable?
3. What do you feel is the ideal atmosphere for worship at First Community?
4. Do you feel comfortable bringing your friends to First Community? Why? What should cease or begin to help?
5. Is there a certain time, other than Sunday morning, that is more convenient for your family to attend?

# SONG REVIEW WORKSHEET DEVELOPED AND SHARED BY KEITH D. SCHWANZ

## Song Review Worksheet Instructions

### Theological Review: Table 1

Hopefully you will find very few songs that will be disqualified by your initial review. Every box in Table 1 must be checked or the song should not be used in corporate worship because of its theological deficiency.

Any conflict with Scripture will disqualify a song.

There are some songs that claim a privilege or experience exclusive to one person. This type of individualistic song is by definition not suitable for corporate worship.

- "You took the fall and *thought of me, above all*."[1]
- "Thank You for giving Your life *just* for me."[2]

### Theological Review: Table 2

All songs that pass the review in Table 1 are examined in greater detail in Table 2. Since you are looking for *theological substance* in a song for corporate worship, look for *an explicit reference* when assessing the different theological issues. Do not check a box if the theological issue is merely implied. The goal is not to make as many check marks as you can but to ascertain how robust the song is theologically.

Only put a check in the "Quotes a Scripture passage(s)" box if it is a direct quotation or very direct paraphrase.

At least two checks should be made in Table 2 for the song to qualify it for further review.

### Lyric and Melody Review: Table 3

The issues raised in Table 3 will help you assess the literary and melodic quality of the song. You should have at least five boxes in Table 3 checked for the song to qualify for use in corporate worship.

Look for literary devices that stir the imagination.

- "Guide me, O Thou great Jehovah, / Pilgrim through this barren land" (allegory).[3]
- "Lord, the light of Your love is shining" (alliteration).[4]
- "*Born* Thy people to deliver, / *Born* a Child and yet a King, / *Born* to reign in us forever, / Now Thy gracious kingdom bring" (anaphora).[5]

- "O for a thousand tongues to sing" (hyperbole).[6]
- "My heart an altar, and Thy love the flame" (metaphor).[7]
- "You are strong when you feel weak, in your brokenness complete" (paradox).[8]

Note when a song's theme progresses toward a climax—from "Long my imprisoned spirit lay" to "My chains fell off" to "No condemnation."[9] A song may have a musical or emotional peak without the text itself moving to a climax. Put a check in this box only if the *text* progresses toward a climax. Songs with a refrain often are not textually climatic since every stanza leads to the same refrain.

## Song Review Worksheet

| Song title: | |
|---|---|
| Source/Number: | Reviewed by: |

## Theological Review

Put an **X** in the box for every statement that is true.

Table 1

| | |
|---|---|
| Compatible with Scripture. | |
| Does not suggest a privilege or experience that is exclusive to one person. | |

If *both* boxes in Table 1 are checked, continue with the review. Otherwise, the song fails to qualify for use in corporate worship.

Table 2

| | |
|---|---|
| Explicit reference to the Trinity. | |
| Explicit reference to an attribute(s) of God. | |
| Explicit reference to God as Creator. | |
| Explicit reference to the gospel: the life, death, and/or resurrection of Jesus. | |
| Explicit statement that salvation is by grace through faith in Jesus Christ. | |
| Confesses the need for forgiveness of sin. | |
| Confesses the need of a pure heart. | |
| Declares the lordship of Jesus Christ. | |
| Declares the transforming power of the Holy Spirit. | |
| Uses baptismal images or references. | |
| Uses eucharistic images or references. | |
| Explicit reference to the eternal reign of God. | |
| Encourages the church to participate in the *missio Dei*. | |

| | |
|---|---|
| Quotes a Scripture passage(s).<br>*Reference(s):* | |
| Speaks as the community (we/us), not the individual (I/me). | |
| TOTAL **X**s FOR TABLE 2 | |

### Lyric & Melody Review

Put an **X** in the box for every statement that is true.

**Table 3**

| | |
|---|---|
| Stirs the imagination through literary devices such as metaphor, simile, paradox, alliteration, anaphora, and so on. | |
| Theme progresses toward a climax. | |
| Phrases follow usual speech patterns; grammar is not discarded for sake of rhyme. | |
| Avoids the use of archaic language. | |
| Avoids gender exclusive language. | |
| Avoids the use of the male pronoun for God, except where Jesus is the antecedent. | |
| Natural accents of the words match the accents of the melody. | |
| The melody is singable by the congregation (not soloistic). | |
| TOTAL **X**s FOR TABLE 3 | |

If you have at least 2 **X**s in Table 2 and at least 5 **X**s in Table 3, explore the liturgical setting that best suits this song by completing Table 4. Otherwise, the song fails to qualify for use in corporate worship (unless a specific context justifies an exception).

### Liturgical Review

**Table 4**

Mode of Communication (Select One)

| | |
|---|---|
| *I / we* speak about *God* to *us*—**proclamation**. | |
| *I / we* speak about *me / us* to *us*—**affirmation**. | |
| *I / we* speak about *me / us* to *God*—**petition**. | |
| *I / we* speak about *God* to *God*—**praise**. | |

Primary Story (Select One)

| | |
|---|---|
| My/our encounter(s) with God. | |
| God's story. | |

Best Fit in a Service Order (select one or two)

| | | | | | |
|---|---|---|---|---|---|
| Gathering | | Invitation | | Praise | |
| Call to Worship | | Creed | | Confession | |
| Assurance | | Prayer | | The Word | |
| Dedication | | Baptism | | Communion | |

| Thanksgiving | | Healing | | Offering | |
| Lament | | Adoration | | Sending | |

Use in the Christian Year (Select All That Apply)

| Advent | | Christmas | | Epiphany | |
| Lent | | Holy Week | | Easter | |
| Ascension | | Pentecost | | Ordinary | |

Comments:

# APPENDIX 3
# A SAMPLE LITURGY FOR INFANT BAPTISM
(Adapted from the *Book of Common Prayer*)

---

**Minister:** Who presents this child for baptism?

**Parents:** We present N. (name of child) to receive the sacrament of baptism.

**Minister** (to parents, sponsors, or godparents): Will you be responsible for seeing that the child you present is brought up in the Christian faith and life?

**Parents and godparents:** *We* will, with God's help.

**Minister:** Will you by your prayers and witness help this child to grow into the full stature of Christ?

**Parents and godparents:** We will, with God's help.

## The Baptismal Covenant

As parents and godparents, let us affirm the faith into which you are living and will train and nurture N.

Today I invite all those who would like to affirm their baptism to stand and repeat these vows as an expression of our continued commitment and desire to confess Jesus Christ as Lord.

**Minister:** Do you believe in God the Father?

**People:** I believe in God, the Father almighty, Creator of heaven and earth.

**Minister:** Do you believe in Jesus Christ, the Son of God?

**People:** I believe in Jesus Christ, his only Son, our Lord.

> He was conceived by the power of the Holy Spirit and born of the Virgin Mary.
>
> He suffered under Pontius Pilate, was crucified, died, and was buried.
>
> He descended to the dead.
>
> On the third day he rose again.
>
> He ascended into heaven, and is seated at the right hand of the Father.
>
> He will come again to judge the living and the dead.

**Minister:** Do you believe in God the Holy Spirit?

**People:** I believe in the Holy Spirit,

> the holy catholic church,
>
> the communion of saints,
>
> the forgiveness of sins,
>
> the resurrection of the body,
>
> and the life everlasting.

**Minister:** Will you continue in the apostles' teaching and fellowship, in the breaking of bread, and in the prayers?

**People:** I will, with God's help.

**Minister:** Will you persevere in resisting evil, and, whenever you fall into sin, repent and return to the Lord?

**People:** I will, with God's help.

**Minister:** Will you proclaim by word and example the good news of God in Christ?

**People:** I will, with God's help.

**Minister:** Will you seek and serve Christ in all persons, loving your neighbor as yourself?

**People:** I will, with God's help.

**Minister:** Will you strive for justice and peace among all people, and respect the dignity of every human being?

**People:** I will, with God's help.

## Prayers for the Candidates

**Minister:** Let us now pray for N., who is to receive the sacrament of new birth (and for those [this person] who *have* renewed *their* commitment to Christ).

**Minister:** Deliver *them*, O Lord, from the way of sin and death. Open *their hearts* to your grace and truth. Fill *them* with your holy and life-giving Spirit. Keep *them* in the faith and communion of your holy church. Teach *them* to love others in the power of the Spirit. Send *them* into the world in witness to your love. Bring *them* to the fullness of your peace and glory. Grant, O Lord, that all who are baptized into the death of Jesus Christ your Son may live in the power of his resurrection and look for him to come again in glory; who lives and reigns now and forever. *Amen.*

## Thanksgiving over the Water

**Minister blesses the water:** We thank you, Almighty God, for the gift of water. Over it the Holy Spirit moved in the beginning of creation. Through it you led the children of Israel out of their bondage in Egypt into the Land of Promise. In it your Son Jesus received the baptism of John and was anointed by the Holy Spirit as the Messiah, the Christ, to lead us, through his death and resurrection, from the bondage of sin into everlasting life.

We thank you, Father, for the water of baptism. In it we are buried with Christ in his death. By it we share in his resurrection. Through it we are reborn by the Holy Spirit. Therefore in joyful obedience to your Son, we bring into his fellowship those who come to him in faith, baptizing them in the name of the Father, and of the Son, and of the Holy Spirit.

**Minister touches the water:** Now sanctify this water, we pray you, by the power of your Holy Spirit, that those who here are cleansed from sin and born again may continue forever in the risen life of Jesus Christ our Savior. To him, to you, and to the Holy Spirit, be all honor and glory, now and forever. *Amen.*

## The Baptism

**Minister:** N., I baptize you in the name of the Father, and of the Son, and of the Holy Spirit. *Amen.*

**Minister:** Let us pray. Heavenly Father, we thank you that by water and the Holy Spirit you have bestowed upon *these* your servants the forgiveness of sin, and have raised *them* to the new life of grace. Sustain *them*, O Lord, in your Holy Spirit. Give *them* an inquiring and discerning heart, the courage to will and to persevere, a spirit to know and to love you, and the gift of joy and wonder in all your works. *Amen.*

Let us welcome the newly baptized and those today who have affirmed their faith.

**Minister and People:** We receive you into the household of God. Confess the faith of Christ crucified, proclaim his resurrection, and share with us in his eternal priesthood.

· · ·

See http://www.bcponline.org/ for complete liturgies from the *Book of Common Prayer.*

# NOTES

## Chapter 1

1. Later I will discuss how important it is that worship leaders create contextually appropriate services. The tension between placating people and discarding all the familiar liturgies of the saints will be addressed here.

## Chapter 2

1. See introduction for complete text.

2. James F. White, *Introduction to Christian Worship* (Nashville: Abingdon Press, 1990), 29.

3. See Henry H. Knight III, "Worship and Sanctification," *Wesleyan Theological Journal* 32, no. 2 (1997): 5-14.

4. See the Westminster Shorter Catechism, http://www.reformed.org/documents/WSC .html. See also Augustine, *On Christian Teaching*, translated with an introduction and notes by R. P. H. Green (Oxford: Oxford University Press, 1997), 8-10.

5. James Smith notes that this is found explicitly in the work of Rene Descartes in the *Meditations*. See James K. A. Smith, *Desiring the Kingdom* (Grand Rapids: Baker Academic, 2009), 42.

6. Ibid.

7. Ibid., 43.

8. Ibid.

9. Ibid., 54.

10. Ibid.

11. Randy Maddox, *Responsible Grace* (Nashville: Kingswood Books, 1994), 69-70.

12. Smith, *Desiring the Kingdom*, 53. There is of course a danger in how this could be heard. It is not the case that simply being habituated is a type of instrumentality that guarantees automatic results. It is the case that many children raised in "Christian" homes remain within Christianity their entire lives. However, it is also the case that some who are shaped and formed as Christians in their youth walk away from their faith as they grow up. The reasons for why this occurs are complex, diverse, and contextual. However, what is at stake here is the notion that people become who they are through habits and practices surrounded by some story of imagination, Christian or otherwise.

13. Smith, *Desiring the Kingdom*, 93.

## Chapter 3

1. The Hebraic imagery in Gen. 2:7 of *nāshām* (breathing) can allude to the breathing of a woman as in labor.

2. See Diane Leclerc, "Sin of the (M)other: A Wesleyan-Holiness Feminist Hamartiology," chap. 5 in *Singleness of Heart: Gender, Sin, and Holiness in Historical Perspective* (Lanham, MD: Scarecrow Press, 2001).

## Chapter 4

1. The phrase "means of grace" is most often connected to the sacraments. This concept will be explored in greater detail in section III. Within the beauty of the sacraments, the service of the Word and Table is a means of grace, a healing and transforming event.

2. See John 8:1-11 for entire account.

3. See Mark 10:46-52 for entire account.

4. Smith, *Desiring the Kingdom*, 173.

5. Ibid., 163.

## Chapter 5

1. Thanks to my colleague Dr. Richard Thompson who first helped me to imagine the role of the Spirit as the One who breathes in and then exhales the church each week.

2. Michael Horton, *A Better Way: Rediscovering the Drama of God-Centered Worship* (Grand Rapids: Baker Books, 2002), 24.

3. Stanley Hauerwas, "Liturgical Shape of Christian Teaching: Teaching Christian Ethics as Worship," in *In Good Company: The Church as Polis* (Notre Dame, IN: University of Notre Dame Press, 1995), 157.

4. Susan J. White, *Foundations of Christian Worship* (Louisville, KY: Westminster John Knox Press, 2006), 15.

## Chapter 7

1. See also my chapter "What Is the Point of God's Mission?" in *Missio Dei,* eds. Keith Schwanz and Joseph Coleson (Kansas City: Beacon Hill Press of Kansas City, 2011). There I suggest that the final emphasis of God's mission and healing in the world is that God may be all in all at the consummation of the kingdom.

2. Ibid., 121.

3. Brent Peterson, "What Becomes of the Consummation of the Kingdom of God, and Christian Hope?" in *God Reconsidered: The Promise and Peril of Process Theology,* ed. Al Truesdale (Kansas City: Beacon Hill Press of Kansas City, 2010), 131.

## Section II

1. John Wesley, Sermon 39, "Catholic Spirit," sec. 4, *Sermons II,* ed. Albert C. Outler, vol. 2, *The Bicentennial Edition of the Works of John Wesley,* hereafter cited as *Works* (Nashville: Abingdon Press, 1976– ), 85.

## Chapter 8

1. See introduction for complete text.

## Chapter 9

1. The Lord's Day is the celebration of Christ's resurrection that begins and anticipates the renewal of all of creation. Christ's resurrection is a day celebrating the conquest of the dominion of sin and death. "The weekly observance of the Lord's Day announces that the just and unending dominion of God has already begun in the coming of Christ" (Laurence Hull Stookey, *Calendar: Christ's Time for the Church* [Nashville: Abingdon, 1996], 40). However, there are many congregations also worshipping on different days of the week for many good reasons. Many people must work on Sundays and thus cannot attend. Making allowance for such people is right and proper. As cultural shifts occur, faithful Christian communal worship can occur at different times throughout the week. However, caution should be taken when a worship time is chosen simply for the convenience of not interrupting our weekend plans.

2. See my fuller conversation about the lectionary on page 107. The lectionary is groupings of common scriptural texts that many Catholics and Protestants follow. These texts are often collected around a common theme and regularly pay attention to the certain day or season of the church year. Each week there are four lessons (passages): an Old Testament text, a psalm, an epistle, and a gospel text. It is also noteworthy that the formation of the lectionary and that of the church year developed together in Christian worship.

3. Technology provides many ways groups can work together in the sharing and collaboration of ideas.

## Chapter 10

1. See appendix 1 where I have included a list of questions that can be used as a beginning template for gathering information.

## Chapter 11

1. Robert Webber, "152 What Is the Christian Year?" in *The Services of the Christian Year,* vol. 5, *The Complete Library of Christian Worship* (Peabody, MA: Hendrickson, 1993), 80.

2. See Gary Lee Waller, *Celebrations and Observances of the Church Year: Leading Meaningful Services from Advent to All Saint's Day* (Kansas City: Beacon Hill Press of Kansas City, 2009).

3. Liturgical colors, like the church year and Scripture readings in worship (lectionary), have developed over time. In the light of this history, the church should guard against any type of legalism that claims Christian tradition as its basis. The colors can be a meaningful way to celebrate and mark the seasons. For a further history on liturgical colors, see Stookey, *Calendar: Christ's Time for the Church*, 155-57.

4. See Geoffrey Wainwright, "Beginning with Easter," *The Reformed Journal* 38, no. 3 (March 1988): 13-17.

5. Don E. Saliers, "The Church Year and Congregational Life," *Reformed Liturgy and Music* 20, no. 2 (Spring 1986): 92-94

6. Martin Connell, *Eternity Today: On the Liturgical Year* (New York: Continuum, 2006), 1:110-11.

7. There is not unanimous agreement on all the motivations for the selection of December 25. See Connell, *Eternity Today*, 1:101-3.

8. Connell, *Eternity Today*, 1:152-55.

9. White, *Introduction to Christian Worship*, 66.

10. Webber, "152 What Is the Christian Year?" 80.

11. See Connell, *Eternity Today*, 2:60-75.

12. Ibid., 58.

13. Martin Connell observes that such fasting seeks to make persons more aware of the love of God. These Lenten disciplines "are meant to keep hearts beating and engaged in the world, to keep them from turning to stone, and to keep the senses alert for the fullest revelation of the gifts of God" (Ibid., 57-58).

14. John D. Grabner, "Triduum: Practical Considerations," *Reformed Liturgy and Music* 24, no. 1 (Winter 1990): 12-15.

15. The gospel lectionary text in year A is John 13:1-15 (it is also an alternative in years B and C), the washing of the disciples' feet.

16. Craig Hovey, *To Share in the Body* (Grand Rapids: Brazos, 2008), 81.

## Chapter 12

1. Wesley, Sermon 39, "Catholic Spirit," *Works*, 2:82.

2. See Wesley, Sermon 101, "The Duty of Constant Communion," *Works*, 3:427-39.

## Chapter 13

1. Romans 1:18-20 affirms that God has revealed Godself to all people. This general revelation is also known as *natural theology*. While Christians should be thankful for this general revelation, in God's providence, God revealed more of Godself through the Old Testament texts and most powerfully in the revelation of Jesus Christ as the incarnate Son of God.

2. See Smith, *Desiring the Kingdom*, 176.

3. Unfortunately, I think Smith undermines the role creatures play by the Spirit in participating in the new creation God is bringing on the earth by his parenthetical rejection of creatures creating.

4. Philip asked the eunuch, "'Do you understand what you are reading?' He replied, 'How can I, unless someone guides me?' And he invited Philip to get in and sit beside him" (Acts 8:30*b*-31).

5. Timothy Roche, "The Devil and Andrea Yates," *Time*, March 11, 2002, http://www.time.com/time/magazine/article/0,9171,1001989,00.html (accessed July 22, 2011).

6. Jim Fodor, "Reading the Scriptures: Rehearsing Identity, Practicing Character," in *The Blackwell Companion to Christian Ethics*, eds. Stanley Hauerwas and Samuel Wells (Oxford: Blackwell Publishing, 2004), 141.

7. Thanks to my colleague Dr. Jay Akkerman, whose passion for excellence in Scripture reading is an inspiration to me and shaped some of these practices in reading excellence. There are many resources for assisting the public reading of Scripture. Resources both from religious institutions and from the field of mass communications can be helpful. One website specifically offering assistance to lectors (those who read the Scriptures) is by Peter P. Kenny, 1999-2003, at http://www.theology.ie/lector.htm.

8. Roy A. Rappaport, *Ritual and Religion in the Making of Humanity* (United Kingdom: Cambridge Press, 1999), 37.

9. In my experience, most readers sound less like Shakespeare and more like Ben Stein in *Ferris Bueller's Day Off.*

10. Walter Brueggemann, *Finally Comes the Poet: Daring Speech for Proclamation* (Minneapolis: Fortress, 1988), 1.

11. Ibid., 4.

12. Ibid., 68.

## Chapter 14

1. Central Board of Finance of the Church of England, "The Order for Holy Communion Rite A," in *The Alternative Service Book 1980* (Beccles: William Clowes, 1980), 119. This is an adapted version of the prayer from the *Book of Common Prayer.*

2. White, *Foundations of Christian Worship*, 29.

3. See Smith, *Desiring the Kingdom*, 194.

4. This is referring to the epiclesis in the eucharistic prayer.

5. Henry H. Knight III, "Worship and Sanctification," *Wesleyan Theological Journal* 32, no. 2 (1997): 9.

6. Remember the emphasis of *anamnēsis* is being present to that which has gone before. This emphasis also plays a dynamic part of the celebration of the Lord's Supper.

7. Maddox, *Responsible Grace*, 177-87.

8. "But you are a chosen race, a royal priesthood, a holy nation, God's own people, in order that you may proclaim the mighty acts of him who called you out of darkness into his marvelous light" (1 Pet. 2:9).

9. First Corinthians 2:15-16 and Phil. 2:5 celebrate the church having the mind of Christ. This is not a possession of the church but a picture of the transformation of the church to more fully be the body of Christ.

10. This is a prayer I adapted from a prayer created by Dr. Roger Hahn, who drew upon the *Book of Common Prayer* and other prayer books in creating the general form of this prayer.

11. Pastor Kent Conrad opened my eyes to this important aspect of worship. Many times as the church prays for the needs of the world, God, by the Spirit, desires to use each local congregation to "be the answer to the prayers and petitions of the world."

12. See David B. Burrell, *Deconstructing Theodicy: Why Job Has Nothing to Say to the Puzzle of Suffering* (Grand Rapids: Brazos Press, 2008).

13. Morris Weigelt and E. Dee Freeborn, *Living the Lord's Prayer: The Heart of Spiritual Formation* (Kansas City: Beacon Hill Press of Kansas City, 2006).

## Chapter 15

1. See Smith, *Desiring the Kingdom*, 171.

2. Ibid., 172.

3. Martin Luther, *D. Martin Luthers Werke: Kritische Gesamtausgabe; Tischreden* (Weimar: Hermann Böhlaus Nachfolger, 1921), 6: no. 7034; trans. and quoted in *What Luther Says*, comp. E. M. Plass (St. Louis: Concordia, 1959), no. 3091.

4. See appendix 2, "Song Review Worksheet." This was developed by Keith D. Schwanz and helps to discern the proper use and place of songs.

## Chapter 16

1. Creedal quotations are from *The United Methodist Hymnal* (Nashville: United Methodist Publishing House, 2003), 7.

2. Alexander Schmemann, *For the Life of the World* (Crestwood, NY: St Vladimir's Seminary Press, 1988), 25.

3. Brent D. Peterson, "Eucharist: The Church's Political Response to Suffering and Vocational Empowerment to Suffering Love," *Wesleyan Theological Journal* 43, no. 1 (Spring 2008), 149.

4. Smith, *Desiring the Kingdom*, 192.

5. "Kenosis" is a term often defined as "self-emptying." Philippians 2:5-9, titled "The Christ Hymn," also describes how "Christ emptied himself for love of the Father and the world."

6. Some may still protest that the only motivation for tithe envelopes is for tax purposes and there is a type of holiness in anonymity. I still find my father's logic compelling and people are not required to seek the reduction for a giving contribution. People with such convictions could also return the deduction to the church.

7. Malachi 3:8-10 describes those failing to pay tithes as robbing God. All Christians must heed the charge and discipline of Malachi. See also Lev. 27:30-33 and Num. 18:21-28.

8. Thanks to Dr. Neil MacPherson for this great liturgical practice.

## Section III

1. Matthew 28:19 in the Great Commission commands, in the making of disciples, to baptize. Matthew 26:26-28, Luke 22:19, and 1 Cor. 11:24 celebrate Christ's imperative to eat and drink in remembrance of him.

2. See Wesley, Sermon 101, "The Duty of Constant Communion," *Works*, 3:434.

3. *The Babylonian Captivity of the Church*, trans. A. T. W. Steinhäuser, Frederick C. Ahrens, and Abdel Rosss Wentz, in vol. 36, *Luther's Works* (Philadelphia: Muhlenberg Press, 1959), 124.

4. Ibid., 67.

5. James F. White, *The Sacraments in Protestant Faith and Practice* (Nashville: Abingdon, 1989), 18.

6. The *Catechism of the Catholic Church* states clearly, "It follows that 'the sacrament is not wrought by the righteousness of either the celebrant or the recipient, but by the power of God' (St. Thomas Aquinas, *STh* III, 68,8). From the moment that a sacrament is celebrated in accordance with the intention of the Church, the power of Christ and his Spirit acts in and through it, independently of the personal holiness of the minister. Nevertheless, the fruits of the sacraments also depend *on the disposition of the one who receives them*" (part 2, sec. 1, chap. 1, para. IV, sec. 1128, http://www.vatican.va/archive/ccc_css/archive/catechism/p2s1c1a2.htm [accessed on August 12, 2011, emphasis mine]).

7. Brent D. Peterson, "A Post-Wesleyan Eucharistic Ecclesiology: The Presence of Christ in the Eucharist as the Memory of the Facing Event Between Christ and the Church," in *Proceedings of the 2011 Annual Meeting of the North American Academy of Liturgy* (Notre Dame, IN, 2011), 190.

8. Lawrence E. Mick, "Baptism in the Medieval West," in *The Sacred Actions of Christian Worship*, in vol. 7, *The Complete Library of Christian Worship*, ed. Robert E. Webber (Nashville: Hendrickson, 1993), 110.

9. Augustine of Hippo, Sermon 169,11,13, Sermons, vol. 5, in pt. 3 of *The Works of St. Augustine: A Translation for the 21st Century*, trans. Gerald Bonner, et al. (New York: New City Press, 1992), 231.

## Chapter 18

1. Hovey, *To Share in the Body*, 29.

2. John Wesley, "A Treatise on Baptism," *The Works of John Wesley*, 3rd ed., ed. Thomas Jackson, hereafter referred to as *Works* (Jackson) (London: Wesleyan Methodist Book Room, 1872; reprinted, Grand Rapids: Baker, 1979), 10:190.

3. Ibid., 193.

4. Ibid., 188.

5. Ibid., 191.

6. Wesley, Sermon 74, "Of the Church," *Works*, 3:49.

7. In 1 Cor. 12 Paul celebrates how God created diversity for the health and wholeness of the entire body.

8. John D. Zizioulas, *Being as Communion: Studies in Personhood and the Church* (Crestwood, NY: St. Vladimir's Press, 1985), 57. See also pp. 15-19 and 49-61.

9. The *Book of Common Prayer* is the title to prayer books used mostly in the Church of England (Anglican Church). This prayer book was used by John and Charles Wesley. John abbreviated the *Book of Common Prayer* and fashioned *The Sunday Service of the Methodists in North America* (1784), which he gave to Thomas Coke and Francis Asbury for the worship of Methodists in America.

10. Susan White notes that as baptism was a person's entrance into the body of Christ, it was also his or her empowerment to participate in the church's mission in the world as the body

of Christ; hence, baptism has often been spoken about as "the ordination rite of the laity" (Susan White, *Foundations of Christian Worship*, 72.)

11. Susan White notes that the Christian tradition was skewed by those who misunderstood Augustine (*Foundations of Christian Worship*, 81).

12. White, *Sacraments in Protestant Practice and Faith*, 55.

13. Ibid.

14. Wesley, "A Treatise on Baptism," *Works* (Jackson), 10:193.

15. Maddox, *Responsible Grace*, 75. Maddox references Wesley's Letter to John Mason (21 Nov. 1776), *The Letters of the Rev. John Wesley, A.M.*, 8 vols., ed. John Telford (London: Epworth, 1931), 6:239-40. Cf. Sermon 59, "God's Love to Fallen Man," *Works*, 2:434.

16. Distinct from the Reformed tradition, Wesley also affirmed that God's healing salvation is for all and not simply for the elect, as some restricted predestined group. Prevenient grace is the foundation for the belief within Wesley of universal atonement, offered to all who would respond.

17. Wesley, "November 21, 1776," *Works* (Jackson), 12:453.

18. "I believe, till I was about ten years old I had not sinned away that 'washing of the Holy Ghost' which was given me in baptism; having been strictly educated and carefully taught, that I could only be saved 'by universal obedience, by keeping all the commandments of God;' in the meaning of which I was diligently instructed" (Wesley, "May 24th, 1738," *Works* [Jackson], 1:98). What is most intriguing is that this reflection occurs at the beginning of Wesley's testimony about the assurance he received in his Aldersgate experience.

19. White, *Sacraments in Protestant Practice and Faith*, 56.

20. See below for a larger discussion on catechism and confirmation. Catechism is the intentional training and discipleship for infants who have been baptized and people who have not been baptized. Confirmation is an official ritual where people baptized as infants can stand during a baptismal service and pledge their commitment to live into the covenant and salvation they were brought into.

21. Rob L. Staples, *Outward Sign and Inward Grace: The Place of Sacraments in Wesleyan Spirituality* (Kansas City: Beacon Hill Press of Kansas City, 1991), 186. Staples also illumines this crucial point from Ole Borgen: "The work begun in Baptism must therefore issue forth in subsequent repentance, faith, and obedience, which are demands binding on all who have received God's grace, by whatever means, according to their state, abilities, and circumstances. As the child is taught and achieves the understanding of reason and uses the grace he has received, he will steadily grow in grace and holiness and consciously and willingly embrace a life of holiness when he is able" (Ole Borgen, *John Wesley on the Sacraments* [Nashville: Abingdon, 1972], 170).

22. Staples, *Outward Sign and Inward Grace*, 166.

23. Matthew 18:6 warns those who lead children astray. Verses 1-6 articulate Jesus' elevation and celebration of a child's faith.

24. Wesley, "A Treatise on Baptism," *Works* (Jackson), 10:193.

25. See Acts 16:15 where Lydia's household was baptized; Acts 18:8 Crispus's household; and 1 Cor. 1:16 Stephanas's household. Certainly the biblical mandate to baptize infants is not explicit, but nowhere does Scripture forbid or discourage it.

26. Staples, *Outward Sign and Inward Grace*, 269.

27. White, *Introduction to Christian Worship*, 217.

28. "This is Your Baptismal Liturgy: A Resource for Understanding the United Methodist Ritual of Holy Baptism" (General Board of Discipleship, United Methodist Church, 2001), 17.

29. Ulrich Zwingli, "Of Baptism," *Zwingli and Bullinger*, ed. G. W. Bromily (Philadelphia: Westminster Press, 1953), 156.

30. White, *Introduction to Christian Worship*, 213.

31. Staples, *Outward Sign and Inward Grace*, 268.

## Chapter 19

1. Recall from chap. 11 that the Easter Vigil was a service in the hours of darkness of Holy Saturday and before the sunrise on Easter Day.

2. Lawrence E. Mick, "Preparation for Baptism: The Catechumenate," in *The Sacred Actions of Christian Worship*, vol. 7, *The Complete Library of Christian Worship*, ed. Robert E. Webber (Nashville: Hendrickson, 1993), 109.

3. There are occasions when people desire to be baptized or have their children baptized, but their physical health or that of their children is deteriorating in such a fashion that they do not have time to wait for one of the ordinary scheduled times. In these cases, it is certainly permissible for baptisms to take place in homes, hospitals, or wherever people may be. However, for Wesleyans it is important to state that the desire for baptism should not be motivated out of a fear that not being baptized dooms a person to hell.

4. See appendix 3, where the baptismal liturgy from the 1979 *Book of Common Prayer* (New York: The Church Hymnal Corporation, 1979), 299-314, is offered as a template.

5. Ibid., 302.

6. Ibid., 305-6.

7. Ibid., 306-7.

8. Ibid., 307.

9. Accompanying this meal was the kiss of peace and the prayers of the faithful.

## Chapter 20

1. Transubstantiation affirms that bread and wine become the body and blood of Christ in their *species* or *substance* of the bread and wine: trans- (cross or change) substances. While the bread and wine's accidents or outward appearance (color, taste, smell) do not change, the substance or essence (what the thing really is) changes into the body and blood of Christ. This theory draws upon an Aristotelian understanding of things having accidents and species or substance. So the Roman Catholic Church affirms that if the bread or wine would be viewed under a microscope, it would still look like bread and wine, but it was really in its essence or substance the body and blood of Christ.

2. See Staples, *Outward Sign and Inward Grace*, 217-18.

3. Ibid., 222.

4. Daniel Brevint (1616-95) originally published this work in 1673. John and Charles Wesley included Brevint's work as an introduction to their *Hymns on the Lord's Supper* (Bristol: Farley, 1745).

5. Brevint, *The Christian Sacrament and Sacrifice*, sec. IV.3, in J. Ernest Rattenbury, *The Eucharistic Hymns of John and Charles Wesley: To Which Is Appended Wesley's Preface Extracted from Brevint's Christian Sacrament and Sacrifice Together with Hymns on the Lord's Supper* (London: Epworth, 1948; reprint [updated grammar], Cleveland: OSL Publications, 1990), 151.

6. Wesley, *Hymns on the Lord's Supper*, no. 59, sts. 1-3, p. 49 (italics mine).

7. Charles Wesley, "O the Depth of Love Divine," st. 4 (1745) (Hymn no. 627 in *The United Methodist Hymnal*). It is intriguing that this hymn was written the same year as the publication of the *Hymns on the Lord's Supper*.

8. Ibid., no. 91, st. 3, p. 78 (italics mine).

9. Borgen, *John Wesley on the Sacraments*, 59.

10. Wesley, *Hymns on the Lord's Supper*, no. 81, st. 1, p. 69 (italics mine).

11. As noted in chap. 3, this verse exposes the importance of Christ's command to partake of the Eucharist, which the Wesleys did not take lightly. The Wesleys did not view this command as a legalistic burden but a gracious invitation to life.

12. *United Methodist Hymnal*, 10.

13. See Wesley's sermons "The Means of Grace" (Sermon 16, *Works*, 1:396-97) and "The Duty of Constant Communion" (Sermon 101, *Works*, 3:427-39).

14. *United Methodist Hymnal*, 10.

15. *Didache*, in R. C. D. Jasper and G. J. Cuming, *Prayers of the Eucharist: Early and Reformed* (Collegeville, MN: Liturgical Press, 1990), 23.

## Chapter 21

1. Wesley, "June 27th, 1740," Journal 4, in *Journal and Diaries II (1738-1743)*, ed. W. Reginald Ward and Richard P. Heitzenrater, *Works*, 19:158.

2. The Lord's Supper is a confirming ordinance; it is the offering of sanctifying grace. This is the normal grace offered at the Table, hence, the claim that ordinarily the Lord's Supper is the sacrament of sanctification.

3. John Wesley, Sermon 101, "The Duty of Constant Communion," *Works*, 3:429. This sermon was adapted largely from the nonjuror Robert Nelson's 1707 Sermon, "The Great Duty of Frequenting the Christian Sacrifice."

4. Rule following often captures the imagination of calling the sacraments an *ordinance*.

5. See Brent D. Peterson, "The Science of the Sacraments: The Being and Becoming of Persons in Community," *Wesleyan Theological Journal* 44, no. 1 (Spring 2009), 181-99.

6. Wesley, Sermon 121, "Prophets and Priests," *Works*, 4:78.

7. Frank Baker, *John Wesley and the Church of England* (Nashville: Abingdon, 1970), 242.

8. See Exod. 13:3-10. Thanks to my colleague Stephen Riley for this insight.

## Chapter 22

1. This prayer was chosen for its faithfulness to the larger Christian tradition and its continuity with the *Book of Common Prayer* and the eucharistic theology of John Wesley. See "The Great Thanksgiving," as part of the Word and Table: Service I in *The United Methodist Hymnal*, 9-11.

2. *United Methodist Hymnal*, 9-11.

3. Ibid., 9.

4. Ibid., 10.

5. See earlier conversation on the Lord's Prayer on p. 125.

## Appendix 2

1. Larry LeBlanc and Paul Baloche, "Above All" (Colorado Springs: Integrity's Hosanna! Music; Florance, AL: LenSongs Publishing, 1999), CCLI no. 2672885.

2. Dennis Jernigan, "Thank You Lord" (Muskogee, OK: Shepherd's Heart Music, Inc., 1991), CCLI no. 577439.

3. William Williams, "Guide Me, O Thou Great Jehovah" (1745), trans. William Williams and Peter Williams (1771).

4. Graham Kendrick, "Shine, Jesus Shine" (Tunbridge Wells, UK: Make Way Music, 1987), CCLI no. 30426.

5. Charles Wesley, "Come, Thou Long-Expected Jesus" (1744).

6. Charles Wesley, "O for a Thousand Tongues to Sing" (1739).

7. George Croly, "Spirit of God, Descend Upon My Heart" (1854).

8. Martin Smith, "Shout to the North" (Curious? Music UK, 1995), CCLI no. 1562261.

9. Charles Wesley, "And Can It Be?" (1738).

# BIBLIOGRAPHY

Augustine. *On Christian Teaching*. Translated with an introduction and notes by R. P. H. Green. Oxford: Oxford University Press, 1997.

Baker, Frank. *John Wesley and the Church of England*. Nashville: Abingdon, 1970.

Borgen, Ole. *John Wesley on the Sacraments*. Nashville: Abingdon, 1972.

Brevint, Daniel. "The Christian Sacrament and Sacrifice." In *The Eucharistic Hymns of John and Charles Wesley: To Which Is Appended Wesley's Preface Extracted from Brevint's Christian Sacrament and Sacrifice Together with Hymns on the Lord's Supper*, by J. Ernest Rattenbury, 145-63. London: Epworth, 1948. Reprint (updated grammar), Cleveland: OSL Publications, 1990.

Brueggemann, Walter. *Finally Comes the Poet: Daring Speech for Proclamation*. Minneapolis: Fortress, 1988.

Burrell, David B. *Deconstructing Theodicy: Why Job Has Nothing to Say to the Puzzle of Suffering*. Grand Rapids: Brazos Press, 2008.

Connell, Martin. *Eternity Today: On the Liturgical Year*. Vols. 1-2. New York: Continuum, 2006.

Fodor, Jim. "Reading the Scriptures: Rehearsing Identity, Practicing Character." In *The Blackwell Companion to Christian Ethics*. Edited by Stanley Hauerwas and Samuel Wells. Oxford: Blackwell Publishing, 2004.

Grabner, John D. "Triduum: Practical Considerations." *Reformed Liturgy and Music* 24, no. 1 (Winter 1990): 12-15.

Hauerwas, Stanley. "Liturgical Shape of Christian Teaching: Teaching Christian Ethics as Worship." In *In Good Company: The Church as Polis*. Notre Dame, IN: University of Notre Dame Press, 1995.

Hovey, Craig. *To Share in the Body*. Grand Rapids: Brazos, 2008.

Jasper, R. C. D., and G. J. Cuming. *Prayers of the Eucharist: Early and Reformed*. Collegeville, MN: Liturgical Press, 1990.

Knight, Henry H., III. "Worship and Sanctification." *Wesleyan Theological Journal* 32, no. 2 (1997): 5-14.

Leclerc, Diane. *Singleness of Heart: Gender, Sin, and Holiness in Historical Perspective*. Lanham, MD: Scarecrow Press, 2001.

Luther, Martin. *The Babylonian Captivity of the Church*. Translated by A. T. W. Steinhäuser, Frederick C. Ahrens, and Abdel Ross Wentz. Vol. 36, *Luther's Works*. Philadelphia: Muhlenberg Press, 1959.

Maddox, Randy. *Responsible Grace*. Nashville: Kingswood Books, 1994.

Mick, Lawrence E. "Baptism in the Medieval West." In *The Sacred Actions of Christian Worship*. Vol. 7, *The Complete Library of Christian Worship*. Edited by Robert E. Webber. Nashville: Hendrickson, 1993.

_____. "Preparation for Baptism: The Catechumenate." In *The Sacred Actions of Christian Worship*. Vol. 7, *The Complete Library of Christian Worship*.

Peterson, Brent D. "Eucharist: The Church's Political Response to Suffering and Vocational Empowerment to Suffering Love." *Wesleyan Theological Journal* 43, no. 1 (Spring 2008): 146-64.

_____. "A Post-Wesleyan Eucharistic Ecclesiology: The Presence of Christ in the Eucharist as the Memory of the Facing Event Between Christ and the Church." In *Proceedings* of the 2011 Annual Meeting of the North American Academy of Liturgy. Notre Dame, IN, 2011.

_____. "The Science of the Sacraments: The Being and Becoming of Persons in Community," *Wesleyan Theological Journal* 44, no. 1 (Spring 2009): 181-99.

_____. "What Becomes of the Consummation of the Kingdom of God, and Christian Hope?" In *God Reconsidered: The Promise and Peril of Process Theology*, edited by Al Truesdale, 131-39. Kansas City: Beacon Hill Press of Kansas City, 2010.

_____. "What Is the Point of God's Mission?" In *Missio Dei*, edited by Keith Schwanz and Joseph Coleson, 115-21. Kansas City: Beacon Hill Press of Kansas City, 2011.

Roche, Timothy. "The Devil and Andrea Yates." *Time*, March 11, 2002. http://www.time.com/time/magazine/article/0,9171,1001989,00.html (accessed July 22, 2011).

Saliers, Don E. "The Church Year and Congregational Life." *Reformed Liturgy and Music* 20, no. 2 (Spring 1986): 92-94.

Schmemann, Alexander. *For the Life of the World*. Crestwood, NY: St. Vladimir's Seminary Press, 1988.

Smith, James K. A. *Desiring the Kingdom*. Grand Rapids: Baker Academic, 2009.

Staples, Rob L. *Outward Sign and Inward Grace: The Place of Sacraments in Wesleyan Spirituality*. Kansas City: Beacon Hill Press of Kansas City, 1991.

Stookey, Laurence Hull. *Calendar: Christ's Time for the Church*. Nashville: Abingdon, 1996.

Wainwright, Geoffrey. "Beginning with Easter." *The Reformed Journal* 38, no. 3 (March 1988): 13-17.

Waller, Gary Lee. *Celebrations and Observances of the Church Year: Leading Meaningful Services from Advent to All Saints' Day*. Kansas City: Beacon Hill Press of Kansas City, 2009.

Webber, Robert. "152 What is the Christian Year?" In *The Services of the Christian Year*. Vol. 5, *The Complete Library of Christian Worship*. Peabody, MA: Hendrickson, 1993.

Weigelt, Morris, and E. Dee Freeborn. *Living the Lord's Prayer: The Heart of Spiritual Formation*. Kansas City: Beacon Hill Press of Kansas City, 2006.

Wesley, Charles, and John Wesley. *Hymns on the Lord's Supper*. Bristol: Farley, 1745.

Wesley, John. *Journal and Diaries II (1738-1743)*. Edited by W. Reginald Ward and Richard P. Heitzenrater. Vol. 19, *Works*.

_____. *Sermons*. Edited by Albert C. Outler. Vols. 1-4, *The Bicentennial Edition of the Works of John Wesley*. Nashville: Abingdon Press, 1976–. Abbreviation: *Works*.

_____. *The Sunday Service of the Methodists in North America*. Strahan, 1784. Reprinted, Nashville: United Methodist Publishing House, 1992.

_____. *The Works of John Wesley*. Edited by Thomas Jackson. 14 vols. 3rd ed. London: Wesleyan Methodist Book Room, 1872. Reprint, Baker: Grand Rapid, 1979. Abbreviation: *Works* (Jackson).

Westminster Shorter Catechism, http://www.reformed.org/documents/WSC.html.

White, James F. *Introduction to Christian Worship*. Nashville: Abingdon Press, 1990.

_____. *The Sacraments in Protestant Faith and Practice*. Nashville: Abingdon, 1989.

White, Susan J. *Foundations of Christian Worship*. Louisville, KY: Westminster John Knox Press, 2006.

Zizioulas, John D. *Being as Communion: Studies in Personhood and the Church*. Crestwood, NY: St Vladimir's Press, 1985.

Zwingli, Ulrich. "Of Baptism." In *Zwingli and Bullinger*. Edited by G. W. Bromily. Philadelphia: Westminster Press, 1953.

## Worship Book Resources

*Book of Common Prayer*. New York: Church Hymnal Corporation, 1979.

"This Is Your Baptismal Liturgy: A Resource for Understanding the United Methodist Ritual of Holy Baptism." General Board of Discipleship, United Methodist Church, 2001.

*The United Methodist Hymnal*. Nashville: United Methodist Publishing House, 2003.